KT-387-501

KA 0275759 1

“I Married Me a Wife”

"I Married Me a Wife"

Male Attitudes Toward Women in the American Museum, *1787–1792*

Arthur Scherr

LEXINGTON BOOKS
Lanham • Boulder • New York • Oxford

LEXINGTON BOOKS

Published in the United States of America
by Lexington Books
4720 Boston Way, Lanham, Maryland 20706

12 Hid's Copse Road
Cumnor Hill, Oxford OX2 9JJ, England

British Library Cataloguing in Publication Information Available

Library of Congress Cataloging-in-Publication Data

Scherr, Arthur, 1951–
I married me a wife : male attitudes toward women in the American museum, 1789–1792 / Arthur Scherr.
p. cm.
Includes bibliographical references.
ISBN 0-7391-0044-0 (alk. paper)
1. Sex role—United States—History—18th century. 2. Man–woman relationships—United States—History—18th century. 3. Men—United States—History—18th century—Attitudes. 4. American museum.
I. Title.
HQ1075.5.U6S38 1999
305.3′0973′09033—dc21 99-33389
CIP

Printed in the United States of America

The paper used in this publication meets the minimum requirements of American National Standard for Information Sciences—Permanence of Paper for Printed Library Materials, ANSI/NISO Z39.48–1992.

Contents

Chapter 1. Introduction 1

Chapter 2. Mathew Carey and the *American Museum* 23

Chapter 3. 1787: A Year of Constitution-Making 51

Chapter 4. Marriage, Manners, and Morals 87

Chapter 5. Turn and Return: The *American Museum* Views "The Fair Sex," 1788-1792 117

Chapter 6. Conclusion 169

About the Author 185

Chapter 1

Introduction

Inspired by burgeoning feminism, in the late 1960s the academic community began an intensive investigation into the oppression American women had endured in a white–male–dominated society. A plethora of both scholarly and fictional works on this theme found an enthusiastic audience. Following this trend, many recent historians who study the period from 1760 to 1800 argue that the eighteenth-century American middle-class patriarchy enjoined women to act as mindless servants, virtual slaves, and powerless sexual objects. They impugn patriarchal middle-class male pundits, who prescribed that women fulfill roles comprising virtuous, "notable housewifery," "Republican motherhood," and "true womanhood," terms which respectively depicted the prototypical woman in seventeenth-, eighteenth-, and nineteenth-century literature.

Sympathetic scholars charge that middle-class white male spokesmen have invariably disparaged women as lamentably irrational, oversensitive creatures, fit only to bear and raise children, and incapable of, or not meant for, the cerebration required for an advanced education, especially in the sciences and mathematics. The "Goodwoman," the "notable housewife," obeyed her father and his later surrogate, her husband, in all matters.

Mary Beth Norton, a prominent historian, argues that eighteenth-century women were defined vis-à-vis men, in terms of their roles as wives, mothers, daughters, and sisters. Female identity was determined by males.

Through the course of the century, "men's attitudes toward women changed little; they persisted in seeing their wives and daughters in traditional patriarchal terms. In men's eyes, women were properly viewed as dependents of a specific marital household."[1] Another major social historian, Carroll Smith-Rosenberg, in a study of the "hysterical woman" based on sources extending from 1785 to 1895, largely focuses on the Northern middle-class stereotype of women as "emotional, pious, passive and nurturant." She concludes:

> The American girl was taught at home, at school, and in the literature of the period, that aggression, independence, self-assertion and curiosity were male traits, inappropriate for the weaker sex and her limited sphere. Dependent throughout her life, she was to reward her male protectors with affection and submission.

Lower-class town dwellers and farm women accepted and tried to emulate these middle-class urban values, according to Smith-Rosenberg.[2]

The first decade of the Republic under the Constitution, the 1780s and 1790s, is especially important for evaluating the role of literate and articulate males in establishing female identity in a new nation searching for stability under an untried, experimental form of government. Did representative democracy, speaking through its magazines and newspapers, propose a sphere of political autonomy and equality for women? This is a query that journalism scholar Karen K. List answers with a resounding negative in a recent article, "The Post-Revolutionary Woman Idealized: Philadelphia Media's 'Republican Mother,'" in *Journalism Quarterly*. After a survey of fifteen Philadelphia magazines published in the 1780s to 1790s, including Mathew Carey's *American Museum*, the subject of our study, and three newspapers, the *Aurora*, *Porcupine's Gazette,* and *The Gazette of the United States*, List concludes that these vehicles of the middle-class intelligentsia "failed to convey the idea that women could be autonomous; they seemed to understand women's sphere only from the perspective of enhancing female educational opportunities to benefit men and children, with little recognition that this—at the same time—might enhance women's status in the home." Her examination of the periodical literature revealed that "American culture generally did not value female autonomy." Both fiction and nonfiction, with few exceptions, depicted women as puerile and excessively emotional. In List's opinion, these ideas reflected a dismal reality: "Most women were not experiencing anything of the Revolution's promise . . . . She was likely to be considered innately inferior to her husband and incapable of any serious thinking."[3]

In form as well as content, Professor List argues, the media displayed a subliminal misogynist bias. Even ostensibly objective news reports invariably portrayed "women present as observers, but not participants." In the 1790s, Philadelphia's violently partisan press only supported women's independent political action when it conformed to the newspaper's own stance. List aptly remarks: "That sort of support of women's autonomy appeared so superficial and self-serving as to be meaningless." List's examination of the *Aurora* and *Porcupine's Gazette*, which she restricted only to the brief period from 1797 to 1799, revealed a "focus on bosoms throbbing—either with ardor or fear—not on brains."[4] Thus, List's findings lend support to the feminist view that males have always ignored the positive intellectual, emotional, and social attributes of women.

Similarly, Linda Kerber, a prominent historian of "woman's sphere" in the Revolutionary War era, asserts that middle-class male opinion leaders were self-serving and condescending in the roles they assigned to women in the new republic. She astutely notes wartime "deflection of women's patriotism into benevolence" rather than political activism. Women sewed shirts and collected money for the Continental Army because that was the only way their activity in the political arena "could be made plausible to the millions of women whose lives were defined by their domestic responsibilities." In other words, middle-class women had, to an extent, internalized negative male stereotypes about their political and intellectual disempowerment. Kerber concludes:

> Western political theory had provided no context in which women might comfortably think of themselves as political beings . . . . The *man* of Enlightenment theory was literal, not generic. The only reference to women in *The Federalist Papers* would be to the dangers that the private intrigues of courtesans and mistresses pose to the safety of the state.[5]

Women obtained little respect from men and lacked outlets for protest, according to most historians, even in an era when all *men* were supposedly created "equal." Many scholars conclude that the idea that women were helpless and rightfully dependent on men for fulfilling their needs was widely inculcated in the late eighteenth century, by women writers as well as men.[6] Eighteenth-century female authors often concurred with the view of oversolicitous, patriarchal males that women lacked the emotional discernment to repel lustful rakes and seducers. One female novelist wrote tersely in 1805, "Not possessing that quick precision and force of intellect which is the peculiar prerogative of men," the young maiden "too often listens to the plighted vow, and listening, is undone." Still, women writers often advised woman to be submissive and resigned in their relations with men. Most female essayists agreed that a father could dictate his daughter's choice of a husband; they complied with the male dogma that a wife should always try to please her husband and never rebel against his desires and commands. This seemed especially the case after 1800, when the Industrial Revolution and the Second Great Awakening, as well as the conservative reaction to the French Revolution, inspired movements to constrict women's personal and moral freedoms and social liberties.[7]

At this time, the concept of "woman's sphere" was evolved to define the activities women might perform without entering provinces and occupations that were designated men's responsibility. Apparently, even well-intentioned women accepted the subordinate, traditional role of domestic homemaker and comforter to which men had relegated them. One young lady, writing in the Philadelphia *Port Folio* in 1802, instructed her sisters, "Our state in society is a dependent one, and it is ours to be good and amiable, whatever may be the conduct of the men, to whom we are subjected." Similarly, Mrs. Ann Taylor's *Practical Hints to Young Females, on the Duties of a Wife, a Mother, and a Mistress of a Family*, printed in Boston in 1816, willingly conceded "the superiority of the other sex." Her standard advice book for young women, *Correspondence between a Mother and her Daughter at School*, taught that the proper "sphere" for a woman was the home rather than the world of business. "*Men* have much to do with the world without," she wrote. "*Our* field of action is circumscribed; yet, to confine ourselves within its humble bonds," was both women's duty and beneficial to humanity.[8]

Although during the 1790s some magazines earnestly attempted to view women as more autonomous beings—expert household managers, mothers, and independent actors—male more often than female authors propounded these opinions. Middle-class women were publicly and privately committed to inculcating republican virtue and patriotism in their sons, and wrote them hortatory letters during the 1780s and 1790s. They won masculine praise for these efforts. But, despite their desire to enhance women's reputation, to depict them as industrious and virtuous rather than idle and extravagant, female reformers admitted that woman's sphere was private and family-centered while man's was public and business-oriented. Professor Norton optimistically concludes that the confluence of wartime experiences and republican ideology during the Revolutionary War era increased women's self-esteem and social status. Nevertheless, despite the belief in women's intellectual equality and in their political and social contributions as mothers, "none of the orthodox republican thinkers formally challenged the basic assumption that women's destiny was to marry and bear children, and that girls should be trained solely for that goal. They continued to view women largely within the context of household and family." These reformers, who include within their ranks such "radicals" as Judith Sargent Murray, thought that Mary Wollstonecraft went too far when she focused on women as individuals in her *Vindication of the Rights of Women* (1791), "even if they were still to be primarily wives and mothers," Norton observes.[9]

In general, during the 1790s women voiced little opposition to "male" commands that they play a subordinate role in the social, intellectual, and political spheres. This was true even of "revolutionaries" like Wollstonecraft and Murray. Although Mary Wollstonecraft advocated woman's self-respect, liberty, and equality, she emphasized that these qualities would enhance her value in marriage as a "*help meet*" to her husband. She thought marriage could be meaningful if women were prepared to act as companions of men, not merely compliant sexual objects. As Janet W. James notes, "Mary Wollstonecraft had no wish to take women out of the home." Nor was she eager to demand a place for female intellectuals like herself. Even Wollstonecraft's views were essentially conservative.[10]

Like James, American historians examining public opinion about women in the early republic tend to concentrate more on women's educational and cultural activities, and the views of English and European thinkers, than on American (particularly American *male*) attitudes. This is especially true of Mary Sumner Benson's detailed, path-breaking study, *Women in Eighteenth Century America*.[11] Therefore, a careful examination of a periodical edited by a *man* for a substantial number of years, Mathew Carey's *American Museum,* published in Philadelphia from January 1787 until December 1792, may fill an important gap in our understanding of male ideas about women at the turn of the nineteenth century.

Many female historians regard the 1790s as a key period in the male redefinition of women's social position. By 1790, as a result of the influence of the American Revolution and republican ideology, women's role as the educative "Republican Mother" complemented, without supplanting, her earlier functions as "notable housewife" and docile male companion. As Mary Beth Norton puts it, "Men, too, recognized that women acting in a domestic capacity could have a beneficial effect upon the republic," by teaching their children, particularly their sons, the virtues of American liberty and self-government. Women's social value was greatly enhanced during the war years, during which they were extolled as maternal guardians of private (and ultimately public) "manners" and morality: "When coupled with a simultaneous reevaluation of housewifery, the emphasis on motherhood was to lead to a broad reassessment of women's status in the United States." As the parent entrusted with her children's education in patriotism and "republican virtue," the mother's responsibility was enormous.[12]

On the other hand, even enlightened reformers like Dr. Benjamin Rush, Susanna Rowson, and Judith Sargent Murray assumed that the primary purpose of a better education was to help woman fulfill her role as homemaker and—especially in the South—delicate, prudish "lady": "domestic wife and delicate saint," as Patricia McAlexander calls her.[13] More sympathetically, Norton merely admits that most post-Revolutionary feminists could accept no greater public role for woman than the fulfillment of her "obligation to create a supportive home life for her husband and particularly in her duty to raise republican sons who would love their country and preserve its virtuous character."[14] Apparently education would not help women develop an autonomous identity, but merely enable them to better serve within their patriarchal society.[15]

A few scholars—notably Herman Lantz in his content analysis of periodicals, Nancy F. Cott in her study of female "passionlessness," and Carroll Smith-Rosenberg in her review of late nineteenth-century female hysteria—suggest that women exercised covert, "subtle" power over their husbands or manipulated male value systems and stereotypes in a way that restrained male coerciveness. Their strategy was desperate. Deprived of the vote, these investigators contend, women feared they would also be deprived of the exercise of their own wills. They argue that this message was conveyed by male-oriented books, newspapers, and magazines even in the Revolutionary decades of the 1780s to 1790s, when Americans strove to establish a reputation for freedom and liberalism as citizens of a rising new republic. Writers like William Kenrick (1725-1779), an Englishman with a rakish reputation whose tract, *The Whole Duty of Woman*, nevertheless epitomized a prudishly sexist, conservative viewpoint, are depicted as representing *American* men in many of these studies. "Thy kingdom is thine own house, and thy government the care of thy family," he advised, warning women to stay out of politics. "Let the laws of thy condition be thy study and learn only to govern thyself and thy dependents." Kenrick insisted that modesty, humility, lack of curiosity, and dearth of education or desire for knowledge were the optimal modes of conduct for a woman.[16]

Apparently, historians who have studied women's issues of the 1790s have failed to detect much evidence of aggressiveness or self-assertion in their everyday behavior. Norton says, "Women as well as men expected wives to subordinate themselves to their spouses." Especially in pre-Revolution years, wives agreed that their proper social role was obedience to their husbands; they even justified their treatment using Biblical references. Norton feels they acquiesced passively in their meek status during the eighteenth century: "White American wives had an unambiguously subordinate mental role, but—at least until the very end of the century—there are few or no indications that they resented their status." Rather, they accepted and internalized traditional humiliating male stereotypes of their behavior and abilities. "White women in all likelihood believed themselves inferior to men," Norton observes. "This hypothesis is borne out by an examination of a variety of contemporary sources."[17] Norton then proceeds to discuss what *women* were writing about themselves in letters, essays, and journals. Although they may have derived negative self-perceptions from middle-class white male stereotyping, we are not told exactly what *male* writers were writing about them. Moreover, historians often fail to use newspapers and magazines, which are among the few sources which might carry "objective" information on women's everyday lives, to discern whether and to what extent their allegedly poor self-image was reflected in their actions.

A study of southern plantation wives with conclusions more extreme than Norton's employs a similar technique. In *The Plantation Mistress* (1982), Catherine Clinton argues that male founders of women's academies were inspired by a desire to divert women from demanding the suffrage and social equality. She also asserts that women internalized male demands for modesty and submissiveness, epitomized by the "Southern lady." As she brusquely puts it: "Southern gentlemen enshrined and adorned their females, while women were willing to exemplify these 'ladylike' virtues. Oppression was exercised not only through sanctions against rebellion but internally, as women's compliance with the silencing stereotypes determined their own self-censuring behavior."[18] By contrast, a recent essay on the Philadelphia Young Ladies Academy, founded by Dr. Benjamin Rush and other leading male physicians, lawyers, and ministers during the 1780s, concludes that historians have exaggerated the importance of both refinement and "republican motherhood" as educational ideals of the decade: women were being trained in writing and bookkeeping, and their education was more than mere ornamentation.[19] Men may have partially abandoned stereotyping, at least during the 1780s to 1790s, when they attempted to include all groups, to some extent, within an harmonious fledgling republic.

Although some of these volumes exhibit an impressive amount of research, they often fail to convey much information on what *men* were actually saying and writing about women and their role. Historians like Norton and Clinton make it clear that women thought their place was to remain at home and obey their husbands. But they avoid any extended discussion of what *men* perceived about *women*, and what they advocated as women's goals and identities, especially for the significant decade of the 1790s, when the Constitution and its "republican experiment" were just getting underway. As Janet W. James explains, advice manuals of the 1790s vigorously "condemned any derelictions from household duty" by women and "undertook to inculcate the proper attitudes and conduct for the married state in all its phases from courtship through motherhood." Among the middle classes, "to all appearances, the young lady or the well-bred matron of 1800 was the replica of her mother and grandmother in her ideas of what the world expected of her, and no more likely than her forbears to question them."[20] But the most conservative advice manuals were generally written by women—Hester Chapone (1772), Jane West (1806), and Ann Taylor (1816).[21]

With a few exceptions, such as Jan Lewis, who emphasizes the depiction of women as wives and sexual partners in her study of late eighteenth-century media, historians stress the Revolutionary creation of the ideal "Republican Mother." In a seminal article in the *American Historical Review* in 1984, Norton argues that women gained status from the Revolution, which "initiated a public dialogue on the subject of women and their proper roles." The Revolution inspired public discussion of women's effect on political society rather than on members of the immediate family. "Americans argued about such subjects as woman's basic nature, the proper aims and content of women's education, and the intellectual abilities of females," Norton points out. "The new interest in women flowed directly from a combination of wartime experiences and republican ideology." In its search for social solidarity and republican consensus, the post-Revolutionary generation of the 1790s carefully delineated its perception of women's public role. Since republican ideology emphasized the contribution of all citizens to society, Norton concludes, "the Revolutionary generation . . . became the first to define a public role for American women." Professor Norton exalts women's function as singularly unselfish beings, dedicated mothers and wives in a self-centered, male-dominated society. While male family members pursued egotistic goals, the Republican mother devoted herself to the well-being of the entire community with her charitable activities. After the Revolution, Norton says, "women became the keepers of the nation's conscience, the only citizens specifically charged with monitoring the traditional republican commitment to the good of the entire community."[22] One of the objectives of our study of the *American Museum* will be to discover if the pieces it published in fact expounded this paradigm of women as custodians of national morality and self-sacrificing ideals. In Norton's view, as "Republican Mothers," women became the most important members of the state.

This conclusion is an exaggeration of Linda Kerber's own interpretation. Though she invented the "Republican Mother" concept, Kerber's claims for the impact of the Revolution on men's view of women are far less grandiose. Kerber does find that, after 1789, male magazine editors rejected articles that poked fun at the "fair sex"; they also printed admiring biographies of great women. She makes the important point that the America depiction of women as "Republican Mothers" was the first time women gained an independent role in political theory; she blames Europeans like Jean-Jacques Rousseau for inspiring prejudices against educated, aggressive, "masculine" women, even in liberal, reformist circles, where such provincial attitudes were particularly egregious. With the exception of the Marquis de Condorcet, even the *philosophes* of the Enlightenment refused to perceive women as autonomous beings who existed apart from "their roles as mothers and wives."[23] Most political theorists rejected or ignored the hypothesis that women may have played a political role at the beginning of society. They were primarily concerned with existing regimes. Even the liberal pamphleteers Catherine Macaulay and Mercy Otis Warren (though not her more eccentric, possibly psychotic brother James) accepted female subordination.[24]

Adherents of the "Republican Mother" ideal merely upheld woman's right to comment on political matters, but not to vote or hold office. As Kerber explains, "Her political task was accomplished within the confines of her family." The model republican woman was a mother, and she was devoted to "civic virtue," which she most aptly practiced in the home. Somewhat unconvincingly, considering their lack of political power, Kerber argues that a mother's domestic roles embodied a "political purpose": "The Republican Mother was a device which attempted to integrate domesticity and politics."[25]

Comparing American women to "deferential [male] citizens" in a pre-democratic United States, Kerber confesses that women—even her "Republican Mothers"—remained a peg below men on the political scale. Yet she feels that poor white men's replacement by women in the deferential role constituted an improvement in women's position: "As the restrained, deferential democracy of the republic gave way to an aggressive, egalitarian democracy of a modern sort among men, women invented a restrained, deferential but nonetheless political role." Ironically, though they lacked political rights, women taught their husbands and children the meaning of political virtue. At the same time, an unappreciative egalitarian male society required deferential women in order to prosper, just as the South required slave labor. But women's deference manifested itself as "service: raising sons and disciplining husbands to be virtuous citizens of the republic." Although Kerber argues that women "invented" this role, it is likely that men seeking to restrict their autonomy conceived this empty façade of power, as Elaine Forman Crane suggests: "It is not impossible that at least some exponents extolled republican motherhood as a means of deflecting or containing the ambitions of women for a political role." (The latter view would be acceptable to those like Joan Hoff- Wilson who deplore "male sex-stereotyping of women.")[26]

In his book *Inventors of the Promised Land*, Lawrence J. Friedman briefly assesses a precursor of the *American Museum* (subject of our study), the *Columbian Magazine*, published in Philadelphia from 1786 to 1792. Friedman finds that its writers anticipated the theme of "True American Womanhood" that, as Barbara Welter points out, became prevalent after 1800. Mathew Carey was a member of the five-man editorial board of the *Columbian Magazine* for its first three months of publication, September to December 1786. He left in January 1787 to become founding publisher of the *American Museum*.[27]

Although Friedman's *Inventors of the Promised Land* primarily discusses the years from 1800 to 1850, he casts a backward glance at the *Columbian Magazine*'s view of women in the early 1790s. Men stressed women's role as devoted mothers who inculcated patriotism in their children. The theme of True American Womanhood eulogized her domestic, family-centered duties. Unlike Kerber, Friedman portrays the idea as of male origin. He cites random passages in which the *Columbian Magazine*'s essayists noted that patriotic women's responsibilities were "soft, sentimental, and in the area of the hearth." His analysis of what he calls "true American womanhood" from 1800 to 1835 depicts women as men's pawns:

> The male patriot's vision of True American Womanhood was, therefore, a creature who could exhibit decorative, moral, or sentimental qualities at a moment's notice. Yet she was not to invoke these qualities at her own discretion—only when men called upon her or needed her to compensate for their coarse, masculine qualities.[28]

Although Friedman's view is extreme, it corresponds with the conclusions of Clinton, Welter, and Hoff-Wilson.

Friedman concerns himself with disproving the "American myth" of freedom and equality from colonial times to the present. His chapter on views of women in the eighteenth century relies on Barbara Welter's essay, "The Cult of True Womanhood," a minor classic since its publication in 1966. In Welter's view, the Industrial Revolution precipitated the decline of women's social status: middle-class women were relegated to the home, where they waited for their salaried husbands to return from a hard day's work. The home was no longer a center of domestic production and socially egalitarian community, and the middle-class woman was accordingly reduced in stature to a frail, decorative ornament, financially and psychologically dependent on her husband. Lower-class women were similarly dependent, working in the factories till they found a mate. As Welter puts it, "The attributes of True Womanhood, by which a woman judged herself and was judged by her husband, her neighbors and society, could be divided into four cardinal virtues—piety, purity, submissiveness, and domesticity." Her unflattering description of "woman's place" went unchallenged for almost a decade. Gerda Lerner reiterated Welter's views in her article, "The Lady and the Mill-Girl."[29]

Beginning in the 1970s a new emphasis on woman's autonomy and independent sexuality emerged in the scholarly literature. First, Carl Degler, analyzing medical opinion on women during the Victorian Era, then Barbara

Berg, Patricia McAlexander, and Laura McCall investigating women's political activities and literature for earlier periods, called into question Welter's thesis of the passive, male-dominated female, identifiable only through her role as wife, daughter, or mother.[30]

Following Degler's path-breaking article in the *American Historical Review* in 1974, demonstrating that many middle-class American women enjoyed sex, and that female sexuality was accepted and even encouraged by many male physicians in Victorian America, his study, *At Odds: Women and the Family in America from the Revolution to the Present* (1980) took the story back into the eighteenth century. Starting with the truism that most intellectuals depicted women as more erotic and libidinous than men during the period from the Middle Ages to the Victorian Era, Degler found that marriage manuals during the seventeenth and eighteenth centuries placed great emphasis upon the sexual arousal, pleasure, and satisfaction of women. Depicting the clitoris as the female analogue of the penis, one manual advised the reader that this female genital should be stimulated to encourage "the action excited in coitus until the paroxysm alters the sensations." *Aristotle's Master Piece*, a work of erotic pseudo-gynecology that circulated widely in the eighteenth and early nineteenth centuries, similarly took for granted the sexual feelings of women. Although at least one hundred editions of the book were printed before 1830, there were no complaints about its content in any newspaper or periodical. According to Degler, until about 1850 the idea that women had strong sexual needs, as well as the prurient male assumption that "women's sexual desires were insatiable seems to have lingered on, too, though disguised as an admonition to women and a warning to men."[31]

It was not until the 1840s and 1850s that male physicians wrote books that disparaged or denied women's sexual response. In Degler's view, historians have not understood that these new puritanical theorists were *prescribing* normative sexual behavior for women, rather than *describing* their actual practices. "Some historians who later read this literature often took these [medical] writings to be expressions of the actual practices and common beliefs of the time rather than what they were: a new ideology of sexual behavior, which was being advanced to counter the traditional one, which had recognized and encouraged women's sexuality," Degler argues. "Some of the interpretations by modern historians of that new literature were in error." The increasingly straitlaced nature of the society's sexual literature was stressed by other scholars as well. John and Robin Haller concluded, "Love manuals written during the first half of the nineteenth century treated women as potentially equal partners in the marriage bed, but they were not nearly as explicit in their discussion of sex as those of the previous century."[32] Apparently, the final decades of the eighteenth century, the period to be examined here, marked a time of transition between an epoch of sexual liberty and freedom of discussion about sex and an increasing prudishness and clandestine attitude toward sexuality more characteristic of many writings of the Victorian Period.[33]

On the basis of a study of novels and the fictional short stories in *Godey's Lady's Book*, the most popular magazine in antebellum America, Laura McCall argues that female sexuality was recognized as an accepted fact during the period 1820 to 1860. She thereby disputes Welter's thesis that women's magazines considered "purity and piety" indispensable female attributes. She finds little evidence, in her content analysis of *Godey's* magazine from 1830 to 1860, that women's magazines advocated the "four cardinal female virtues—piety, purity, submissiveness, and domesticity." Patricia McAlexander contests the relevance of Welter's ideas for the 1790s. She insists that late eighteenth-century literature about women's traits and optimal sexual role upheld diverse views: "There was a strong disagreement regarding the proper role for women; indeed, America seems to have participated fully in an intense cultural dialogue on the subject occurring throughout the western world."[34] Although McAlexander and McCall's views have many similarities, McCall's emphasis on women's sexuality is more pronounced.

In two articles, McCall demonstrates that novels and short stories in the period from 1820 to 1860 were replete with examples of the expression of erotic sentiments between the sexes. Sentimental novels, read by men as well as women, taught "a reverence for sexual expression as the ultimate symbol of love and personal sharing."[35] *Godey's Lady's Book,* as well as other examples of "prescriptive literature," praised female sexuality, portraying women as strong, autonomous figures capable of "assertive behavior." McCall feels that the magazine's popularity and influence justify careful analysis of its depiction of women (1830 to 1860) "in order to determine whether in fact it preached a doctrine of feminine submission and a limited, home-based way of life."[36]

McCall applied the four cardinal virtues invented by Welter to the characters in *Godey's*, and found that its articles did not encourage women to be passive and domesticated, nor even religious. Moreover, in contrast to the opinions of scholars like Frank L. Mott and Ann Douglas, she concluded that the issue of "the moral purity of most characters was not developed at all." McCall's analysis of 150 randomly chosen fictional pieces even discovered depictions of "passionate and voluptuous women." Though *Godey's* frowned on extramarital sexual relations, its motives were far from prudish, since "it was often implied that sexual pleasure, within the confines of marriage, was a healthy and suitable sentiment." *Godey's* did not urge women to find their sole gratification in the household. Some stories "depicted marriage in a very unfavorable light," with middle-class wives unhappy in a lonely house with nothing to do. Some of the essays demanded greater work opportunities for female doctors and midwives. Rather than urge women to submit to male domination, *Godey's* articles argued that women were often superior to men in their capacity for independent action and were equally competent in business and politics. McCall concludes that the vast majority of women in her sample exhibited positive traits—intelligence, physical strength, independence, and emotional maturity.[37]

Contrary to the general interpretation of antebellum women found in most scholarly studies, McCall detects few suggestions in *Godey's* (the publisher was Louis Godey) that the ideal woman should be pious, pure, submissive, and domestic. She even reaches the daring conclusion that the "prescriptive literature" of the period did not really condemn assertive female behavior: this was only a myth propagated by historians. McCall also notes a growing tendency of feminist scholars—Nancy Cott and Mary Kelley among them—to depict Victorian women writers as protesters against the *status quo* rather than docile figures in their private lives. But she is most impressed with her own "systematic approach" and its superiority to the earlier, "shallow" efforts of previous historians to examine the prescriptive literature.[38]

What is needed for the period of the 1780s to 1790s is a study similar to what McCall has done for *Godey's Lady's Book.* We should examine a magazine that prints stories—fiction and nonfiction alike—that delineate woman's everyday life and man's everyday opinion of her. This has not been done for any of the extant periodicals for that period. It would be most enlightening to analyze what an important magazine thinks constitutes the most interesting, and representative, *actions* of women—by means of the articles and essays it prints about them—and, if possible, the male *reactions* to these female lives. Courtship, marriage, motherhood—we would expect these to be most prominent in magazine articles about women. But these topics only comprise the *form* of what we seek to discern about male attitudes toward women. We need to carefully analyze the *content* of magazine articles, in a kind of *explication de texte*, to ascertain what the writer is really trying to convey to the reader about his/her opinion of the women of the time and their activities. Our study will attempt to apply this concept to one of the most popular and important journals of the decade, Mathew Carey's *American Museum.*

By comparison with the Colonial and Victorian eras, the period I wish to examine, the 1780s to 1790s, comprises a virtual "No-Man's Land" for the cultural historian. Although my source—the *American Museum,* a monthly published from January 1787 to December 1792—is a "middle-class" document, which only the literate and basically well-educated would bother to read and comprehend, this is true of virtually all the literary fare of that time, and, with trifling exceptions, of more recent times as well. Thus, we are interested, not primarily in the poorest or most oppressed women, although they occasionally do appear in the pages of the *American Museum*, but in an essentially bourgeois *mentalité* and middle-class lifestyle.

An in-depth study of one male-edited magazine's opinions on women over a period of several years is necessary, since most historians have relied merely on one or two examples, as if that were sufficient to condemn all males as misogynists. Undeniably, women derived many negative self-concepts from laws that denied them a legal identity, particularly in the case of married women. But it often happens that laws lag behind social opinion and social practice. Perhaps middle-class American men in the 1790s did not have so poor an opinion of female talents, or so obsessive a desire to keep women in submission, as many historians tell us, or women at the time apparently perceived.

Though full-scale investigation is not our purpose here, Mathew Carey's Philadelphia monthly, the *American Museum*, may serve to epitomize what *men* were writing about the normative status of women in the 1790s as well as their actual behavior. Considered by scholars "among the best of eighteenth-century American magazines," as John Tebbel puts it, the *Museum* earned a reputation as one of the most carefully edited, comprehensive, and representative, as well as long-lived, periodicals published in the eighteenth-century United States.[39] Persisting from 1787 to 1792, with a special volume appearing in 1799, the *American Museum* reprinted political and economic documents and essays as well as original pieces, stressing nationwide and retrospective coverage. After 1790, about one-third of the pieces were original, and there was more short fiction. Women often played prominent roles as heroines in these short stories.[40]

The dean of historians of American journalism, Frank L. Mott, recognized the superiority of Carey's magazine to its competitors and its indispensability for the student of eighteenth-century culture: "The *Museum* is perhaps the most important American magazine file of its century: it is invaluable for a study of the society, economics, and politics of 1787 to 1792, and it is far more American in materials than most of its contemporaries."[41]

Carey chose his material from the years preceding, during, and after the Revolution as well as from contemporary authors. Each issue averaged one hundred pages, while his competitors' ran only about sixty-four. Small print and octavo pages allowed Carey sufficient space to satisfy the interests of his 1,250 readers, including such statesmen as George Washington. Frank Mott ranks Carey "the ablest magazine editor of his time," while Lyon Richardson, stressing the journal's diversity, calls it "a true museum." The magazine published poetry, satirical essays, and commentaries on politics, education, and abolitionism. Moreover, as Tebbel points out, it "devoted considerable space to advising women about their role in society."[42] Intensive examination of the *American Museum's* pages should provide abundant data on male attitudes toward women in the 1790s.

As Janet W. James points out, most recent women's historians—Anne Firor Scott, Linda Kerber, Nancy Cott, and Mary Beth Norton—use *family correspondence* as the primary means for illuminating women's social history. In contrast, James and Mary Sumner Benson, like myself, prefer to employ written works and magazine articles. Although women's letters are undoubtedly valid and valuable sources, they constitute a *particular* rather than a *general* object of study, and are obviously of limited use and information where *public male attitudes* are the topic. For this reason, periodicals like the *American Museum*, which addressed a wide readership, are indispensable sources of male opinion and deserve thorough study by scholars.[43]

Although James and Benson restrict themselves to printed sources, they have not fruitfully pursued them as a means of discovering men's views of women in relation to their everyday experiences. Perhaps this was not their purpose. Indeed, they seem basically concerned with evaluating the prescriptive literature—the "highbrow culture" of the time. James discusses the views of New England clergy and prudish female advisers to the "fair sex" at great length in her trenchant study. For the most part, her book is about *women's opinion of women*; it does not especially concentrate on the male point of view. Moreover, to anticipate our findings, the *American Museum* places less emphasis on woman's role in educating children than we might expect after reading Dr. James and the plethora of studies which emphasize the "Republican Mother"; it attends more to her role as the male's wife and sexual mate (or potential mate).

An innovative scholar, Mary Sumner Benson anticipated the idea of the "Republican Mother," finding that in the 1780s Americans more often discussed young women's education at school and their later duties in the home than "marriage as an institution and the choice of a husband." Contrary to what I have found in the *American Museum*, Benson did not detect much emphasis in the literature on the theory and practice of courtship. Surprisingly, she found little discussion of social and sexual relationships. Like later adherents of the "Republican Mother" thesis, Benson concludes, "Domestic training in preparation for marriage was usually regarded as the function of the home, not the school." Young women pessimistically accepted marriage as their fate, though they lamented that it would put them under their husbands' control. Nevertheless, Benson surprisingly observes, "There were few elaborate discussions of marriage, nothing at all comparable to the detailed attention given to education."[44] Our survey of the *American Museum* will disclose that, at least for this magazine, such was not the case: Marriage and heterosexual norms, ideals and realities of behavior, frequently received coverage.

Experts respect the *American Museum* as a source for investigating eighteenth-century society. It provides ample (largely male) coverage of the activities and social role of women. Therefore, it constitutes a suitable starting point for a thorough examination of American men's attitudes toward women in the 1790s. Its essays deal with the realities of female behavior as well as stereotyped male ideals. Perhaps a close reading of the *American Museum*—together with a brief concluding comparison of its ideas with those of a few contemporary journals—will help us to more accurately discern male opinions of women in the 1790s. Our inquiry seeks to determine whether middle-class male rhetoric stridently invoked female docility and ascribed low intelligence and irrationality as women's typical characteristics, in a deliberate male effort to dominate them by instilling feelings of insecurity, inferiority, and low self-esteem.[45] The question remains a topic of academic and popular controversy.[46]

Notes

1. Mary Beth Norton, "The Evolution of White Women's Experience in Early America," *American Historical Review* 89, no. 3 (June 1984): 610.

2. Carroll Smith-Rosenberg, "The Hysterical Woman: Sex Roles and Role Conflict in 19th-Century America," *Social Research* 39, no. 4 (Winter 1972): 656.

3. Karen K. List, "The Post-Revolutionary Woman Idealized: Philadelphia Media's 'Republican Mother,'" *Journalism Quarterly* 66, no. 1 (Spring 1989): 68, 67.

4. List, "Post-Revolutionary Woman Idealized," 70. See also List, "Magazine Portrayals of Women's Role in the New Republic," *Journalism History* 13 (Summer 1986): 64-70.

5. Linda K. Kerber, *Women of the Republic: Intellect and Ideology in Revolutionary America* (Chapel Hill: University of North Carolina Press, 1980), 111 (first quote), 105 (second quote). For a different view, arguing that Jefferson meant for women and blacks to be included within the phrase of the Declaration of Independence that stated that "all men are created equal," see Allen Jayne, *Jefferson's Declaration of Independence: Origins, Philosophy and Theology* (Lexington, Ky.: University Press of Kentucky, 1998), 123-126.

6. See especially Joan Hoff Wilson, "The Illusion of Change: Women and the American Revolution," in Alfred F. Young, ed., *The American Revolution: Explorations in the History of American Radicalism* (Dekalb, Ill.: Northern Illinois University Press, 1976), 383-445, and "Dancing Dogs of the Colonial Period: Women Scientists," *Early American Literature* 7, no. 3 (Winter 1973): 222-235; Elaine F. Crane, "Dependence in the Era of Independence: The Role of Women in a Republican Society," in *The American Revolution: Its Character and Limits*, Jack P. Greene, ed., (New York: New York University Press, 1987), 253-275; and Janet W. James, *Changing Ideas About Women in the United States, 1760-1825* (New York: Garland, 1981), 65-119. On the other hand, Mary Beth Norton, *Liberty's Daughters: The Revolutionary Experience of American Women, 1750-1800* (Boston: Little, Brown, 1980), argues that the experience of the Revolution advanced women's political consciousness and spurred their quest for equality.

7. James, *Changing Ideas About Women*, 121-159; the quotation, from Caroline Matilda Warren's *The Gamesters* (1805), is in James, *Changing Ideas About Women,* 142.

8. Philadelphia *Port Folio*, 2 (May 8, 1802), 137, quoted in James, *Changing Ideas About Women*, 137; other quotes are in James, *Changing Ideas About Women,* 143 (first quotation), 156 (second quotation). For other interpretations of the early Victorian woman's "sphere," see Mary Kelley, *Private Woman, Public Stage: Literary Domesticity in Nineteenth Century America* (New York: Oxford University Press, 1984); Gerda Lerner, "The Lady and the Mill Girl: Changes in the Status of Women in the Age of Jackson, 1800-1840," in *A Heritage of Her Own: Toward a New Social History of American Women*, Nancy F. Cott and Elizabeth H. Pleck, eds. (New York: Simon and Schuster, 1979), 182-196; Patricia J. McAlexander, "The Creation of the American Eve: The Cultural Dialogue on the Nature and Role of Women in Late Eighteenth-Century America," *Early American Literature* 9, no. 3 (Winter 1975): 252-266; and Barbara Welter, "The Cult of True Womanhood: 1800-1860," *American Quarterly* 18, no. 2, pt. 1 (Spring 1966): 151-174.

9. Norton, *Liberty's Daughters*, 247-250; quote at 250.

10. James, *Changing Ideas About Women*, 94. See also McAlexander, "American Eve," 256.

11. Mary Sumner Benson, *Women in Eighteenth Century America: A Study of Opinion and Social Usage* (New York: Columbia University Press, 1935).

12. Norton, *Liberty's Daughters*, 245. See also Ruth H. Bloch, "American Feminine Ideals in Transition: The Rise of the Moral Mother, 1789-1815," *Feminist Studies* 4 (Jan. 1978): 101-126, and Bloch, "The Gendered Meanings of Virtue in Revolutionary America," *Signs* 13, no. 1 (Autumn 1987): 37-58, for a similar view.

13. McAlexander, "American Eve," 257.

14. Norton, *Liberty's Daughters*, 298.

15. For an extreme statement of this view applied to the antebellum South, see Catherine Clinton, *The Plantation Mistress: Woman's World in the Old South* (New York: Pantheon Books, 1982), 123-138. Clinton argues, "The campaign to improve women's education was linked to a heightened awareness of the importance of their reproductive role, rather than to any improvement in their political or economic status." *Plantation Mistress*, 124. Linda K. Kerber, "The Republican Mother: Women and the Enlightenment—An American Perspective," *American Quarterly* 28 (Summer 1976): 187-205, and Bloch, "American Feminine Ideals," apply this view in a more temperate manner to the 1790s.

16. William Kenrick, *The Whole Duty of Woman* (9th ed., Philadelphia, 1794; Evans #27181), 19; see the *Dictionary of National Biography* for his life. Herman R. Lantz et al., "Pre-Industrial Patterns in the Colonial Family in America: A Content Analysis of Colonial Magazines," *American Sociological Review* 33, no. 3 (June 1968): 413-426; Lantz et al., "The Preindustrial Family in America: A Further Examination of Early Magazines," *American Journal of Sociology* 79, no. 3 (November 1973): 566-588; Lantz et al., "The American Family in the Preindustrial Period: From Base Lines in History to Change, *American Sociological Review* 40, no. 1 (Feb. 1975): 21-36; Nancy F. Cott, "Passionlessness: An Interpretation of Victorian Sexual Ideology, 1790-1850," may be found in *Signs: A Journal of Women in Culture and Society* 4, no. 2 (Winter 1978): 219-236, and in *A Heritage of Her Own*, Cott and Pleck, eds., 162-181; Smith-Rosenberg, "Hysterical Woman."

17. Norton, *Liberty's Daughters*, 64-65, 117.

18. Clinton, *Plantation Mistress*, 97.

19. Margaret A. Nash, "Rethinking Republican Motherhood: Benjamin Rush and the Young Ladies' Academy of Philadelphia," *Journal of the Early Republic* 17, no. 2 (Summer 1997): 171-191.

20. James, *Changing Ideas*, 127, 135.

21. James, *Changing Ideas*, 39-40, 126-127.

22. Norton, "Evolution of White Women's Experience," 616-618; Jan Lewis, "The Republican Wife: Virtue and Seduction in the Early Republic," *William and Mary Quarterly* 44, no. 4 (Oct. 1987): 689.

23. Kerber, "Republican Mother," 196-197. For a recent restatement of this theme, emphasizing the "republican mother" concept's roots in evangelical religion,

sentimental and Romantic novels, Lockean psychology, and Scottish "civil jurisprudence," see Rosemarie Zagarri, "Morals, Manners, and the Republican Mother," *American Quarterly* 44 (June 1992): 192-215, and Zagarri, "The Rights of Man and Woman in Post-Revolutionary America," *William and Mary Quarterly*, 3d Ser., 55, no. 2 (April 1998): 203-230.

24. Kerber, *Women of the Republic*, 13, 28, 30-31, 80, 227, 251-257; Crane, "Dependence in the Era of Independence: The Role of Women in a Republic," 255-258.

25. Kerber, "Republican Mother," 202-203.

26. Kerber, "Republican Mother," 203; Crane, "Dependence in the Era of Independence: The Role of Women in a Republic," 267-268, quote at 268; Hoff-Wilson, "Dancing Dogs," 226. Kerber unconvincingly concludes that men perceived the idea of "Republican Motherhood" as a threat to their political power. It was a "revolutionary invention" that "justified an extension of women's . . . participation in the civic culture." "Republican Mother," 204. She extends to the present the adversarial connection between men and the "Republican Mother": "The ambivalent relationship between motherhood and citizenship would be one of the most lasting, and most paradoxical, legacies of the revolutionary generation." Kerber, "Republican Mother," 205.

27. Lawrence J. Friedman, *Inventors of the Promised Land* (New York: Knopf, 1975), 112-113; Barbara Welter, "The Cult of True Womanhood, 1820-1860," *American Quarterly* 18 (Summer 1966): 151-174. For information on the *Columbian Magazine*, see Frank L. Mott, *A History of American Magazines, 1741-1850* (Cambridge, Mass.: Harvard University Press, 1966), 94-99. See also William J. Free, *The Columbian Magazine and American Literary Nationalism* (The Hague: Mouton, 1968), 26.

28. Friedman, *Inventors of the Promised Land*, 116. See also Mott, *History of American Magazines*, 64-67.

29. Welter, "Cult of True Womanhood," 152; Gerda Lerner, "The Lady and the Mill Girl: Changes in the Status of Women in the Age of Jackson, 1800-1840," *Midcontinent American Studies Journal* 10 (Spring 1969): 5-14, reprinted in Cott and Pleck, eds., *A Heritage of Her Own*, 182-196. For similar interpretations, see also Marlene LeGates, "The Cult of Womanhood in Eighteenth-Century Thought," *Eighteenth-Century Studies* 10 (Fall 1976): 21-39, which is primarily concerned with European views of women as potentially rational. Their "amiability" and virtue were male constructs and under male control. See Ann Douglas, "The Fashionable Diseases: Woman's Complaints and their Treatment in Nineteenth Century America," *Journal of Interdisciplinary History* 4 (Summer 1973): 25-52, and Douglas, *The Feminization of American Culture* (New York: Knopf, 1977); Keith Melder, "Ladies Bountiful," *New York History* 48 (July 1967): 233-254; and Sylvia Strauss, *'Traitors to the Masculine Cause': The Men's Campaign for Women's Rights* (Westport, Conn.: Greenwood Press, 1982), a discussion of British reform, finds that as late as the 1840s, even among male liberals, "the ideal of womanhood, despite the concession of better education, was distinctly Dickensian; that is to

say, women were to be gentle, self-sacrificing, docile creatures whose prime function it was to minister to men." Strauss, *Traitors*, 139.

30. Carl N. Degler, "What Ought to Be and What Was: Women's Sexuality in the Nineteenth Century," *American Historical Review* 79, no. 5 (Dec. 1974): 1467-1490; Degler, *At Odds: Women and the Family in America from the Revolution to the Present* (New York: Oxford University Press, 1980); Barbara Berg, *The Remembered Gate: The Origins of American Feminism: The Woman and the City, 1800-1860* (New York: Oxford University Press, 1978); McAlexander, "Creation of the American Eve"; Ellen K. Rothman, *Hands and Hearts: A History of Courtship in America* (New York: Basic Books, 1984); Laura McCall, "'The Reign of Brute Force is Now Over': A Content Analysis of *Godey's Lady's Book*, 1830-1860, *Journal of the Early Republic* 9, no. 2 (Summer 1989): 217-236; McCall, "'With All the Trembling, Rapturous Feelings of a Lover': Men, Women, and Sexuality in American Literature, 1820-1860," *Journal of the Early Republic* 14, no. 1 (Spring 1994): 71-89.

31. Degler, *At Odds*, 251; John S. Haller, Jr., and Robin M. Haller, *The Physician and Sexuality in Victorian America* (Urbana, Ill.: University of Illinois Press, 1974), 92-94; Otho T. Beall, "*Aristotle's Master Piece* in America: A Landmark in the Folklore of Medicine," *William and Mary Quarterly* 20, no. 2 (April 1963): 207-222.

32. Haller and Haller, *Physician and Sexuality*, 96; Degler, *At Odds*, 253.

33. For the seamier side of Victorian sexuality, see Ronald Pearsall, *The Worm in the Bud: The World of Victorian Sexuality* (Harmondsworth, Eng.: Penguin Books, 1983).

34. McAlexander, "Creation of the American Eve," 253; McCall, "'Reign of Brute Force,'" 217-222.

35. McCall, "Men, Women, and Sexuality," 82. For a similar view, see Karen Lystra, *Searching the Heart: Women, Men, and Romantic Love in Nineteenth-Century America* (New York: Oxford University Press, 1989).

36. McCall, "'Reign of Brute Force is Now Over,'" 221.

37. McCall, "'Reign of Brute Force is Now Over,'" 225, 226, 231; Mott, *American Magazines, 1741-1850*, 580-598; Douglas, *Feminization of American Culture*.

38. McCall, "'Reign of Brute Force is Now Over,'" 234, 236. Kelley, *Private Woman, Public Stage*; Nancy F. Cott, *The Bonds of Womanhood: 'Woman's Sphere' in New England, 1780-1835* (New Haven: Yale University Press, 1977).

39. John Tebbel, *The American Magazine: A Compact History* (New York: Hawthorn Books, 1969), 12-13, quote at 13.

40. Mott, *American Magazines, 1741-1850*, 103.

41. Mott, *American Magazines, 1741-1850*, 30.

42. Frank L. Mott, *American Journalism: A History, 1690-1960*, 3d ed. (New York: Macmillan, 1962), 139-140; Lyon N. Richardson, *A History of Early American Magazines, 1741-1789* (New York: Thomas Nelson and Sons, 1931), 272; Tebbel, *American Magazine*, 13.

43. James, *Changing Ideas About Women*, xxviii. All of the writers cited in this paragraph have already been mentioned except for Anne Firor Scott, *The Southern*

Lady: From Pedestal to Politics, 1830-1930 (Chicago: University of Chicago Press, 1970).

44. Benson, *Women in Eighteenth-Century America*, 168-169.

45. We will briefly survey the following magazines in our conclusion: the *Columbian Magazine* (1786-1792), which Carey also began in Philadelphia; Boston's *Massachusetts Magazine* (1789-1796), founded by Isaiah Thomas, a great newspaper editor and book publisher; and Philadelphia's *Lady's Magazine*, which lasted only from 1792 to 1793, and was edited by the relatively unknown W. Gibbons. These magazines were chosen because they were contemporary with the *American Museum* and devoted substantial attention to "women's issues." See Mott, *American Magazines, 1741-1850*, 30-31, 65-66, 94-99, 108-111.

46. Carroll Smith-Rosenberg, "Dis-Covering the Subject of the 'Great Constitutional Discussion,'" 1786-1789," *Journal of American History* 79 (Dec. 1992): 841-873, esp. 856-873, briefly assesses the *American Museum*'s attitudes toward women from a radical feminist viewpoint—mixed with poststructuralism—opposed to my own. Linda Kerber's recent essay, "'I Have Don . . . Much to Carrey on the War': Women and the Shaping of Republican Ideology After the American Revolution," in *Women and Politics in the Age of the Democratic Revolution*, Harriet B. Applewhite and Darline G. Levy, eds. (Ann Arbor: University of Michigan Press, 1990), 227-257, ascribes a more powerfully autonomous role to women after the Revolution than in her previous studies. Though she concludes that the American Revolutionaries erected a modified patriarchy that did little to improve the condition of women, she finds that Judith Sargent Murray and other unheralded individuals, mostly Quakers, intermittently voiced a demand for women's rights. In contrast to female French Revolutionary militants, American women acted as individuals rather than collectively.

Chapter 2

Mathew Carey and the *American Museum*

The most recent biographer of Mathew Carey (Jan. 28, 1760-Sept. 16, 1839), editor of the *American Museum*, has called him "the greatest publisher in America in the first two decades of the nineteenth century," and "a central figure in the politics of his time." Especially after the War of 1812, Carey sought to reconcile differences between contending parties—the Democrats and the Federalists—much as he had earlier attempted to assuage conflicts between men and women in the pieces he published decades earlier in the *American Museum*. In general, Carey's consistent aim throughout his publishing career was "to promote national unity and public welfare."[1] He was respected as a nationalist and a promoter of American manufactures as well as an economic theorist, printer, publisher, and a major bookseller.

Born in Dublin, Ireland, Carey was the son of Christopher Carey, a middle-class Roman Catholic banker who had earlier served in the British Navy and as an army contractor. Carey's younger brother, James, joined him in Philadelphia in the 1790s. James published the radical democratic newspaper, the *United States Recorder,* until 1799, when the government quashed it under the Sedition Act . Both Mathew and his brother were well-educated. But as a result of a childhood fall, Mathew was lame for the rest of his life, and suffered from shyness as a boy. He had always wanted to be a printer and bookseller. He entered this trade against his father's wishes, apprenticing himself to Thomas McDonnel, whom he joined, at the age of seventeen, as co-publisher of the radical, pro-American and anti-English *Hibernian Journal*. Carey's first essay was a diatribe against the practice of dueling. In 1779, enraged by the oppression of Irish Catholics, he wrote a pamphlet in their defense that aroused the anger of the British as well as conservative Catholics. His father discreetly smuggled him to Paris, where his pro-American reputation gained him the friendship of Benjamin Franklin and the Marquis de Lafayette. He worked briefly at Franklin's printing press at Passy, returned to Dublin in 1780 and edited such anti-English newspapers as the *Freeman's Journal* and (in 1783) the *Volunteer's Journal*, which was subsidized by his father. The newspaper favored Irish independence, and libeled the Duke of Rutland (Lord Lieutenant of Ireland) and the British House of Commons. Carey led an anti-Protestant demonstration at Daly's Theatre and was imprisoned in London's Newgate. Threatened with renewed prosecution, in September 1784 Carey fled to the United States.[2]

Arriving in Philadelphia almost penniless, Carey was befriended by Lafayette, who was visiting the United States. He gave Carey four hundred dollars, which the latter repaid in 1824, when an impoverished Lafayette made a final tour of America. George Washington and Benjamin Franklin also assisted Carey, who began a newspaper, the *Pennsylvania Herald*, on January 25, 1785. In an effort to stimulate circulation, Carey employed an unique journalistic technique, publishing transcripts of the assembly debates (which he took down in shorthand). His paper supported the "Republican" (conservative) party in the legislature, and for this reason, as well as his newspaper's astonishing economic success, his competitor, Colonel Eleazar Oswald, editor of the radical ("Constitutionalist") party paper, the *Independent Gazetteer*, envied and detested him. Oswald ridiculed the Irish in general and Carey's lameness in particular. But when Carey published a biting satire on Oswald called *The Plagi-Scuriliad* in January 1786, Oswald challenged him to a duel, in which Carey was severely wounded in the thigh of his crippled leg and bedridden for a year. Meanwhile, his newspaper gained renown as an advocate of a stronger national government and greater harmony and unity between contending factions.[3]

Ambitious to acquire a nationwide readership, Carey, joined by four other printers, launched the monthly *Columbian Magazine* in September 1786. Carey wrote many of the articles, including a brief biography of General Nathanael Greene in the first issue. The magazine was highly successful and praised by General Washington. But the profits were too meager to satisfy Carey, who left the project in December 1786, after only three months, to begin *The American Museum, or Repository of Ancient and Modern Fugitive Pieces, &c., Prose and Poetical*, whose first issue appeared in January 1787. In search of a national audience, Carey assured his readers that his selections would consist of American newspaper articles of lasting worth, as well as classical literature and excerpts from popular advice books, mixed with original poems and essays by the best American writers on political, economic, and cultural subjects. Although after his first year he could claim about 1,250 subscribers, numbering among them Washington, Franklin, Jefferson, Hamilton, and Madison, many of his accounts were not paid. Nevertheless, his claim that the *American Museum* was an unprofitable venture is dubious, since in 1792 he put out a third edition of volume one. He explained, in his first issue's message "To the Reader":

> It is with some degree of diffidence that I venture to solicit the patronage of the public for the present undertaking, destitute as it is of originality.... I frequently regretted that the perishable nature... entailed oblivion [upon the worthwhile articles contained in newspapers].

He said that Franklin, who was president of the Pennsylvania executive council, felt the same way, and that this had inspired the undertaking.[4]

After printing the last issue of the *American Museum* in December 1792, Carey began a risky and speculative, but eventually prosperous career as a publisher and bookseller. He published radical works of the Enlightenment such as Mary Wollstonecraft's *A Vindication of the Rights of Woman* (1794) and the Marquis de Condorcet's *Outline of an Historical View of the Progress of the Human Mind* (1796), as well as Helen Maria Williams's more conservative *Letters Containing a Sketch of the Politics of France* (1796). He was painfully aware that great stamina was required to succeed as a publisher in the new republic. When his younger brother James meandered between Baltimore, Richmond, and Savannah struggling to set up a printing enterprise, Mathew reproached him: "Nothing but perseverance will do in so arduous an undertaking as the Establishment of a News Paper, and I am fearful that you do not possess enough of that Quality to secure you from wandering." Historian Michael Durey perceives Carey as an experimental, radical printer, an émigré who "was probably the most prolific publisher and certainly the greatest risk-taker in the publishing world."[5]

Though Carey complained that he had set the subscription rates for the *American Museum* too low (as he put it, "two dollars and forty cents per annum, for which I gave two volumes containing each from 500 to 550 pages"), in addition to enduring remiss subscribers who "lived in remote situations," he had actually printed too many copies. Carey also insisted that the Post Office Act of 1792, which failed to include magazines within its purview and thereby subjected them to the same exorbitant rates charged personal letters, forced him to close down the magazine.[6] But whether or not he profited from publishing the *American Museum*, its reputation as the finest journal in the country, and the praise he received from President Washington and leading Federalists, helped him in future enterprises. Carey also used the knowledge of book distribution he had gained as publisher of the *American Museum* when he later began book publishing on an unprecedented scale in the new nation.[7]

Carey's first major book venture, *A Short Account of the Malignant Fever* (Philadelphia, 1793), which examined the disastrous yellow fever epidemic in Philadelphia in the summer of 1793, combined an entrepreneurial spirit and compassion for the sick. Following his on-the-spot report, *A Desultory Account of the Yellow Fever*, *A Short Account* was very popular, going through four editions extending into 1794. Carey exported copies of these books overseas without waiting for orders, knowing that the topic was sensational and newsworthy. Indeed, *A Short Account* was translated into French, German, Dutch, and Italian. Carey and his friend, banker Stephen Girard, were members of a health committee that assisted victims of the contagion. Seeking to inform the public on critical yet obscure medical topics as well as to make profits, in 1793 Carey published several books concerned with yellow fever and rabies. His business partners' descendants, Lea and Febiger, publish medical books exclusively. They are the oldest publishing house in America. Over the course of his career, Carey published forty-five medical books, some with hand-colored plates that became landmarks of American book arts.[8]

Suffering financial disappointment in publishing magazines such as the *Columbian* and the *American Museum*, which, he said, netted him only four hundred dollars by the end of 1792, Carey decided that bookselling was the way to wealth. He formulated innovative marketing and sales techniques. Importing large quantities of books from Dublin, London, and Edinburgh, he expanded his Philadelphia bookstore into one of the largest in the country. In 1794-95 Carey branched out into publishing as well as bookselling. One of the first publishers to rely on unanticipated purchases instead of prior subscription sales, Carey daringly printed two multi-volume, costly works in large numbers: William Guthrie's *A New System of Modern Geography* (2 vols., 1794) and Oliver Goldsmith's *History of the Earth, and Animated Nature* (4 vols., 1795). Carey gambled that works so ornate and elaborate would be able to find a market in Philadelphia as well as London. His venture failed.[9]

Carey was saved from debtors' prison by the famous Parson Mason Locke Weems, an ordained Anglican minister who made his living as a traveling book salesman in rural Virginia and Maryland. He was to become famous as the author of *The Life of Washington*, with its legendary cherry-tree episode. Carey hired Weems to sell the Guthrie and Goldsmith volumes in the South and West, a task only he had the proficiency in salesmanship to accomplish. Hiring subagents to advertise the volumes in taverns and village stores, he succeeded in selling the high-priced books in the trading towns south and west of Philadelphia and saved Carey from bankruptcy. However, when Carey entrusted Weems with undertaking subscriptions for specific books and selling books he sent him on consignment, the results were disappointing. Carey's books were too erudite and dull for most rural Americans. At Weems's suggestion, he published more popular titles, such as almanacs and chapbooks. But Weems himself, with his *Life of George Washington*, first published at Baltimore in 1800, authored the first nineteenth-century bestseller. Carey bought his copyright in 1809 and published it after Weems had sold more than sixteen editions of 5,000 copies each.[10] However, Carey's publishing empire was still insecure, especially its "southern network."[11]

Continuing to embark on original enterprises, Carey published the first American atlases in 1794-1795. They contained maps of the United States and Europe; the latter were designed to help readers comprehend the strategies of French Revolutionary military campaigns. He followed these with pocket atlases. In 1802 he published the first American guidebook with road maps, and titled it *The Travellers' Directory*. As early as 1790 Carey had exhibited his risk-taking nature, publishing the first Roman Catholic Bible in America, the Douay translation of the Vulgate in quarto. He charged six dollars per copy by subscription, putting out an edition of five hundred. He sought to recoup his financial fortunes in 1800 by reproducing the King James Bible in quarto, in a style similar to the standard Edinburgh edition.[12]

Carey's shifting political loyalties may have cost him business. During the 1790s he had supported a stronger national government and proposed the expansion of American trade and manufactures. An ardent advocate of the new U.S. Constitution, he had endeared himself to Washington, Hamilton, and other Federalist leaders, earning their support for the *American Museum*. But during the 1790s Carey's sympathies turned toward the emerging Jeffersonian Republican party. As an Irish Catholic, he hated the British government, with which the Federalist party had become identified. Despite his support for Hamilton's centralizing economic program, by 1794 he had chosen the Anglophobic adherents of the French Revolution, the Democratic-Republicans. He published the *American Remembrancer* (1795-1796), a subtle attack on the Federalist-sponsored Jay Treaty. Carey went so far as to denounce Washington for ratifying the law. He composed an *Address to the House of Representatives* (1796), urging the defeat of the Treaty. He and his brother James, editor of the radical Democratic *United States Recorder*, were links between Jefferson and the Irish community.[13]

As a result of his switch to the Democrats, Carey found himself engaged in a scurrilous feud with "Peter Porcupine," the Federalist pamphleteer from England, William Cobbett. When Cobbett attacked him in the press and his Federalist creditors hounded him in 1799, Carey thought of selling his publishing house and retiring to the country. But his successful counterattack on Cobbett saved his bank credit at a time when he was dangerously overextended. After Jefferson won the presidency in 1801, Carey's political power increased. He won a seat on the board of directors of the Bank of Pennsylvania, and never again had to worry about loans. But he earned the enmity of left-wing Jeffersonians when he supported the recharter of the Hamiltonian Bank of the United States in 1811, and after the Bank's recharter in 1816.[14]

The War of 1812 tested Carey's hopes for national unity and the increased economic growth of his adopted country. He was angered by New England Federalist opposition to the war and its merchants' illicit trade with Great Britain during the conflict. At the same time, he hoped to conciliate the conflicting parties and sections and promote union at war's end. In 1814 he wrote *The Olive Branch*, a lengthy work that criticized both the Democratic and Federalist parties for insufficient patriotism and urged them to unite in prosecuting the war and building a stronger national government to promote future economic growth. The book was very popular, running to ten editions in the years from 1814-1816, and sold more copies than any other political work in the United States before 1820. Chiding President Madison and his fellow Democrats for what he considered their sheepishness in enforcing the Embargo Act and their apathy toward Eastern disaffection during the War of 1812, Carey advocated draconian measures that curbed the freedom of speech of disunionists and supporters of the British. He feared that the New England states might secede when the Hartford Convention met in December 1814. *The Olive Branch* criticized Madison's inactivity in the face of this threat. Since Carey praised the average New Englander for being a patriotic farmer and attributed disunionist sentiments primarily to mercantile leaders and hireling Federalist journalists and politicians, his book may be viewed as a nonpartisan appeal for national unity. At the same time, Carey warned that old-fashioned Jeffersonian states'-rights, Antifederalist ideas were now being turned against nationalism by their Federalist opponents. He praised the War of 1812 as a righteous conflict on behalf of neutral rights and against the impressment of American seamen by the British Navy. Despising those New Englanders who opposed the war, refused to fight, and traded with the enemy, as those in Massachusetts and Vermont did, he depicted them as "Jacobins" and disorganizers.[15]

Despite *The Olive Branch's* antipathy to Federalist disunionists, Carey urged Madison to encourage their support by appointing moderate Federalists to his Cabinet and calling a Unionist convention to offset the Hartford Convention. During the war Carey was at the height of his power as a publisher, and possessed the nation's most effective and widespread system for the sale and distribution of books. Extracts from *The Olive Branch* were printed in newspapers and magazines. Thomas Jefferson wrote Carey, praising the book for "exhibiting to both [parties] their political errors." In denouncing the states'-rights, parochialist element in both parties that opposed measures of political and economic nationalism, Carey aroused the ire of William Duane, the radical Jeffersonian editor of the Philadelphia *Aurora*, a newspaper that opposed the recharter of the Bank of the United States and taxes to fund a larger navy. Historian Edward C. Carter II believes that the Democrats gained votes in state and national elections in 1815-1816 as a result of *The Olive Branch*'s publication. When Carey died in 1839, newspaper obituaries heaped special praise on the role *The Olive Branch* had played in spreading nationalist sentiments and conciliating the Federalist and Democratic-Republican parties after the War of 1812.[16]

Although *The Olive Branch* was indeed a bestseller, Carey had long since achieved economic security. After 1800, relying less on his southern and rural western markets and more on his northern and urban markets, he reaped greater profits. Following the emergence of political parties during the 1790s, few printers were likely to achieve economic independence by lobbying with political leaders for government contracts, since few officials possessed abundant patronage. Moreover, the increase in the number of printers residing at the capital decreased the likelihood of profit. During the national government's stay in New York City from 1789-1790, six New York printers shared its printing, consisting of a mere twenty-six official publications. After the capital moved to Philadelphia in 1791, eight Philadelphia printers, including Carey, who obtained few assignments from the Washington Administration, shared seventy-three printing jobs. Most of the work went to the firm of Francis Childs and John Swaine of New York, who opened a shop in Philadelphia in order to keep their previous virtual monopoly of government contracts. By 1795, the number of U.S. government printing jobs had grown to one hundred thirty-one, and there were thirty-four printer/publishers to produce them. Ten years later, Philadelphia had fifty-one printer/publishers. Although the "politicization of print," as Rosalind Remer calls it, discouraged printers from relying solely on official patronage for support, government printing contracts were still preferable to printing for individual patrons or relying on a single political party for business. As in the colonial period, government contracts provided printers with an economic safety net and public prestige. Fortunately for Carey, President Jefferson, admiring his work and his devotion to republicanism, granted him several government printing contracts.[17]

During the 1790s, Carey's political writings and his letters to friends and family in Ireland revealed boundless enthusiasm and determination, despite the *American Museum*'s cessation. At a time when printers and booksellers were both involved in publishing, Carey was a bookseller, printer, and publisher. Like his quest to balance agrarian and manufacturing interests under a strong republican government's stewardship on the national level, Carey's undertaking to build a flourishing printing and bookselling business in his adopted country showed his confidence that his ambitions would be realized on a personal level. Notwithstanding the considerable risk involved, Carey's goal was to provide the new nation with books, finding titles that would sell easily and printing them cheaply enough to compete with widely available imported editions. He required a busy retail establishment from which to vend his wares, and buoyant, far-flung markets where they might be sold. He needed a wide assortment of books with a guaranteed steady sale, obtaining them by exchanging his holdings with other publishers.[18]

Seeking to secure a stable profit margin, Carey became a founding member of the Philadelphia Company of Printers and Booksellers, a trade association to fix the price of books sold, which met for the first time on July 4, 1791. Carey served on the executive committee of the Company during its brief life from 1791-1794. Only a few members of the union published books consistently through the 1790s: Carey; Joseph Cruikshank; Thomas Dobson (first American publisher of the *Encyclopedia Britannica*); Benjamin Johnson; Henry and Patrick Rice; and William Young. Each of these men was listed in the Philadelphia directory as a printer/bookseller or bookseller/stationer. Although Carey simultaneously pursued the crafts of publisher, bookseller, and printer, the Company's membership was less versatile, and the organization dissolved in 1794 as a result of conflicts of interest between printers and publishers. Eight years later (February 1802), Carey organized the Philadelphia Company of Booksellers, whose primary interests were publishing and book-selling. Members of the company agreed to publish books under its logo.[19]

Also in 1802—perhaps the busiest year of his career—Carey secured the contract for publishing the laws of Pennsylvania, with the help of his agent, veteran Philadelphia newspaper publisher Francis Bailey, whom Carey rewarded with the printing job, permitting him to use his printing shop at Lancaster. In the same year Carey finally gained a long-sought appointment to the board of directors of the Bank of Pennsylvania.[20]

Eventually, Carey entirely relinquished job printing for publishing. He distributed to others the production of most of the books and pamphlets he published, employing both local and country printers. As early as June 1794, Carey had begun to transform himself from a moderately successful printer and bookseller to a prosperous publisher. He sold imported books, American books he obtained through exchanges with other booksellers, and books he published himself.[21]

Promoting the expansion of Philadelphia's public school system, which effected increased literacy and hence an augmented market for published matter, prominent Philadelphia printers like Carey and William

Duane demanded greater popular access to public education. Furthermore, they were eager to supply American textbooks for the budding public school system. Reprints of English and domestic schoolbooks became a mainstay of the infant American publishing trade; Carey even mailed a copy of one of his firm's "republican" textbooks to President-elect Jefferson for his "examination."[22]

Although Carey claimed he believed that a publisher should be cautious in what he chose to publish and publish copies in moderate numbers, he often failed to follow his advice. As a result of overproduction, he was constantly in debt, either putting out too many copies of a particular book or too many titles as a whole. Ultimately, Carey gained economic independence by publishing Bibles in various formats and fonts, leaving the type standing so that he could print copies on demand. His financial success was derived from this one book, a book that would always find a market and which, when produced cheaply—as he did by use of the standing type—could successfully compete with British imports.[23]

Perhaps Carey's most lucrative venture was the production of Bibles. After publishing the first Catholic Bible in the United States in 1790, he printed and sold at a cheap price an elegant quarto King James family Bible in 1800, replete with beautiful illustrations, making a great profit. Setting out to dominate the nation's Bible business, after the success of his King James Bible he purchased the standing type for a duodecimo school Bible. Carey printed regular editions of these Bibles until 1820, offering them in catalogs. He listed the Bibles by numbers so that they could be identified according to their formats, bindings, and other "extras," such as psalms and Apocrypha. His success in selling Bibles from 1800-1820 lifted him out of debt and enabled him to undertake larger publishing ventures.[24]

In addition to the *American Museum*, Carey's publication of separate works of fiction contributed to the growth of a sense of American literary nationalism as well as to his personal fortune. He published and republished poems like John Trumbull's mock-heroic epic about the unfortunate Tory, *M'Fingal*, first published in 1775 and expanded in 1782. He republished this work when he arrived in the United States, first in a chapbook (i.e., pamphlet) edition in 1787 and then in a larger format in 1791. In 1789 he published a collection of poems by another "Hartford Wit," David Humphreys, and he later distributed several anthologies of American verse, such as the *Columbian Muse* (1794). Although Carey's most recent biographer concludes that "no publisher did more to encourage American writers in the federal period," by the 1790s Carey turned more to English authors, who were more popular than American. He began to specialize in cheap American editions of English novels, and published almost 1,100 books (mostly by English writers) from 1785 to 1821, an average of about thirty annually. One of his most successful ventures was an American edition of Susanna Rowson's best-selling novel, *Charlotte Temple*, which he published in 1794, three years after it appeared in England. Despite his desire to encourage American productions, Carey knew he had to give his readers what they wanted.[25]

After 1820, Carey limited his business activities and increased his involvement in social and political affairs. He had always been prominent in Philadelphia organizations, creating the Hibernian Society for the Relief of Emigrants from Ireland in 1792 and helping to found the first Sunday-school society in the United States in 1796. After the business Panic of 1819, he formed an organization in support of a protective tariff, the Philadelphia Society for the Promotion of National Industry. In Carey's view, the United States' promising economic growth rate and the active state and federal government promotion of roads and canals evinced a unique opportunity to set a republican example for a world too familiar with tyranny. He wrote dozens of articles and pamphlets in favor of a higher tariff during the 1820s, in addition to lending his support to the building of railroads, canals, and other internal improvements. In 1821 Carey turned the management of his printing business over to his son, Henry Charles Carey, another avid economic nationalist, and his son-in-law Isaac Lea, and devoted all his energies to social issues. Avidly concerned to achieve social justice, he gained a reputation in Philadelphia for charity and philanthropy. When he died in 1839 at the age of seventy-nine, his funeral procession was, except for the multimillionaire banker Stephen Girard's, the largest the city had ever seen. Among Carey's last acts was his fight to preserve the Union against South Carolina's threat of nullification in the 1830s. He composed a series of twenty-five pamphlets denying that a state could declare a law of Congress "null and void" within its borders.[26] He had never wavered in his goal, first pronounced in the pages of the *American Museum*, to promote the cause of national unity between the Union's genders and sections.

****

The *American Museum* quickly achieved distinction for a diverse array of essays, political literature, brief narratives, and poetry. During its life as a monthly periodical, from January 1787 to December 1792, it experienced a change in its title. From 1787 to1788 Carey called it *The American Museum, or Repository of Ancient and Modern Fugitive Pieces, &c. Prose and Poetical*. When Carey changed its title in 1789 he sought to reflect the journal's change in its editorial policy, providing more original contributions (about one-third of the magazine's contents) and more short fiction, making it more like "magazines in general," as he explained in the preface to volume eight. After 1789, the magazine assumed a much longer, more comprehensive title: *The American Museum, or, Universal Magazine; Containing Essays on Agriculture–Commerce–Manufactures–Politics–Morals–and Manners. Sketches of National Characters–Natural and Civil History–and Biography. Law Information–Public Papers–Proceedings of Congress–Intelligence. Moral Tales–Ancient and Modern Poetry, &c., &c.*[27]

Dedicating his first issue "To the Patrons of Liberty, Virtue, Art and Science," Carey offered his second volume to the Marquis de Lafayette, who had often befriended him. Carey's bibliographer, William Clarkin, calls the *Museum* "one of his most successful productions." The *Museum* lasted six years, a substantial time for those days, and received the commendations of leading political figures like George Washington, John Dickinson, and William Livingston; it boasted Alexander Hamilton, Thomas Jefferson, Benjamin Franklin, and James Madison among its subscribers. According to historian Robert W. Sellen, this distinguished roster of readers suggests that the *Museum* "became a kind of forum for the exchange of ideas among Americans of prestige and influence."[28] It is therefore appropriate to utilize its articles and essays to gauge popular attitudes toward women among the literate male population.

Some experts regard the *American Museum* as the first U.S. literary magazine, a distinction with which others might credit the *Columbian Magazine*, despite its emphasis on nonfiction. Carey was willing to help American writers in their quest for autonomy and artistic independence from England. He printed poems and essays by Philip Freneau, Francis Hopkinson, John Trumbull, David Humphreys, and many others, in tandem with political and economic essays expounding nationalist opinions.[29]

Political materials predominated during the first few years of the *American Museum*'s life. Extolling the preservation of great documents and historical works and their diffusion among a new generation, Carey retrospectively printed Thomas Paine's *Common Sense* (1776) in his first issue, as well as Benjamin Rush's more recent essay, "The Revolution is Not Over" and Benjamin Franklin's "Consolation for America." These were extremely patriotic, nationalistic essays, supporting the Revolution and its fruition in the new United States Constitution. The *Museum* printed the Constitution in September 1787, shortly after it appeared in the daily newspapers and before any other magazine, with favorable Federalist commentary by nationalist Tench Coxe. Unlike its competitor, *The Columbian*, the *Museum* tended to print more pro- than anti-Federalist articles, and it generally devoted more space to the debate over the Constitution than any other magazine. Carey professed impartiality, but printed only a few Antifederalist tracts. On the other hand, the *Museum* printed each of the *Federalist Papers*, selected pro-Constitution satires by Hugh Henry Brackenridge from his newspaper, the *Pittsburgh Gazette*, and Francis Hopkinson's poem, "The New Roof" (August 1788). Carey's support of the Federalists continued through 1792. He praised Hamilton's fiscal system and the creation of the Bank of the United States. However, his Anglophobia led him to leave the Federalist party in 1795, when he published the *American Remembrancer*, a series of articles in opposition to the pro-British Jay's Treaty negotiated by the Washington Administration. In 1799, seeking to defuse tensions aroused by the undeclared war between the United States and Revolutionary France, which was simultaneously fighting the British, Carey brought out *The American Museum, or, Annual Register of Fugitive Pieces, Ancient and Modern For the Year 1798*, which was printed for him on June 20, 1799. This is, not altogether correctly, sometimes referred to as the thirteenth volume of the magazine, though there is really no connection between them.[30]

Like the *Columbian Magazine* and many others, the *American Museum* commented on the social customs of the period, although unfortunately, unlike the *New-York Magazine*, it seldom reviewed plays. It castigated the evils of dueling, to which Carey had been opposed since youth, even before Oswald severely wounded him in a duel. Drunkenness was also decried in its pages. Carey took the liberal, "enlightened" side of such issues as Black slavery, printing an English translation of a lengthy French essay entitled "The Negro Equalled by Few Europeans," as well as the constitution and list of officers of the Pennsylvania Society for the Abolition of Slavery. The *Museum* also espoused penal reform and proposed uniform state licensing procedures for physicians.[31]

His contributors' insistence that thrift, frugality, and the punctual payment of taxes were the best ways to maintain national stability, republicanism, and public virtue was consistent with Carey's support of domestic manufacturing and a popular boycott of foreign luxuries. The *Museum* tried to encourage discussion of extensive pubic education projects like a "federal university" and supported free public schools to advance equality of opportunity. Many of its writers, such as Francis Hopkinson and Benjamin Rush, rejected the study of "dead languages" like Greek and Latin. This idea accorded with the emergent democratic credo.[32]

Both the *American Museum* and its competitors devoted a modicum of attention to discussing the proper education for women. Noah Webster's *American Magazine* favored "female instruction" in English, arithmetic, and geography, but proposed to prohibit their reading passionate, prurient literature like novels. Benjamin Rush added penmanship, vocal music, dancing, history, and moral essays to the list of subjects proper for female edification. More than other magazines, the *American Museum* forthrightly defended women's prerogative to read and write whatever they wished.[33]

Male chauvinism and sexism occasionally manifested themselves in these journals. For instance, in 1788 Webster's *American Magazine* advised in "An Address to the Ladies":

> To be *lovely* you must be content to be *women*; to be mild, social, and sentimental—to be acquainted with all that belongs to your department—and leave the masculine virtues, and the profound researches of study to the province of the other sex.

Webster thought that women were neither physically nor emotionally equipped for a life of diligent study.[34] As Frank L. Mott dryly comments about the general white male middle-class attitude towards women at this time: "Women were being advised how to be perfect ladies so continually that at least some of them must have grown weary of it."[35]

It is hoped that our examination of the writing in the *American Museum* may help us discern the extent to which Carey's magazine followed these stodgy formulas. Nevertheless, the editors of all these periodicals often thought they were catering to women's literary preferences. They were striving for their fiscal support, no matter how quaint or condescending we may consider their statements that women were incapable of undergoing "the rigour of intense study," as *The Lady's Magazine, or Repository of Entertaining Knowledge* remarked in 1792.[36]

Most magazines engaged in an endless discourse on women's fashions from as early as the 1750s. The *American Museum* joined them in insisting that women adopt simpler, more "American" styles of dress and avoid purchasing or imitating extravagant, ornate, "aristocratic" European fashions.[37] On the whole, Mott concludes, despite their often dull contents and their tendency to reprint old material, the *American Museum* and its contemporaries are "invaluable as a mirror of the current ideas of writing and literary taste, and as a picture of the social and political life of America during the years they cover." Moreover, they managed to consolidate much of the most important American writing of the time between their covers.[38]

In terms of political coverage, the *American Museum* demonstrated its editor's sophistication, transcending ethnic and parochial boundaries to achieve a national and nationalistic outlook. Not only did the *Museum* support the Federalists against the Antifederalists, one of its most prominent themes in the realm of American foreign policy after the national government became operational was advocacy of a strong union that would promote security and prosperity at home and attain respect and public credit abroad. While advocating the expansion of American foreign trade, the *American Museum* maintained that the United States's moral, economic, and geographical superiority to and isolation from Europe justified political isolation from the Old World's wars and problems, and its rulers' oppression of the unprivileged. As the editor, Carey urged, through his selections and later by means of his contributors' original essays, that Americans develop a national character independent of Great Britain, the former Mother Country, the prerequisite of true national greatness. Articles published in the *American Museum* reflected both American resentment and suspicion of undemocratic, monarchical European governments and a patriotic desire that the United States expand its territory and commerce. The *Museum*'s early nationalist and Federalist stance expounded the views of the Washington Administration and the U.S.'s "governing group," as Robert W. Sellen calls it, helping to spread nationalistic "ideas among Americans of the sort we now call opinion molders."[39]

In its political as well as social (and gender-related) expressions of opinion, by promoting American republicanism in opposition to European monarchy and extolling American exceptionalism (uniqueness) and isolation from foreign influences, the *American Museum* helped shape traditions and attitudes which survived for centuries in American culture.

Carey consciously modeled his magazine on (John) *Almon's Remem-*

brancer of London, a distinguished monthly compilation of previously published essays, poetry, and short fiction. The *American Museum* was likewise conceived to give prominence to pieces from American newspapers which rose above ephemera and deserved a national audience, as well as original poems and essays by the foremost American writers on political, economic, and cultural subjects. Though Carey aimed to distribute his magazine nationally, his objective was impeded by the immature state of business, transportation, and communication in the young republic. Unfortunately, disgruntled subscribers often withheld payment to express their anger at delays and irregularities in receiving copies, forcing Carey to sue them in court. Carey claimed he made no profit from the *American Museum* despite its popularity and its outstanding reputation because the subscription costs were too low to support the expense of national distribution. In his *Autobiography*, published after his death, Carey lamented the financial failure of his most important enterprise. He sketched a somber picture of his experience:

> Never was more labour bestowed on a work, with less reward . . . . I was times without number, obliged to borrow money to go to the market, and was often unable to pay my journeyman on Saturday . . . . My embarrassments arose from three sources. The subscription was too low. It was only two dollars and forty cents per annum, for which I gave two volumes containing each from 500 to 550 pages . . . . more than half of my subscribers lived in remote situations . . . their remittances so extremely irregular . . . . I printed, moreover, quite too many copies.

Ostensibly a man of high moral standards, Carey uprightly refused to raise the magazine's price or reduce its size in order to cut costs. Impressed by his integrity, James Green observes, "In the end the magazine made no money at all, even though its reputation could not have been higher." The last straw for Carey was the Post Office Act of 1792, which raised the postage for magazines to the same rate as that for letters, whereas under the Confederation they had been lower. Ironically, not only had President Washington's patronage—which consisted of little more than verbal praise—been unable to save the magazine, his administration's Postmaster General, Timothy Pickering, who proposed the law, had administered the *coup de grace*.[40]

On the other hand, Carey's complaints of financial hardship were probably exaggerated. He *must* have profited from the *Museum*, whose circulation, he boasted in the preface to volume two, had increased from less than twenty to about 1,250. He even brought out second and third editions of the first volume in 1788, 1789, and 1792, attesting to its continued popularity. Probably the inequity of the Post Office Act of 1792, together with the remissness of subscribers, made his mind up to finally embark on a more venturesome career as a bookseller and book publisher.[41]

When Carey first began the *Museum*, however, he was determined that it prosper. In 1787 he adopted innovative techniques of advertising his wares, distributing broadsides (leaflets), a bold new method in those days. In a personal plea for patronage, he emphasized the magazine's low price:

> Sir,
> Give me leave respectfully to solicit your patronage for the *American Museum*—a periodical publication, lately established in this city, and calculated to serve the cause of liberty and virtue. To evince the utility and advantages of this work, it may be sufficient to observe, that in the four numbers already published (which cost subscribers only 6s. and non-subscribers 7/6) there have been given entire the following publications:
>
> *Common Sense*, sold for: 2/6
> *M'Fingal* " " 5/0
> *Address to the Armies of America* " " 2/6
> *Poem on the happiness of America* " " 2/6

Although Carey thought the subscription price of $2.40 or eighteen shillings per year for twelve numbers (two volumes), a year's issue, was a bargain, he was aware that hard money was scarce in the United States, which might make payment difficult for his customers. In June 1788, therefore, he announced that he would accept in exchange, "for the accommodation of the friends of literature and science . . . during the present scarcity of specie . . . all kinds of seasonable country produce in payment of sub-scriptions." At this early stage of his business, Carey was willing to compromise with his customers for the sake of future profits.[42]

An additional indication that Carey, ambitious for the success of the *Museum*, probably achieved it despite his later complaints, was his international clientele. Within the continental United States, booksellers distributed the *American Museum* and other Carey publications in New York City, Boston, New Haven, Lancaster, Elizabethtown, New Brunswick, Baltimore, Charleston, and Savannah; and at London, Dublin, Bordeaux, and Amsterdam abroad.[43] As late as 1799, Carey informed prospective customers that complete sets of the *American Museum* were still in print "in twelve octavo volumes, from January 1787, till December 1792, [and] may be had of the publisher hereof, and of Charles Debret, London."[44] An avid entrepreneur, he believed that a market existed for the *American Museum* as late as six years after it had ceased publication.

Eager to exploit the *Museum*'s reputation in order to gain new customers, for the frontispiece of his June 1788 volume Carey printed a testimonial from George Washington himself. Though Washington was not elected president till later in the year, he was still the most popular man in the United States, and he radiated praise. "The *Museum* has met . . . with universal approbation from competent judges," he wrote. "I will venture to pronounce, as my sentiment, that a more useful literary plan has never been undertaken in America, or one more deserving of public encouragement." Washington concluded enthusiastically: "I heartily desire, copies of the *Museum*, might be spread through every city, town, and village in America." Perhaps Washington's acclaim was partly responsible for the printing of second editions of the *Museum*'s 1788 volumes in 1789, 1790, and 1792.[45]

After Carey renamed the periodical the *American Museum, or Universal Magazine* in January 1789, he seemed more intent on gaining official patronage for his journal, dedicating volume five, covering the first half of 1789 (January to June) to Pennsylvania Governor Thomas Mifflin, and volume six, for the half-year from July to December 1789, to President Washington and the members of the Senate and the House of Representatives. He had earlier dedicated volume four to the President.[46]

Nevertheless, while he flattered men in power, Carey continued to experience difficulty with delinquent subscribers. He sent his brother John to Boston in 1789 with a form letter requesting that they pay. Subscribers in Philadelphia paid $2.40 annually, those outside paid ten cents more. Half the annual cost was payable at the time of subscribing. A volume was published every six months, for a total of two volumes per year.[47] The volume for July to December 1792 (number twelve) was the final one, although, as already mentioned, W. & R. Dickson of Lancaster printed a single, similar volume for Carey called *The American Museum, or, annual Register of Fugitive Pieces, ancient and modern, for the year 1798*, in 1799.[48]

In this final issue of the *American Museum*, Carey reiterated what had been his avowed purpose from the outset of his newspaper career, when he stated his desire for reconciliation with Eleazar Oswald, who had severely wounded him in a duel. He stated his desire to present a balanced picture of the Franco-American controversy and the political dispute between the Democratic-Republicans and the Federalists. Much of the 1798 issue was devoted to reprinting newspaper articles that had appeared in 1796 and 1797, critical of John Adams's presidential candidacy and his alleged preference for monarchy. Other essays denounced British violations of America's neutral rights on the high seas and condoned France's adoption of the British policy of seizing American shipping trading with the enemy. Carey's preface explained his intention to present a balanced picture, with an equal number of essays pro and con. Though he failed to make clear which party he supported, he said his own biases had been outweighed by his crusade for impartiality and conciliation between the young republic's contending parties:

> The selection of political essays, was attended with some difficulty. I saw I was in danger of being too much influenced by the natural and unavoidable bias in favour of those opinions and principles which I held myself. I used every effort to avoid this error. I sincerely sought to make an impartial choice, and bring forward the best written productions on both sides, leaving to the reader to decide between the adverse opinions. It is not for me to say whether or not I have succeeded. On that point I await the public verdict. But this much I may venture to assert, that if I have failed, it has not been intentionally.

Aware that his goal of objectivity would be difficult to achieve, Carey nevertheless persevered in trying to present both sides of the issue, as he had done in his discussion of relations between the genders in the past.

As always, his aim was the achievement of national unity. He rejected the support of violent partisans:

> It were idiocy, or worse, to suppose or expect that a work on the plan I have pursued in the selection of the contents of this, should meet with the approbation of either of the parties, the clashing of whose political opinions has arrayed the citizens of the United States in hostile bands against each other. Far from expecting the praise or approbation of men of this description, I deprecate it. Were they to commend, I should suspect that I had failed of accomplishing the end I had proposed.[49]

Literary scholar Albert H. Smyth, a late-Victorian intellectual greatly impressed by the versatility and scope of the articles appearing in Carey's magazine, extolled the *American Museum* as the first Philadelphia periodical to "reflect faithfully the internal state of America," especially in political affairs. By comparison Carey's previous venture, the *Columbian Magazine*, "avoided the serious political problems of the times, and granted too much of its space to agricultural improvements and the beginnings of manufactures." Bestowing perhaps excessive praise, Smyth, accepting the truth of Carey's comment that he never profited from publishing the *American Museum*, sympathetically concluded, "in those years of personal penury and public turmoil, Matthew [*sic*] Carey laid the foundation of the American system of social science."[50]

The following discussion of the *American Museum* is concerned with one particular aspect of its legacy to "American social science," as Smyth calls it: as depicted in its pages, how did middle-class white American men view women in the late 1780s and early 1790s?

Mathew Carey's Feminism

Carey's proto-feminist views were the result of both economic self-interest and personal inclination. His wife, Bridget Flahavan, the twenty-one-year-old daughter of a local Roman Catholic businessman who had been bankrupted by the Revolution, was an "industrious, prudent, and economical" woman. She was a responsible partner whom he trusted with the management of his publishing business when he had to leave town.

They were married on February 24, 1791, and lived happily together for nearly thirty-nine years. Of their nine children, six lived into adulthood. Bridget reputedly exercised a restraining influence on Carey's hot temper. Her maturity and competence undoubtedly fostered his favorable opinion of women.[51]

An astute publisher, Carey was undoubtedly aware that half his reading public consisted of women. He sought to print works that would appeal to them. In 1794 he published the first American edition of Mary Wollstonecraft's *A Vindication of the Rights of Woman* (1792). He always kept in stock books like *The Lady's Pocket Library* (1792), a digest of the standard advice and comportment manuals. He published sentimental novels to entertain his female and proto-feminist market. One of his most important publications was Susanna Rowson's famous American novel, *Charlotte Temple, A Tale of Truth.* Carey printed the first American edition in 1794, pirated from the 1790 London edition. The novel emphasized the triumph of virtue over evil, the latter personified by the male seducer. As the principal American publisher of this novel, which was enormously successful in the United States, Carey, who in 1812 wrote a correspondent that he had already sold over fifty thousand copies, probably made thousands of dollars in profits. He also printed an assortment of music books and children's books, including several editions of Adgate's *Philadelphia Harmony* (1797) and various versions of *Aesop's Fables*, published in 1801, 1810, 1811, and 1812, some containing charming wood engravings. Though Carey's *Lady's Pocket Library* included Dr. John Gregory's prescriptive, patriarchal bestseller, *A Father's Legacy to His Daughters* (1765), which preached women's subordination to fathers and husbands, Carey added a footnote to his edition qualifying Gregory's statement that women in England did not have the option of marrying for love, arguing that this did not apply to America, where love ruled.[52]

After the American Revolution, the ideal of the "Republican Mother," who raised her children in accordance with a republican culture's "manners" and patriotic behavior, became prominent in journalistic rhetoric. The new magazines shared this view—Carey's *Columbian Magazine* (1786) and *American Museum* (1787-1792), as well as Noah Webster's *American Magazine* and Hugh Henry Brackenridge's short-lived *United States Magazine*. They often explicitly addressed their journals to women as well as men, acknowledging the presence of a female readership in formal statements of purpose and in their selection of articles.[53]

In his old age, Carey's interest in social reforms to benefit women extended beyond lip service. He became an earnest advocate of the well-being of poor working women. After turning over the management of his printing business to his son Henry Charles Carey in 1821, he devoted his energies to social issues and philanthropy. While advocating a protective tariff and the development of American manufactures, Carey demanded decent working conditions for women in the factories. He sympathized with laborers thrown out of work by the Panic of 1819. Rejecting the common middle-class belief that the poor were inherently lazy, Carey favored the support and extension of public charities. In *Essays on the Public Charities of Philadelphia* (1824; 4th edn., 1829) and *Address to the Wealthy of the Land* (1831), he demanded greater social justice.[54]

Especially fearful of the spread of prostitution among poor women in the 1830s, Carey recommended improving the abysmal working conditions and wages of young women in the factories as a deterrent. "Their numbers and their wants are so great, and the competition so urgent, that they are wholly at the mercy of their employers," he wrote. He widely publicized the plight of the "needlewomen" (seamstresses) in the factories. At the same time, he favored the employment of female labor in industry because he thought it would make women productive, income-earning citizens and heighten their self-esteem. In *Essays on Political Economy* (1822), written before he became aware of greedy employers' injustices against young women, Carey concluded that young female factory operatives were "thus happily preserved from idleness and its attendant vices and crimes," while the whole community profited from their enhanced purchasing power. He defended the rights of poor working women in his pamphlets, *The Wages of Female Labour* (1829) and *The Case of the Seamstresses* (1833). He printed these tracts, which were especially concerned with the dismal working conditions facing women who sewed uniforms for the federal armed forces, along with several pamphlets on behalf of striking shoemakers, to support his fellow laborers' struggle to earn a living wage, even though he knew these publications would not yield him any profit.[55] Unlike many of the nation's political and social leaders, including its early presidents, Carey did not exclude the "fair sex"—particularly its poorer, downtrodden members—from his thoughts and his programs for reform.

Among Carey's final literary productions were his "Rules for Husbands and Wives," published in a collection of essays in 1830. While he certainly evinced paternalistic sentiments here, its tone was sufficiently enlightened for recent scholars to label it pro-feminist. Carey's first rule was: "A good husband will always regard his wife as his equal; treat her with kindness, respect and attention; and never address her with an air of authority, as if she were, as some husbands appear to regard their wives, a mere housekeeper." These views were similar to those that had often appeared in the *American Museum* more than thirty years before, as was the exhortation to mutual accommodation implicit in his directive that the optimal husband "will cheerfully and promptly comply with all her [his wife's] reasonable requests, when it can be done, without loss, or great inconvenience." On the other hand, some of Carey's instructions to the wife were offensively condescending. He commanded that "she . . . never attempt to rule, or appear to rule her husband. Such conduct degrades husbands—and wives always partake largely of the degradation of their husbands." In his fourth edict he urged that the wife transform herself into a clairvoyant automaton to please her spouse: "She will in every thing reasonable, comply with his wishes—and, as far as possible, anticipate them."[56]

Nevertheless, Carey's assumption that woman was man's intellectual equal, who could perceive reason as well as he and perhaps better despite her inferiority in physical strength and socioeconomic power; his respect for the wife's caretaking responsibilities, and his insistence on improving women's working conditions, earned him a place among his generation's male protofeminist opinion molders.

Notes

1. James N. Green, *Mathew Carey: Publisher and Patriot* (Philadelphia: Library Company of Philadelphia, 1985), 1. The biographical information on Carey in the following pages is based on Green; Green's biographical sketch, "Carey, Matthew [*sic*], in *American National Biography*, John A. Garraty and Mark C. Carnes, eds., 24 vols. (New York: Oxford University Press, 1999), 4: 381-383; William Clarkin, *Mathew Carey: A Bibliography of His Publications, 1785-1824* (New York: Garland, 1984), and Broadus Mitchell's sketch of Carey in the *Dictionary of American Biography* (hereafter cited as *DAB*). See also Edward C. Carter II, "Mathew Carey and 'The Olive Branch,' 1814-1818," *Pennsylvania Magazine of History and Biography* 81 (Oct. 1965): 399-415. Carey spelled his name "Mathew" in his letters, not "Matthew."

2. Green, *Carey*, 2-4; DAB.

3. Green, *Carey*, 5-6; *DAB*.

4. Green, *Carey*, 7. See also Frank L. Mott, *A History of American Magazines, 1741-1850* (Cambridge, Mass.: Harvard University Press, 1966), 94-103; William

J. Free, *The Columbian Magazine and American Literary Nationalism* (The Hague: Mouton, 1968). For the information about subscriptions and the quotation, see Clarkin, *Carey Bibliography*, 4-5. See also Robert W. Sellen, "The *American Museum*, 1787-1792, as a Forum for Ideas of American Foreign Policy," *Pennsylvania Magazine of History and Biography* 93 (April 1969): 179.

5. Michael Durey, "Thomas Paine's Apostles: Radical Emigrés and the Triumph of Jeffersonian Republicanism," *William and Mary Quarterly*, 3d Ser., 44 (Oct. 1987): 684; Mathew Carey to James Carey, March 6, 1795, Lea and Febiger Collection, Historical Society of Pennsylvania, quoted in Remer, *Printers and Men of Capital*, 49.

6. Carey's *Autobiography*, quoted in Clarkin, *Carey Bibliography*, 5. See also Green, *Carey*, 7, and Mott, *History of American Magazines*, 18, 103.

7. Green, *Carey*, 8, 25; Clarkin, *Carey Bibliography*, 7; Sellen, "*American Museum*," 179-89; Richard B. Morris, *The Forging of the Union, 1781-1789* (New York: Harper and Row, 1987), 24.

8. Green, *Carey*, 8; *DAB.*

9. Green, *Carey*, 10.

10. Green, *Carey*, 11-12.

11. See Rosalind Remer, "Preachers, Peddlers, and Publishers: Philadelphia's Backcountry Book Trade, 1800-1830," *Journal of the Early Republic*, 14, no. 4 (Winter 1994): 497-522, esp. 497-504.

12. Green, *Carey*, 18-19.

13. Green, *Carey*, 17, 25-28; Sellen, *"American Museum,"* 179-184.

14. Green, *Carey*, 27-28; Rosalind Remer, *Printers and Men of Capital: Philadelphia Book Publishers in the New Republic* (Philadelphia: University of Pennsylvania Press, 1996), 37.

15. Carter, "Carey and *The Olive Branch*," 400-412. See also Green, *Carey,* 28, and Steven Watts, *The Republic Reborn: War and the Making of Liberal America, 1790-1820* (Baltimore: Johns Hopkins University Press, 1987), 301-305.

16. Carter, "Carey and *The Olive Branch*," 412-15.

17. Green, *Carey*, 19; Remer, *Printers and Men of Capital*, 1, 33-34; Stephen Botein, "'Meer Mechanics' and an Open Press: The Business and Political Strategies of Colonial American Printers," *Perspectives in American History* 9 (1975): 166-77. For Carey's relationship with Jefferson, see Carey to Jefferson, Dec. 18, 1800, and Jefferson to Carey, Jan. 12, 1801, Thomas Jefferson Papers, Library of Congress. In addition, Carey had an extensive correspondence with Jefferson following the latter's retirement from the presidency.

18. Remer, *Printers and Men of Capital*, 2, 59. By 1850 most publishers specialized in selling the works of particular authors or specific areas of literature (novels, religious books, medical texts). They lacked knowledge of the printing trade, eschewed setting up their own retail outlets, and distributed their own imprints alone. Utilizing an expanding railway network, they reached a nationwide market. Remer, *Printers and Men of Capital*, 9.

19. Remer, *Printers and Men of Capital*, 57-58.

20. Remer, *Printers and Men of Capital*, 35.
21. Remer, *Printers and Men of Capital*, 50-51.
22. Carey to Jefferson, Dec. 18, 1800, Jefferson Papers, Library of Congress; Remer, *Printers and Men of Capital*, 6-7.
23. Remer, *Printers and Men of Capital*, 52.
24. Green, *Carey*, 18-20; Remer, *Printers and Men of Capital*, 172n. After 1800, in their quest for profit Philadelphia's erstwhile political newspaper publishers tended to become apolitical, and book publishers followed suit, producing diverse materials in addition to partisan tracts. Remer, *Printers and Men of Capital*, 38.
25. Green, *Carey*, 21-22.
26. Green, *Carey*, 29-31; Remer, *Printers and Men of Capital*, 1; *DAB*.
27. Clarkin, *Carey Bibliography*, 8; Frank Luther Mott, *A History of American Magazines, 1741-1850* (Cambridge, Mass.: Harvard University Press, 1966), 100-103.
28. Sellen, "*American Museum* as Forum," 180; Clarkin, *Carey Bibliography*, 4-5.
29. Green, *Carey*, 20.
30. Clarkin, *Carey Bibliography*, 4; Green, *Carey*, 26; Mott, *American Magazines, 1741-1850*, 43-44, 51-53; John K. Alexander, *The Selling of the Constitutional Convention: A History of News Coverage* (Madison, Wis.: Madison House, 1990). Mathew Carey, *The American Remembrancer; or, an impartial collection of Essays, Resolves, speeches, &c. relative, or having affinity to, the Treaty with Great Britain*, 3 vols. (Philadelphia: Henry Tuckniss, 1795). See the citation to "Volume XIII" of the *American Museum* in *American Bibliography*, Vol. 12, 1798-1799 (Chicago: Privately printed, 1934), 253.
31. Mott, *American Magazines, 1741-1850*, 56-59; personal examination of the *American Museum* by the author.
32. Mott, *American Magazines, 1741-1850*, 59-60, 63.
33. Mott, *American Magazines, 1741-1850*, 64. See the general discussion of the issue of women's reading in Linda K. Kerber, *Women of the Republic: Intellect and Ideology in Revolutionary America* (Chapel Hill: University of North Carolina Press, 1980), 235-64. Kerber notes that even such protofeminists as Mercy Otis Warren and Judith Sargent Murray denounced middle-class women's preference for reading fiction rather than history and geography, and feared that their infatuation with novels would lead them to neglect their household chores and responsibilities.
34. Noah Webster's *American Magazine* 1 (March 1788): 244-245.
35. Mott, *American Magazines, 1741-1850*, 65.
36. *Lady's Magazine* 1 (July 1792): 69.
37. Mott, *American Magazines, 1741-1850*, 66-67; author's examination of the *American Museum* for the years 1787-1792.
38. Mott, *American Magazines, 1741-1850*, 67.
39. Sellen, "*American Museum*," 189; Green, *Carey*, 25.

40. Clarkin, *Carey Bibliography*, 5 (quotation from Carey's *Autobiography*); Green, *Carey*, 7; Mott, *American Magazines, 1741-1850*, 18-20, 103.

41. Clarkin, *Carey Bibliography*, 5. Clarkin speculates that "Carey neglected to state . . . that he must have made money from it [the *American Museum*]," in light of the number of editions he printed. For a different view, see Green, *Carey*, 7: "In the end the magazine made no money at all, even though its reputation could not have been higher."

42. Clarkin, *Carey Bibliography*, 5-7.

43. Clarkin, *Carey Bibliography*, 7.

44. Clarkin, *Carey Bibliography*, 55.

45. For Washington's statement, see Clarkin, *Carey Bibliography*, 7. See also Green, *Carey*, 8, and Richard B. Morris, *the Forging of the Union, 1781-1789* (New York: Harper and Row, 1987), 24.

46. Clarkin, *Carey Bibliography*, 8.

47. Clarkin, *Carey Bibliography*, 8-10.

48. Clarkin, *Carey Bibliography*, 55.

49. "Preface," dated June 20, 1799, to the *American Museum, or, Annual Register of Fugitive Pieces, Ancient and Modern for the Year 1798* (Philadelphia: Mathew Carey, 1799). In the Preface, Carey informed his readers that he contemplated reviving the annual publication of the *American Museum* if this edition met with a favorable response.

50. Albert H. Smyth, *The Philadelphia Magazines and their Contributors, 1741-1850* (1892; reprinted, Freeport, N.Y.: Books for Libraries Press, 1970), 69-73 (quotation at 73).

51. James N. Green, *Mathew Carey: Publisher and Patriot* (Philadelphia: Library Co. of Philadelphia, 1985), quote at 9; Broadus Mitchell, s.v., "Carey, Mathew," in *DAB*.

52. William Clarkin, *Mathew Carey: A Bibliography of His Publications* (New York: Garland Pub. Co., 1984), xiii; Green, *Carey*, 21, 24. Carey's 1812 estimate is in David D. Hall, "Books and Reading in Eighteenth-Century America," in *Of Consuming Interests: The Style of Life in the Eighteenth Century*, Cary Carson, Ronald Hoffman, and Peter J. Albert, eds. (Charlottesville: University Press of Virginia, 1994), 354-72, at 366. However, Hall believes that fiction's impact on "the common reader and the book trade" in the early nineteenth century was not yet pronounced. *Ibid.* For Carey's remarks on Gregory's book, see Janet W. James, *Changing Ideas About Women in the United States, 1776-1825* (New York: Garland, 1981), 290.

53. Mary Beth Norton, *Liberty's Daughters: The Revolutionary Experience of American Women, 1750-1800* (Boston: Little, Brown, 1980), 246.

54. Green, *Carey*, 29-31.

55. Christine Stansell, *City of Women: Sex and Class in New York, 1789-1860* (New York: Knopf, 1986), 111, 147, 172; Cathy N. Davidson, *Revolution and the Word: The Rise of the Novel in America* (New York: Oxford University Press, 1986), 36, 276n.; Mathew Carey, *Essays on Political Economy* (Philadel-

phia, 1822), 459, cited in Gerda Lerner, "The Lady and the Mill-Girl: Changes in the Status of Women in the Age of Jackson, 1800-1840," in *A Heritage of Her Own: Toward a New Social History of American Women*, Nancy F. Cott and Elizabeth H. Pleck, eds., (New York: Simon and Schuster, 1979), 182-196, quote at 189. Lerner somewhat negatively depicts Carey's view of women, portraying him more as a middle-class promoter of virtue, frugality and the "work ethic" than as a man concerned with the welfare of women and the poor.

56. "Rules for Husbands and Wives" (1830), from Carey's *Miscellaneous Essays* (Philadelphia: Carey and Hart, 1830), excerpted in *Against the Tide: Pro-Feminist Men in the United States, 1776-1990: A Documentary History,* Michael S. Kimmel and Thomas E. Mosmiller, eds. (Boston: Beacon Press, 1992), 73-74.

Chapter 3

1787: A Year of Constitution-Making

Somewhat surprisingly for an urban journal, one of the Philadelphia *American Museum*'s first articles concerned the problem of farm bankruptcy, which had caused such turmoil in the new republic in the years following independence, culminating in Shays' Rebellion in western Massachusetts from 1786 to 1787. Why were farmers so deeply in debt? was a question which many observers of the American scene fearfully asked, as farmers refused to pay their creditors and disturbed court sittings and sheriff's sales of their land for unpaid debts and taxes. Among the reasons were the high taxes in some states, notably Massachusetts, as well as the large amount of imported "luxury" goods Americans were buying from the former mother country, England, which refused to purchase their farm products and discriminated against United States trade in other ways, thereby precipitating a postwar depression.[1]

In this age of burgeoning consumption and consumerism, women seem already to have gained a reputation as ardent shoppers and spenders. In fact, if one believed the essay by "A Farmer," appearing in the *American Museum*'s first issue (January 1787), the "fair sex" were culpable in large part for the plight of the bankrupt farmer. The article begins with the farmer's commending his wife as a hard worker; he regards her as his equal, entitled to reciprocal consideration and credit for his farm's productivity. "I married me a wife; and a very good working young woman she was," he recalls. "We took a farm of forty acres on rent. By industry, we gained a head fast." However, the farmer and his wife raised three daughters: this was the beginning of his problems. When his oldest daughter married, he gave her husband 100 acres of outland as her dowry. She was "a dutiful working girl; and therefore I fitted her out well, and to her mind: for I told her to take the best of my wool and flax, and to spin herself gowns, coats, stockings, and shifts." On this occasion the farmer spent very little of the income he received from the sale of farm products. He generally disbursed only ten dollars a year out of his annual revenue of $150, "for salt, nails, and the like." Unfortunately, he soon found his financial stability threatened by the sudden craze for luxury and extravagance which took place after the Revolution.

When the farmer's second daughter married, his wife insisted that they purchase clothing from the town shops, rather than that his daughter sew her own gown. Inauspiciously, his wife spent several days on a junket, shopping in the city, and returned "with a calico gown, a calamanco [brocaded, glossy woolen fabric] petticoat, a set of stone tea cups, half a dozen pewter tea spoons, and a tea-kettle—things that had never been seen in my house before." Though the farmer did not yet feel economically insecure and was pleased that his daughter was well-dressed at her wedding, there are hints that this episode signifies the beginning of his ruin.

By the time his third daughter is ready for marriage, the farmer's wife and children have become acclimated to an ostentatious lifestyle, with better food, clothing, and furniture than they had been satisfied with before. Instead of saving $150 a year, like other farmers he was deeply in debt and in danger of losing his property. For his third daughter's wedding, nevertheless, the farmer recalls, "[my] wife comes again for the purse; but when she returned [from town] what did I see! a silken gown, silk for a cloak, china tea-geer, and a hundred other things, with the empty purse." Obviously, female irresponsibility and obsessive spending on newly available luxury goods after the privations incident to the Revolutionary War had precipitated the farmer's downfall.

However, the proverbial triad of republican values—"industry, frugality, and virtue"—saved the farmer from ruin. Asserting his patriarchal, dominant role in the family, he determines to sell his produce while purchasing as little as possible in town, and eventually becomes solvent again. "My produce brings (scarce as money is)," he writes during the postwar depression, "as much as it used to do. No one thing to eat, drink, or wear, shall come into my house, which is not raised on my farm, or in the parish, or in the country, except salt." In this story the farmer apparently embodies heroic republican virtue, whereas the women bear the onus for the current problem of rural depression and debt, which the article, significantly entitled, "Cause of, and cure for, hard times," suggests is the outgrowth of their incipient consumerism.[2]

On the other hand, at the outset the farmer describes the women in his family as virtuous and hardworking. Presumably they are corrupted by the materialistic ethos of a mercantile, urban, white male–dominated society, rather than any innate propensity. Therefore the blame for the irresponsible "luxury" of the time, we may conclude, is not woman's alone.

Other essays in this first volume glorified the beneficent influence of women and marriage on a man, and elaborated themes of intergender mutuality, companionate marriage, and marital reciprocity. They tended to deride men as fearful of the autonomous female, a personality who existed in that age as well as ours. Two articles, "Character of a Bachelor" and "Character of a Married Man," printed sequentially, showed a clear preference for the latter, since he contributed to the well-being of his family and society. The bachelor is solitary, concerned only with himself and his belly, afraid of and disrespectful toward women. He eats alone and spends his leisure time in the coffeehouse, "his *sanctum sanctorum* against *bright eyes* and *dazzling complexions*," where he may avoid the temptations of affable, beautiful young women and the pitfalls of possible commitment. The bachelor sought to conceal his fear of the "fair sex." He was a despicable fellow who could only relate to women in the capacity of *master*: "His housekeeper or his laundress, he can speak to without reserve; but any other of the sex, whose condition is above a useful dependent, is his terror." Shamefully attempting to correlate gender with a despised socioeconomic group, the bachelor, seeking to neutralize woman's threat, can only relate to her when she is a member of the servile lower classes. The author has contempt for so spiteful a world view.[3]

In contrast to the lonely, whimsical, egocentric bachelor, the married man was happy and enjoyed pleasurable social relationships. According to the article on a married man in the *American Museum*, his life was virtually a paradise on earth; moreover, he was guaranteed an honored place in Heaven while his posterity kept his benevolence alive down below. The status of marriage conveyed a divine sanction.

Of course, the married man's wife was the being most important to him. She was the source of all his love and "extatic enjoyments": "By an union with the gentlest, the most polished, most beautiful part of the creation, his mind is harmonized; his manners softened; his soul animated by the most tender and lively sensations." As a result of the wholesome, beatific, womanly influence, "Love, gratitude, and *universal* benevolence, mix in all his ideas." A married man's home is more than a castle, it "is his paradise." Primarily because his wife waits there loyally for him, he "never leaves it without regret, never returns to it but with gladness." Rather than being an ambitious man whose life was centered on work and activities outside the home, as he was later depicted, the married man is the willing captive of domesticity and the "extasies" of conjugal love: "The *friend* of his soul, the *wife* of his bosom, welcomes his approach with rapture: joy flushes her cheek—mutual are their transports."[4] Unlike the image of the callous, stern patriarch that is often conjured up when scholars depict relations between husband and wife in the post-Revolutionary era, we see that marriage is described here in idealized, extremely sentimental terms, as a connection embodying reciprocal respect, recognition, and affection.[5] While such portrayals of marriage seem ludicrously romantic, the *American Museum* did not ignore the more somber, grim aspects of woman's life in the 1780s.

Alcoholism has always been something of a dilemma in the United States, but we may be surprised to find a female "drinking problem" admitted in eighteenth-century magazines. An article on drunken women warned that, like men, women who drank excessively were scourges on society as well as self-destructive. The *American Museum*'s essayist bestowed sage advice in a more strident tone than we are familiar with today: "The woman who would avoid disease, pain, loathsomeness, hatred, shame, prostitution—I may add, death and perdition—will avoid strong liquors."[6] Similar admonitions are reserved today for the social problems of cocaine and "crack" addiction. But in the Early Republic the drunkard, though less likely to commit violent crime, was equally stigmatized as a harmful and unproductive member of the community. Notwithstanding the genteel, sentimentalized rhetoric of the period, women as well as men were acknowledged to be part of this social epidemic.[7]

Manifesting a pervasive concern with women's issues, this first edition of the *American Museum* printed a sympathetic account of the fate of a young prostitute, conveying a sense of male guilt at this moral outrage. Tacitly admitting that not all women were asexual, Carey encouraged open discussion of social problems, depicting the dark underside of the romantic facade of heterosexual bliss. "The Prostitute—A Fragment," was a story with a lesson. Charity dictated that the middle-class male assist the young prostitute; she might be the daughter of an old friend! The plight of the young harlot was one of privation and degradation: "The girl before me was an object demanding assistance from five out of the seven works of mercy—she was hungry, thirsty, naked, sick, and a stranger." The wealthy man takes the prostitute to his home, going so far as to deprive another *man*—albeit it is his servant—of his bed:

> There was but one way to administer relief. I clothed her with my surtout—brought her to my chambers—roused up my servant—and insisted on her getting into his bed . . . . She is but a child that providence hath thrown into my way, and must not be neglected.

Unlike the bachelor, this man is willing to distinguish between an unfortunate girl, despite her degraded status, and a menial manservant.

Mixed with his pity for a helpless girl is a note of class conflict, an awareness that socioeconomic inequality, the privileges of the rich and the dearth of opportunity for the poor, especially when they were female, fostered the growth of prostitution and crime. As the author wrote: "Profession she has none: and if she had, she wants what the world calls character—or rather, *she has the worst character in the world—she is unfortunate*!" The writer ends on an optimistic note of fulfilled obligation to the luckless girl: "But I will take care of thee, Magdalen."[8] The man here was naturally seen as the stronger figure.

At times in the pages of the *American Museum,* women were viewed as playing a passive role, merely in relation or reaction to male opinions or initiatives. However, in certain cases the woman, usually as wife, is depicted as assertive, even aggressive, while the husband is delineated as a weakling and a fumbler. An article by "Nitidia," extracted from the *Columbian Magazine*, another of Carey's enterprises, proudly defends woman's traditional pursuit as housekeeper. A wife takes her responsibility for keeping a neat, tidy house very seriously, especially the ritual called "white-washing": mopping the floors, arranging the husband's books and papers, soaking the walls, ceilings, etc., "with brushes, dipped in a solution of lime, called white-wash; to pour buckets of water over every floor," and vigorously scrub the walls and panels. In response to an earlier satire by

Francis Hopkinson, the brilliant Philadelphia essayist, lawyer, musician, and signer of the Declaration of Independence, deriding women's obsession with housecleaning, "Nitidia" praised this activity as a "reasonable prerogative" of every housewife who properly "execute[d] the duties of her station." She pointed out, "Women generally employ their time to better purpose than scribbling." In other words, women's household activities were more useful than men's cerebral vagaries.[9]

On the other hand, "Nitidia" may be regarded as an early exponent of the feminist creed. She charged that men were preventing women from achieving their intellectual potential. "The cares and comforts of a family rest principally on their [women's] shoulders," she explained. "Hence it is, that there are but few female authors: and the men, knowing how necessary our attentions are to their happiness, take every opportunity of discouraging literary accomplishments in the fair sex." She boasted that her lively essay afforded proof of women's literary talent. "We have ladies," she warned, "who sometimes lay down the needle and take up the pen: I wonder none of them have attempted some reply." Paradoxically, "Nitidia" had "taken up the pen" to uphold those household pursuits she claimed men had foisted on women to prevent their attaining intellectual distinction.

Apparently internalizing their housekeeping role, women eagerly defended their social position against men's derision, and counterattacked, calling them "naturally nasty beasts," who could not appreciate a tidy home. According to "Nitidia," the solitary male endangered the environment with his slovenliness. Only their connection with women, "the refined sex," kept "these lords of creation" from "wallowing in filth, and populous cities would infect the atmosphere with their noxious vapours." Her denunciation of the male character was unstinting:

> It is the attention and assiduity of the women, that prevent the men from degenerating into swine. How important, then, are the services we render! And yet for these very services we are made the subject of ridicule and fun:—base ingratitude! nauseous creatures![10]

While "Nitidia" denied that her obsession with enforcing male and household cleanliness amount to being "in a passion," she reached unaccustomed heights of emotion in her rage at "how unreasonably we are treated by the men." Apparently what historian Nancy Cott has referred to as "female passionlessness" did not prevail outside the bedroom. Moreover, such essays as "Nitidia" did not protest women's treatment as "sexual objects," as has been so common in feminist rhetoric since the 1960s, nor were women viewed much in an erotic, sexual context.[11] Rather, women ostensibly were seen as existing in a reciprocal relationship with their husbands, and perhaps other males.

In describing her confrontation with her spouse over his slovenly habits, "Nitidia" capably displays sardonic humor as well as mordant commentary. She recounts an anecdote about the time her "would-be philosopher" husband told her to leave the room while she was mending a dress so that he could "make some important philosophical [i.e., scientific] experiments." Thereupon he cluttered the tables with "all manner of trumpery," diverse materials for his investigation. Though his experiment—whatever it was—failed, he left the "parlour" [living room] a shambles, to be cleaned up by the servants. Much damage had occurred; many pieces of furniture, chinaware, and glass had been destroyed.

"Nitidia's" reaction once again reveals that women were far from "passionless" when they found it necessary to reprimand their husbands. "I would almost as lieve the melted rosin and the vitriol had been in his throat, as on my dear marble health, and on my beautiful carpet," she admits. Nevertheless, she praises her self-control in the presence of her husband. "It is not true, that *women have no power over their feelings* for, notwithstanding this provocation, I said nothing, or next to nothing: for I only observed, very pleasantly, that a lady of my acquaintance had told me that the reason why philosophers are called *literary* men, is because they make a great *litter*—not a word more."[12] It appears that in the 1780s women possessed some mastery of the art of sarcastic humor, like the Audrey Meadows character (Alice) in Jackie Gleason's 1950s television show, *The Honeymooners*.

In an effort to rectify the disaster, "Nitidia" tells us, she waited for her husband, whom she refers to ironically as "My *Precious,*" to leave the house, after which she, somewhat paramilitarily, gathered together all her "forces: brushes, buckets, soap, sand, lime-skins, and cocoanut shells, with all the powers of housewifery." This witty analogy between housecleaning and armed warfare may be designed as much to condemn male militarism as to justify woman's more peaceful, constructive activities. *Her* philosophical experiment, she points out, succeeded, unlike her husband's abortive efforts: "All was well again, except my poor carpet—my vitriolized carpet—which still remained a mournful memento of philosophical fury, or rather philosophical folly."[13]

Unfortunately, "Nitidia's" tribulations were not over. No sooner has she finished cleaning up one mess than her husband returns to announce that he has invited six friends for dinner. Now, despite her fatigued condition, she must prepare a repast! Even worse, the guests, like her husband, were slovenly cigar-smokers. They completed the obliteration of her prized carpet, "which had suffered in the course of experimental philosophy in the morning, [and] was destined to be most shamefully dishonored, in the afternoon, by a deluge of nasty tobacco juice—Gentlemen smokers love segars better than carpets."[14] Although the dedicated housewife loses the battle, her determined efforts to maintain a clean home win the hearts of the *American Museum*'s readers. We are led to conclude that women should be praised for their efforts to maintain a neat home, rather than ridiculed.

However, the tale has greater significance. Its depiction of an incident in the "battle of the sexes" shows woman's intention to defend her identity against male imputations, an identity that may initially have been ascribed to her by males as a means to keep her in a subordinate position. "Nitidia" complains of "the injuries we sustain from the *boasted superiority of men* [my italics]. But we will not be laughed out of our cleanliness." Indeed, the struggle for a tidy home defined the wife's *raison d'être:* "A woman would rather be called any thing than a *slut*—as a man would rather be thought a knave than a fool." (In this context, "slut" referred to an unkempt woman, not a prostitute).[15] While the man, defined by his wits and intellect, would rather be thought "a knave than a fool," a woman, for whom academic pursuits were severely limited, prided herself on her personal cleanliness, in this realm claiming ostensible superiority to the male. As if to emphasize this distinction, "Nitidia" concludes, "when one is about a thorough cleaning, the first dirty thing to be removed is one's husband."[16]

Ironically, women had so thoroughly introjected the role men had ascribed to them that they had turned it to the purpose of asserting female superiority and castigating the male. As with the similar technique by which nineteenth- and twentieth-century African-Americans manipulated the white man's Christianity to fortify themselves for revolt against domination by the "white devils" who designed it originally to subjugate them, "Nitidia's" rationale for her way of life—her "ideology"—is an instance which verifies social anthropologist Clifford Geertz's theory. Geertz contends that ideology is the product of "socio-psychological strains." It indicates that "human thought" is a "public, and not, or at least not fundamentally, a private activity." In effect, ideology is an interaction between "sentiments and institutions . . . modes of interpenetration of culture, personality, and social system." The "role strain theory" of ideology—which has been defined as "a patterned reaction to the patterned strains of a social role"—is certainly apposite to the attempts of women like "Nitidia" to justify themselves against male domination on *male* terms. Oppressed groups (and others) use ideology—patterns of thought and belief that explain social reality in terms easier to comprehend than the actual flux of human events—to alleviate "role strain" and "social desperation," and improve their morale. The harried housewife, farmer's daughter, or adolescent prostitute might be expected to take refuge in the "morale explanation" of ideology: "the ability of an ideology to sustain individuals (or groups) in the face of chronic strain, either by denying it outright or by legitimizing it in terms of higher values." Perhaps the woman's exaggerated claim for the importance of a spic-and-span household (which has persisted into the present) serves this function, enabling her to feel satisfied about her own power in the world and in the family, while men run everything on the outside. This may have been the "ideology" or "world view" that kept the woman of the 1780s from outright revolt. As Geertz lucidly puts it: "Ideology bridges the emotional gap between things as they are and as one would have them be, thus insuring the performance of roles that might otherwise be abandoned in despair or apathy."[17]

On the other hand, woman's obsession with cleanliness and a neat home furnished her a source of self-esteem and an outlet for her anger at the opposite sex's domination. Apparently, it was common for women to denounce male slovenliness, thereby simultaneously unleashing female aggression and belittling the man. This observation takes on added force when we note that "Nitidia" was *not* a woman but a man—indeed, the same Francis Hopkinson who had formerly ridiculed women's interminable quest for cleanliness. He composed "Nitidia" to display his contrition, his earlier essay having caused "no small clamour amongst the ladies."[18] Hopkinson's convincing identification with his female readers suggests the validity of his belief that they would endorse his defense of their alleged obsession with housecleaning projects despite its inconvenience to their slovenly husbands. To judge from homemakers' pervasive insistence on a neat and tidy home down to the present day, he reliably reported the feelings of pride and identity women's thorough internalization of masculine injunctions to maintain an orderly household paradoxically afforded. Indirectly retracting his earlier pejorative comments about their housekeeping habits, Hopkinson, seemingly undismayed by his ensuing loss of face, *refracted* their own views back to them.

Another narrative of female aggression,"The pitiable case of an old bachelor" depicts women as self-assertive, resistant to the sexual advances of the man, and insistent that household norms take priority over male desires. This droll tale of a thirty-eight-year-old unmarried male (rather aged in those days, when the lifespan was about fifty years), who had incessantly been teased and tormented by young women is humorous while it tells much about relations between the sexes. "I've been *twisted* and *twirled* about by the girls, till I'm as thin as a snake," the bachelor laments. Earlier in life he had thought women were attracted by his "gallantry," but now he found they "respect me . . . not for my gallantry or merit—but (the dogs take my grey hairs!) for my advanced age." He gives a good if exaggerated description of male courtship habits in the eighteenth century:

> I had been addressing a young lady steadily for six years—the first year I did nothing but look at and ogle her—the second I chatted with her a little—the third I squeezed her hand, and sighed—the fourth I made proposals of marriage to her—the fifth she consented—and the sixth were to be married, but could not agree on the time or place.[19]

This description reflects the sexual restraint of the time. It suggests that the woman rather than the man was in control of the courtship situation. Recent historians have also concluded that the period of courtship was the time during which the colonial woman exerted most power over the man.[20]

"The old bachelor" depicts the passionate irrationality of an aging man. When his fiancée refuses to marry till August, despite his pleas for a February wedding, he brings his sword to her house, threatening suicide unless she acquiesces, even going so far as to stab himself slightly in the chest. Much to his chagrin, she was indifferent to his suffering: "Instead of fainting or shrieking, she gently laid hold of my arm, and requested me to walk to the fire-place, before I stabbed myself, for *blood was the worst thing in the world to stain a floor and hers was newly washed.*" Her nonchalance disabused him of any romantic notions. "In an instant I felt as if a thousand mosquetoes had laid violent hands on my flesh," he recalls. "My sword fell out of my hand, and I ran home, determined to remain till the day of my death, an Old Bachelor."[21]

As in "Nitidia's" case, the "Old Bachelor" perceives women as showing greater concern about the tidiness of their homes than with their men's comfort. Although woman is depicted as obsessively neat, ironically, man's ostensible animal irrationality and immaturity, symbolized by his "dirtiness," are contrasted with woman's excessive rationality and self-control, epitomized by her passion for household order. This counterpoint, while suggesting that men remained bachelors because women were over-involved with their homes and hobbies, depicts women as possessing autonomous personalities antagonistic to the male, rather than as the passive docile creatures feminist historians contend were considered the norm in the Revolutionary era.[22]

Ironically, if these pieces in the *American Museum* are any gauge, the burgeoning cult of domesticity, characterized by men's insistence that woman's sole place was in the home, backfired at its inception in the 1780s and early 1790s. Literalizing male injunctions, the wife utilized her domestic role as a vehicle of empowerment. To the husband's chagrin (and perhaps his increased mental, emotional, and physical discomfort), she took control of the household regimen. Wifely dominance of the hearth, rather than fostering either uxoriousness or the wife's tractability and subservience to her husband on his return home from his ventures into the grubby world of external moneymaking, perhaps facilitated *disharmony* and conflict among spouses.

Although feminists tend to present the eighteenth century as a period of patriarchy and female repression, judging from the essays appearing in the *American Museum* there was a good deal of discussion about *positive* female attributes. One article, "Comparison between the sexes," directly addressed this matter, praising woman's instincts but doubting the strength of her reasoning ability. Nevertheless, the sympathetic author imputes the latter defect to the limited opportunity society offers women for an education by comparison with men, not to any natural inferiority. Indeed, the author praises women's superior creativity and imagination, as well as the proverbial intuition which renders them natural philosophers. Women's conversation was much more interesting and original than men's. "As to gracefulness of expression, it belongs almost exclusively to women," though unfortunately there were few female authors.[23]

Women had strong and powerful insights about life and morality. They were both more "chaste" and "charming" than men. Their facility in language was "brilliant." Their judgment, conducted by means of intuition rather than reason, was invariably correct and revealed an innate intelligence:

> The perception of woman is as quick as lightning. Her penetration is intuition. I had almost said instinct. By a glance of her eye, she shall draw a deep and just conclusion: Ask her how she formed it? she cannot answer the question. The philosopher deduces inferences . . . but he gets to the head of the stair-case, if I may say so, by slow degrees, and, mounting step by step. She arrives at the top of the stair-case as well as he: but whether she leaped or flew there, is more than she knows herself. While she trusts her instinct, she is scarce ever deceived: she is generally lost, when she attempts to reason.[24]

Though conceding that men "have sounder judgments," the writer sought to prove that this was merely the result of superior education. He believed that, until the age of fourteen, "girls are every where superior to boys." At that stage, the boy proceeds to catch up intellectually, "and he continues to improve, by means of education . . . possibly till thirty." This acute analysis of the educational progress of the sexes has a modern ring; its feminist slant leads one to believe the anonymous author is a woman.

Social privilege, rather than mental superiority, provides the impetus for male intellectual attainments. Man's culture encourages his ambition and striving. While the woman's rudimentary education terminates at adolescence, the male is constantly being stimulated and rewarded for the further pursuit of learning. The essayist understands man's preoccupation with "avarice and ambition"—"the passion for distinction," as John Adams called it. For man, bellicosity and challenge are a way of life:

> He has all the fountains of knowledge opened to him—interest to stimulate him to exercise his part—rivals to emulate—opponents to conquer. His talents are always on the stretch. To this he adds the advantages of travel and even if he should not go abroad, he can enter into an infinite number of houses, from which she is debarred.

The man's greater exposure to education and more varied environments than the woman, permitting him the "continual exercise" of his reason, gave him an unfair advantage over a partner whose social role was comparatively passive and stable.

The nameless author bluntly predicts: "Take a man and a woman, who have never been out of the village in which they were born, and neither of whom knows how to read: I question much if his discretive faculties will be found to be stronger than her's [*sic*]." Thus it was their restricted way of life, enforced by social mores rather than imputed intellectual limitations that prevented women from excelling in the sciences.

Not only did a male-dominated society prevent women from realizing their potential, women's dependence on men exerted a corrupting influence on virtuous, refined feminine sensibilities. Remarking on the inherent "superior sensibility of their souls" and woman's "greater and more refined sentiments" as opposed to man's lust and greed, the author warned that the desire to please the male sometimes corrupted their virtue. "Though the severity, ill-temper, neglect, and perfidy of men, often force women to have recourse to dissimulation,—yet when they have noble [male] characters to deal with, how sincere and ardent is their love!" the writer exclaimed. "How delicate and solid their attachment! Woman is not near so selfish a creature as man. When a man is in love, the object of his passion is, if I may so, himself."[25] The male partner's concern with his own egoistic and physical satisfaction often ruined heterosexual relationships. A woman, on the other hand, would sacrifice her own life out of love for a good man.

In the final analysis, then, social mores unfortunately dictated a subordinate role for the woman. While men seek glory in war, politics, and public affairs, this kind of fame is foreclosed to the female, who must live vicariously *through* her husband. The author delineates a melodramatic picture of a wife or lover desperately waiting for her man's return from the perils of war, obsessed with anxiety, filled with fear of his bloody death. "Time presses, and her grief increases," the narrator remarks, "till worn out at length by too much tenderness, she falls the victim of too exquisite a sensibility, and sinks with sorrow to the grave."[26] Superficially this ending is trite and sentimental. However, in view of the preceding analysis, it appears that the essay's message constitutes a challenge to women: if they allow their lives and emotions to be merely reactive to men rather than proactive, they are not leading autonomous, full lives. Paradoxically, the central idea is one of rebellion rather than docility, one in harmony with the women's movement of the twentieth century. It is especially significant that a man perhaps composed this anonymous article, and that the editor of the magazine, Mathew Carey, was male.

The *American Museum* published much material on women's role in society, perhaps because, then as now, females were avid consumers of magazines. Several periodicals, such as the *Lady's Magazine* and the *Ladies' Monitor*, edited by men, were ephemeral precursors of the "feminization of American culture," as one historian calls it, that occurred in the 1830s.[27] Nevertheless, the *American Museum* was the most prestigious, had the largest circulation, and presented the widest array of viewpoints.

An article on "The happy influence of female society" viewed women in a traditional perspective more characteristic of the later Victorian Era, taking for granted that women's *raison d'être* was to please and serve their husbands and exert a refining influence on their families. Arguing that women had acquired more respect in the enlightened 1780s than in ancient times, when their only role was to gratify barbaric male lust, the author commented, "Many ages elapsed before they [women] were thought of sufficient consequence to become the companions of an hour devoted to society, as well as of that devoted to love." The author's history was accurate, but his recommendations for his own time show that his sentiments were less than progressive. In his view, woman's proper function was to make man feel calm, relaxed, and comfortable after a hard day at work, in his castle-like home, far from the turmoil of society. Women are admired for their beauty and delicacy, the author notes. On the other hand, men are praised for their courage, which women admire but fail to emulate because they are "weak, timid, and defenceless."[28]

Reversing this common assumption, the author points out that despite their strength, men are actually dependent on women. The "enterprising and robust" male has "the greatest need of female softness" to soothe him after the "asperities" of daily business and man-to-man conflict in the marketplace, "and by the lenient balm of endearment, blunt the edge of corrosive care." Men only advanced beyond barbaric coarseness as a result of joining in the "mixed society" of women, which execrable "jealousy" prohibited for most men among the Moslem harems in the Middle East. By participating in *tête-à-tête* with the opposite sex, men acquired "social natures" and "sentimental feelings," which were essential to the survival of civilized society. As the author put it, "Though men may improve themselves in the company of their own sex, the company and conversation of women are alone the school for the heart."[29] In those countries, primarily in western Europe and the United States, where men spent more time with women, men were more "polished and refined." The author contended that only "the company and conversation of the fair" could eliminate male moroseness and gravity, replacing them with "happiness and hilarity."[30] The author readily admitted the beneficial influence of "female society" in soothing the savage male beast and thereby furthering progress.

Manifesting a male persona, the author evinces keen insight into the effect a woman has on man's presentation of self. He points out that men behave in a more reserved manner when in the company of "the fair sex," while with each other they are more brazenly vulgar. "In our sex, there is a kind of constitutional or masculine pride, which hinders us from yielding, in points of knowledge or honour, to each other," he admits, "but we lay it entirely aside in our connexions with women." Eager to please and impress women, men will try to behave in a more humane and cultivated manner, less aggressively than they did with other men. In fact, the author sweepingly concludes, men owe whatever charm, politeness, and "elegance of manners" they possess, "as well [as] the neatness and ornaments of dress" to women.

Unlike other articles, this essay argues that men owe the strength of their rational faculties more to female influence than education. Association with women and the desire to gain their approval "teaches us to obey, where we used to command—and to reason, where we used to be ungovernable." Instead of men's maintaining a rugged veneer, the writer asserts, applying to contacts between men and women David Hume's theories on the role of custom and habit in the learning process, "the virtues we assume, in order to make a better figure in their eyes, become at length habitual to us." Men are very eager to please women, the author observes, because women have devoted their lives to charming, attracting and pleasing men. Here once again is the motif of reciprocal influence and mutuality between the genders that we have already seen.[31]

In the opinion of the author of "The Happy Influence of Female Society," women are responsible for men's cultivation of the fine arts. They exert a catalytic influence, stimulating creative endeavor among the men who sought their favors. "To the society of women, we are indebted for the emulation of pleasing and conferring happiness on others," the writer explains, "and to this emulation, we certainly owe the greater part, if not the whole, of the fine arts." The author goes so far as to depict women as a force for peace in the world, a somewhat novel idea for those times. He graphically and sentimentally portrays women's personal intervention on the battlefield: "Fond of the softer scenes of peace, women have often had the address to prevent, by their arguments and intercession, the direful effects of war; and, afraid of losing their husbands and relations, have sometimes rushed between two hostile armies ready to engage, and turned the horrid scenes of destruction into those of friendship and levity." As far as the author perceived, women shared credit for whatever was valuable in society. He believed that women had a restraining, rational power over men, although he was silent about woman's degree of rationality. In order to please women, men had taken on the accoutrements of civilization and reason, qualities they lacked in dealing with other men.[32]

In addition, the author declared, women exerted a virtually hypnotic power over men, who found them sensually irresistible. Admitting that the man's greater physical strength and psychic "resolution" conferred on him an ostensible natural "superiority," he advised women to utilize their own God-given advantages ("lovely forms" and "soft and engaging manners") to "reduce this seeming superiority of men to a more equal footing." Employing their beauty and persuasive "softness" to seduce men to their point of view, women could exercise a salutary covert power in favor of peace and the arts. Few women were aware of their strong influence on men, especially when the former were young and attractive. "The power of women to bend the stronger sex to their will, is no doubt greatly augmented when they have youth and beauty on their side, but even with the loss of these it is not always extinguished," since ancient history showed that venerable women could succeed in maintaining peace where men had failed.[33]

The author employed historical (sometimes mythical) and recent examples to demonstrate the salutary "ascendancy which women of sense have gained over men of feeling," invariably helping to assuage the wrath of tyrannical kings against their subjects. Nevertheless, it was by "gentle methods"—sexual submissiveness and agreeableness—that women acquired their power over rulers. (He cites Emperor Augustus Caesar and King Henry IV of France as examples). The queens of France from medieval times to the present, he noted, *de facto* ruled the state through the influence they exerted over their husbands, despite the legal prohibition on women's ever actually governing (the Salic law).[34] Unfortunately, only by placating male passions could women achieve influence and authority, according to this theoretical discussion.

Perhaps more importantly, "The Happy Influence of Female Society" reveals that men considered women responsible for much of the good in their society, rather than solely as evil temptresses, like Eve offering Adam the forbidden fruit in the Garden of Eden, a favorite Puritan motif.[35] Without the restraining influence of women, men's brutal passions might run amuck and civilized society become impossible.

The article, "Family disagreements the frequent cause of immoral conduct," evoked a similar theme, but with a more realistic point of departure. While upholding the popular idea that the home was a man's refuge from the tumult of the outside world, a place where he could relax and feel happy with his wife and children, the author pointed out that a husband's bad temper often ruined this potentially idyllic scene. He lamented that frequently men preserved their self-control in the presence of strangers or business associates, only to angrily vent their frustrations at family members. Deploring such a "perversion" of man's proper behavior at home, the author further regretted that arguments between husband and wife often magnified trivial incidents and kindled mutual disrespect. Such spasms of anger, when "the faint affection which remains, is too feeble, to be felt amid the furious operation of the hateful passions," too often led to shattered families.

Even more doleful than its causing "misery" and mutual contempt in the home, the antithesis of what family life *should* be, "family dissension" led to immorality. Discussing this perennial problem of vice and crime in language with a strangely modern resonance, the author remarked that unpleasant family surroundings caused individuals "to pursue their happiness through a devious wild of passion and imagination." "Mature" (post-adolescent) sons will seek pleasure and income by means of crime, fearful of asking their miserly parents for money. Even if matters did not reach such an impasse that the child was jailed, the consequences of a hostile family environment were "always terrible, and destructive of happiness and virtue." Unlike modern social workers and psychologists, the writer is least sympathetic to the children. Betraying a legacy of Puritanism, whose belief in innate depravity did not exempt even infants, the author claims that in disputes with parents, progeny are "usually most culpable" because, with their "violent passions and defective experience," they regard pleasure and disobedience as the most important aspects of life.[36]

However, "Family disagreements the frequent cause of immoral conduct" exhibits a more sophisticated understanding of family conflicts than certain tracts which advocated "breaking the child's will" either by physical or psychological methods. These possessed some popularity among the socioreligious groups that historian Philip Greven calls "evangelicals."[37] In common with the more "enlightened" literature, the author of "Family Disagreements" asserted that the parent must share some of the blame for filial disobedience by failing to be gentle and reasonable at critical moments.

By playing the role of a "limited monarch" rather than a tyrant, the parent might convert the household into a sphere of "joy."[38]

The author did not ignore the question of disobedient daughters, whose "misconduct," perhaps because of the ever-present threat of premarital pregnancy, "is more fatal to family peace," but not more "heinous" than that of their brothers. In seeking to change their situation by fleeing familial misery, daughters tend to lose their "characters, virtue and happiness." The author therefore advises that parents should be gentle with them, try to keep them at home, and allow them "innocent pleasures." At the same time, they must exercise subtle, "unwinking vigilance" over their daughters' activities.[39]

Though at first he castigated the raging husband who disrupted the home, the author of "Family disagreements" warned that the presence of a shrewish, bullying wife posed an equally grave threat to family harmony. In flight from a tormenting spouse, it was only natural for the husband to resort to the company of prostitutes: "When the husband is driven from his home by a termagant, he will seek that enjoyment, which is denied him at home, in the haunts of vice, and in the riots of intemperance." Venereal disease was among the unfortunate byproducts of an unfulfilled marriage ("conjugal infelicity"), the outcome of "that desperate dissoluteness and carelessness in manners, which terminates in the ruin of health, peace, and fortune." Surely such horrible consequences provided sufficient motive for both spouses to make considerable efforts to get along with each other.

The article concludes on a hopeful note: Both joy and virtue in the family depend on "a cordial union," which may be maintained if its members sincerely respect each other. For this purpose, proper decorum and self-control, minimal "familiarity" on all occasions, and suitable "delicacy of manners" and courtesy are essential. Such constraining precautions will usually prevent family passions from erupting into violence, the psychologically astute author concludes. "The human heart is so constituted as to love respect," he explains. "An habitual politeness of manners will prevent even indifference from degenerating to hatred. It will refine, exalt, and perpetuate affection."[40] Men should maintain the same moral and religious stance in both their public and private roles, "in the sight of those from whose applause we expect the gratification of our vanity, ambition, and avarice" in the workplace and our loved ones at home. He reminded his readers that "reciprocal love" was an even more precious reward than public esteem.[41]

Here was a "cult of domesticity" with a twist. A far cry from the invocation to love, loyalty, and romance of more traditional advisory manifestoes, this one proposes the adoption of behavior that is at once both constraining and contrived. Characterized by blunt realism, pragmatic recognition of family crises and tentative proposals for their resolution, this essay in the *American Museum* depicted husband and wife, male and female, as equally flawed, irrational creatures who required the artificial controls etiquette afforded to maintain even a semblance of harmony—and possible building blocks for a more loving, reciprocal future relationship. This article pointedly contrasts the ideal home-as-castle with the reality of household conflict as the breeding ground for delinquency, vice, and crime. It depicts neither man nor woman as especially admirable or rational.

Nevertheless, the *American Museum*'s predominant theme is marital reciprocity and mutual fulfillment. Its "Select Poetry" section, with entries like "The happy fireside" and "The happy pair," expounds an optimistic attitude on relations between the sexes. The latter poem, describing a couple which has been happily married for five years despite their friends' adverse predictions, lyrically states that each party finds contentment in the other's happiness:

> Our cares and our pleasures have still been the same;
> And of sorrow, we're thankful, we know but the name:
> We're mutually pleased in endeav'ring to please,
> And though we're not rich, still we live at our ease.[42]

In a similar vein, "Advice to the married" points out that marriage can be congenial if both spouses practice calm discussion, kind words, and mutual accommodation. There was no suggestion that women must become the husband's passive object:

> In unison sweet let your voices agree,
> While both are maintained in the natural key:
> Thus love shall beat time with a conjugal kiss,
> And your skirmish be only the skirmish of bliss.[43]

At the same time, the *American Museum* dared to depict the harsh, pathological side of some marriages. Unlike the Romantic sentimentalists of the mid-nineteenth century, Carey's writers did not hesitate to analyze a husband's shortcomings. "A Jealous Man," which appeared in the February 1787 issue, sketched paranoid husbands who chronically, obsessively charged their wives with infidelity: "His children he will not love, because he suspects they are bastards. His meat he will hardly touch, mistrusting his wife will mix poison with it."[44] Such stark depictions of an extreme type of irrational *male* reveal the *American Museum*'s awareness that, contrary to the austere, self-controlled, patriarchal stereotype, men as well as women were liable to unwarranted displays of passion.[45]

Though the institution of marriage was invariably portrayed with reverence, writers occasionally depicted the humorous side of the eternal courtship ritual. A successful marital quest was especially urgent for young women, since society in most cases deprived them of an education which could provide the means for economic independence. One essay, "Plan for the establishment of a fair of fairs, or market of matrimony," satirically proposed a carnival-like auction to promote "that most necessary commerce, on which all others must ultimately depend—the commerce of the sexes." This fair would be a place where young women—"the fair sex"—could display their physical and intellectual charms for potential husbands. The article's purport was somewhat puritanical: it denounced women's new fashions in lascivious dress and dancing as being unduly revealing and sexually enticing. The author claimed that women had adopted these new modes in order to attract spouses, since the marriage rate (at least in New England) had declined after the Revolution. But he argued that thus far women's new sexual assertiveness had not procured them many husbands.

Although the essay seemingly takes for granted that marriage was rightfully woman's primary ambition, the author perhaps inadvertently demonstrated females' autonomy and resourcefulness in devising new ways of dressing and dancing even though their ostensible goal was to attract a "lord and master" (as the husband was referred to in the antebellum South).[46] At this time men seemed to lack interest in women: "The ladies have justly complained, that the matrimonial spirit greatly decayed during the war, to the lasting injury of a country, whose welfare depends so much on population." Though demographic statistics show that the 1780s were a decade of rapid population growth, New England's numbers were not keeping pace with the rest of the country.[47]

In the author's words, the young ladies "have invented new modes of dress, calculated to discover almost all their charms to the eyes of their unfeeling lovers; and to reduce all covering to the original fig-leaf of Eve; and introduced new steps and figures in dancing," all in vain. Since men were still showing insufficient interest, the author feared, "with the utmost grief and anxiety, that they [young women] will soon be obliged to increase their allurements, and exhibit their charms in the manner practiced in the new discovered [South Pacific] islands."[48] To judge from this amusing article, young women failed to conform to male ideals of demure, passive femininity. In their search for a mate, they went to stark extremes. This showed that, at least to the writer, they had minds of their own. Unfortunately, like slaves on the auction block, they had to employ their talents in the marriage game, hoping to be "sold" to the highest bidder.

That there was less psychological difference between man and woman than some would pretend was the theme of "On the happiness of domestic life." The author contended that the most pleasurable leisure activity for a man was the enjoyment of his children, which was life-fulfilling rather than unmanly. He denied that fathers eventually found the company of their wives and children tedious and "insipid," precipitating "disgust" and constant family strife. Indeed, the author insisted that the presence of "much domestic misery is no argument that there is no domestic happiness." Unhappy families usually result from coerced marriages between people who have nothing in common. Both husband and wife find true meaning in spending time with their children. More than anything else, marriage and paternity made a man a useful member of the community. As the author sentimentally stated: "He who beholds a woman whom he loves, and an helpless infant looking up to him for support, will not easily be induced to indulge an unbecoming extravagance, or devote himself to indulgence."[49]

To an equal extent with the mother, it was the father's responsibility to teach the son a moral way of life. In the course of doing so, the father himself became a more pristine, moral being. According to the writer: "Many who, in their individual and unconnected state, would probably have spent a life not only useless to others, but profligate and abandoned in itself, have become valuable members of the community, and have arrived at a degree of moral improvement to which they would not otherwise have attained."

In a paean to the joys of domesticity for both sexes, the author laments that "modern times" have "profligately" disparaged the "domestic pleasures." Stigmatizing this view, he concludes that "the truest happiness is to be found at home." Thus, it was not in the hurly-burly of the business world but in the haven of his family that the father, like the mother, found true joy and meaning.[50] Indeed, family life might even save a man from the pitfalls of indolence, depravity, and selfishness, cardinal sins in the ethos of emerging American republicanism.[51]

A sober, discerning examination of relations between the sexes, rather than a stress on man's attraction to woman's physical beauty characterized many of the pieces appearing in the *American Museum*. Female honesty, integrity, and intelligence were more essential than mere sensuality, according to one poem:

> The shape alone let others prize,
> Or features of the fair:
> I look for spirit in her eyes,
> And meaning in her air.
> A damask cheek, a snowy arm,
> Shall ne'er my wishes win;
> Give me the animated form,
> That speaks the mind within.
> A face where awful honor shines,
> Where sense and sweetness move,
> And angel innocence refines
> The tenderness of love.[52]

Female sexuality was accepted, not denied. In this respect, male attitudes during the 1780s were more open-minded than in succeeding decades. For instance, "Lines, address'd to a coquette," was not an angry puritanical diatribe but a witty sally about a passionate woman who wanted to experiment sexually with many men. The poet evinced no self-righteous indignation at the existence of such a woman, but rather feared that in the course of her erotic exploits, she might "torture a heart, not relieve it." In America's monogamous society, after all,

> Tho' interest and custom compel the dear maid
> To bless but one man with her charms,
> Yet nature has given a heart, I'm afraid
> That could wish all the sex in her arms.[53]

Confronted by this potential threat to the stability of male patriarchal society, the author is less apprehensive than one might expect. This suggests men were not such staunch advocates of sexual exclusivity as historians often pretend, but could accept with good humor women who behaved in an aggressive, "masculine" manner. Both their respect for the mature, intelligent, family-oriented wife and mother and their untroubled recognition that other kinds of women existed in America's burgeoning urban society indicate that the male attitude to the "fair sex" was relatively healthy and open-minded, not condescending or unduly harsh.

Then as now, women apparently were avid consumers, delighting in accumulating knickknacks and bric-a-brac with which to decorate their homes. One writer describes the difficulties he experienced with his wife over her obsessive attendance at auctions, similar to present-day flea-markets. Though she had cluttered the house and made his life unbearable, he had no power to restrain her. This was a case where the wife exerted overt rather than "covert" authority in the household. His wife went so far as to buy meat-on-the-hoof, hoarding cattle and sheep in their home. The husband, who narrates the story, regrets his wife's disastrous search for bargains, an instance of the frugal "Puritan ethic" gone haywire:

> Thus by hourly encroachments, my habitation is made narrower and narrower; the dining room is so crowded with tables that dinner can scarcely be served; the parlour is decorated with so many piles of china, that I dare not come within the door; at every turn of the stairs, I have a clock, and half the windows of the upper floors are darkened, that shelves may be set before them.

As if this annoyance were not enough to bear, the wife, violating the unwritten code of the republican household, served him spoiled meat for dinner, merely to gratify her bargain-hunting whims. "Contrary to my taste," the husband reports, "she condemns me to live upon salt provisions. She knows the loss of buying in small quantities; we have therefore whole hogs, and quarters of oxen; part of our meat is tainted before it is eaten, and part is thrown away because it is spoiled; but she persists in her system, and will never buy anything by single pennyworths." Cognizant of bachelorhood's comparative advantages, the husband tells us that a bachelor friend has recommended that he auction off his wife's possessions; but his fellow husbands advise him to remain tolerant of his wife's habits. We gain the impression that the husband is a passive figure, who, despite his "weary" exasperation, will continue to exhibit "patience" toward his domineering mate. He seems comfortable with the "feminine" role. In other respects we find that in this instance, in which the husband complains of the wife's slovenliness, roles have been reversed by comparison with the earlier "Nitidia" essay, where the wife complains of the husband's disorganization and lack of concern about household neatness. The *American Museum*'s general message, then, seems to be that there are no *universal* traits appertaining to the sexes; it is individual particularities that most matter. This is a surprisingly liberal view, one which does not insist on the superior rationality or maturity of the male, despite his patently dominant role in society—which *his* laws have bestowed upon him.[54]

Another story which supports this thesis— that men were not regarded as paragons of all the virtues and invariably superior to women—is the anecdotal "Account of a Swiss captain," which derides *male* rather than *female* vanity, pretense, insincerity, deceit, and childishness. Contrary to the view expounded by many feminists, women were not regarded as the sole possessors of these negative attributes. This tale of a retired Swiss captain with very large whiskers searching for a rich wife conveys a lesson critical for the early republic's political culture: that without *economic independence* no one, either male or female, can enjoy real freedom and dignity. The Swiss captain told a rich young woman with an independent fortune he would do anything she asked, but when she told him she would marry him only if he shaved his whiskers he peremptorily refused and broke off the courtship. The narrator concludes that women must be on the alert for conceited suitors more interested in satisfying themselves than pleasing their mate: "Had all young ladies in like circumstances equal penetration, they might generally rid themselves, with equal ease, of the interested and unprincipled coxcombs by whom they are pestered: they all have their whiskers; and seek for fortunes, to be able to cultivate, not cut them off."[55] For the man as well as the woman hoping to achieve economic security through marriage, existence was fraught with the threat of humiliating servility. Besides, an egocentric man, like a vain woman, would probably make an unsatisfactory spouse.

In most cases, the *American Museum*'s articles in 1787 treated husbands and wives to an equal share of blame for personality conflicts and marital disagreements. "On Trifles," printed in the May 1787 issue, denounced hot-tempered husbands who behaved disrespectfully toward their wives over petty annoyances mostly related to food preparation. Describing the case of "Mr. Sulky" (an aptly allegorical surname) who, piqued that his wife had folded over the pages of one of his books, refused to speak to her at dinner, the author makes clear what he thinks of such conduct: "She [Mrs. Sulky] knew not the cause of his anger, but it was an invariable maxim with him that the wife who did anything besides brushing his clothes, superintending the kitchen, and bearing children, acted a very unbecoming part."[56] Thereby the author denounces such overbearing behavior toward women, although in a sarcastic manner.

In addition, this article portrays wives with independent minds and wills of their own, rebelling against their husbands at certain moments, as when a man wants his wife to buy gold-colored buckles, but she chooses silver ones instead. The author explains:

> Now as she had, in some measure, a sort of *casting vote* in all matrimonial disputes, the husband was obliged to yield; but the argument was renewed every time he looked towards his wife's feet. About the same important affair, there were at last so many disputes, that disputing became a habit, and matrimonial comfort a stranger [my italics].

In depicting the wife as holding the "casting vote," this ludicrous incident suggests that women were subtly engaged in undermining the vestiges of patriarchy in the family, even if they disturbed the harmony of the household by asserting their will. In some ways similar to the way southern slaves malingered and destroyed owners' tools, Mrs. Sulky's passive resistance showed her displeasure with her husband: "One day a knuckle of veal was done to rags, and at night the tobacco was too dry." By this means, the wife deliberately provoked her husband's anger.[57]

However, the author concludes that impulsive, immature men who had led easy, self-indulgent lives displayed an inimical propensity to argue over insignificant "trifles" when things did not go their way. He conjectures, "Men of weak understanding who have laid it down as a mechanical plan of regular life, in which every action has its particular hour and minute, beyond which it cannot be performed are very apt to despise those who would break in upon their rules."[58] Like the middle-class, consumption-oriented wife in the preceding story of the bargain-hunter, the compulsive, time-oriented, entrepreneurial husband is the villain who disturbs marital harmony.[59]

One discerns within the pages of Carey's *American Museum* a perspective on the incipient Industrial Revolution and its businesslike, corporate mentality, which was already beginning to tear apart the old family structure, bringing the department store and the nine-to-five job in its wake.[60] Castigating those purportedly "feminine" qualities of men—their unreasonableness and passions—the author advises them to be sweet-tempered: counsel more often reserved for women. "As a peevish man is a curse to himself, and to all about him," the writer points out, "so a compliant temper, moderated by a due deference for our own opinion, is the surest proof of an excellent and improved understanding; let us be careful that nothing get the better of our tempers."[61] In order to counteract his combative compulsiveness and preserve household tranquility, the burgeoning middle-class industrialized man must cultivate the passive, self-controlled, "compliant" qualities that had traditionally been considered effeminate.

Wives were not exempt from contributing to family conflict. Like their spouses, they could behave selfishly, unreasonably, and in disregard of the common good of the family. An article on the "consequences of extravagance" in the June 1787 *American Museum*, written by a man whose wife was inordinately interested in comparing herself with her neighbors, keeping up with the Joneses and listening to their advice, bears this out. When his wife learned from her neighbors that they did not help their husbands in their businesses, she refused to work with him in his store. Comparing her spouse's social status and standard of living with those of her friends, she harassed him with cruel gibes: "My wife gave me no peace nor assistance. She wondered how I could remain a poor retailer of goods, when men of less abilities than I, were merchants: and, for her part, she would stand no more behind my counter, to be a shop-woman." When he took his wife's advice and became a merchant his wealth increased and his wife hired many servants, after which her "female friends" told her she also required a carriage to properly exhibit herself and her new status. Of course, the husband's difficulties and expenses increased with his income.[62]

As the author of the story made clear, wives were often inclined to manipulate their husbands to get what they wanted. When, "one morning, as we were conversing in bed, she [his usually nagging wife] appeared remarkably loving," he soon discovered her motive: she wanted him to buy her a carriage and horses. After he refused, she went so far as to move out of the house and "sleep for twenty-two nights at the house of one of her friends." He soon acquired an undeserved reputation as a stingy, brutish husband. Even other husbands, his former friends, refused to speak to him, "declaring that a bad husband ought to be put in Coventry [i.e., socially ostracized] by all good ones." Thus this incident reveals that husbands were not uniformly arrayed against wives—rather, they took the woman's side, at least in this case, in disputes with the husband!

Meanwhile, his wife's friends had convinced her that her husband was so miserly because he planned to divorce her and marry a younger woman. At this point she threatened to leave him and their "six small children." Finally, after the husband bought his recalcitrant wife the horses, carriages, servants and other amenities she desired, and revealed to her their cost, she renounced her absurd extravagance, dismissed her spiteful friends, and the family returned to its former habits of "frugality and industry," in accordance with the republican ethos of simplicity and moderation.

Ostensibly, the tale admonishes "undesigning good-hearted women, who are exceedingly mistaken, when they conceive all those their friends, who drink tea with them."[63] For our purposes, the story reveals that all husbands did not invariably unite against all wives in the proverbial "battle of the sexes"; women were often considered a threat to family economy with their excessive regard for social display and emulation, and competition with their neighbors (a fault which, though men undeniably possessed it, is not emphasized in these stories as pertaining to them). However, women will listen to reason and restrain their extravagant tendencies once they are convinced that they endanger the family's survival. Again, women are perceived as being fundamentally rational, although, like men, they have their peccadilloes. They are depicted as self-willed, autonomous beings who will not automatically submit to male dictates and desires. Men's failure to be shocked or angered by such defiance, as they would be in Victorian times, is perhaps owing to the Revolutionary fervor and egalitarian impetus of the Enlightenment. The 1780s were a time when Americans congratulated themselves on the success of their war for liberating themselves from an oppressive monarchy and setting up free, representative governments. Some liberal men believed this self-government and equality should extend to relations between the sexes as well. "It was dangerous for a society with democratic ideals to allow inequality to survive between men and women in the family context," one British historian points out. "The last vestiges of divine right kingship could never be extirpated among men who knew that they could reign as absolute monarchs in the home."[64] To pretend otherwise would be hypocritical, an affront to male as well as female "virtue."[65]

Notes

1. See David Szatmary, *Shays' Rebellion: The Making of an Agrarian Insurrection* (Amherst, Mass.: University of Massachusetts Press, 1980); Robert J. Taylor, *Western Massachusetts in the Revolution* (Providence, R.I.: Brown University Press, 1954).

2. A Farmer, "Cause of, and cure for, hard times," in *American Museum, or Repository of Ancient and Modern Fugitive Pieces, Prose and Poetical* 1, no. 1 (Jan. 1787): 11-13. In all cases, original spelling and punctuation have been retained. Standard accounts of the ethos of virtue, industry, and frugality in eighteenth-

century America include John E. Crowley, *This Sheba, Self: The Conceptualization of Economic Life in Eighteenth-Century America* (Baltimore: Johns Hopkins University Press, 1974), esp. 61-65, 128-129, 133-134, 148-150, and Edmund S. Morgan, "The Puritan Ethic and the American Revolution," *William and Mary Quarterly* 24, no. 1 (Jan. 1967): 3-43. Linda K. Kerber, *Women of the Republic: Intellect and Ideology in Revolutionary America* (Chapel Hill: University of North Carolina Press, 1980), 37-46, discusses the role of women as consumers during the Revolution. On the importance of salt to preserving farmers' meat and pork, see Larry G. Bowman, "The Scarcity of Salt in Virginia During the American Revolution," *Virginia Magazine of History and Biography* 67 (1969): 464-472.

3. "Character of a Bachelor," and "Character of a Married Man," *American Museum* 1 (Jan. 1787): 43.

4. "Character of a Married Man," 43. The idea that the married man was an active conqueror of nature, and his wife merely a hindrance, prevailed among physicians as late as the Victorian Era. See Graham J. Barker-Benfield, *Horrors of the Half-Known Life: Male Attitudes toward Women and Sexuality in Nineteenth Century America* (New York: Harper and Row, 1976).

5. For the patriarchal image of the husband delineated by recent historians, see, e.g., Mary Beth Norton, *Liberty's Daughters: The Revolutionary Experience of American Women, 1750-1800* (Boston: Little, Brown, 1980), 5-7, 48-50, 60-65, 119-120, 235; Kerber, *Women of the Republic*, 203-205; Joan Hoff Wilson, "The Illusion of Change: Women and the American Revolution," in Alfred F. Young, ed., *The American Revolution: Explorations in the History of American Radicalism* (DeKalb: Northern Illinois University Press, 1976); Catherine Clinton, *The Other Civil War: American Women in the Nineteenth Century* (New York: Hill and Wang, 1984); Janet W. James, *Changing Ideas About Women in the United States, 1776-1825* (New York: Garland, 1981), 8-9, 50, 56-57, 144-145; Anne F. Scott, *The Southern Lady* (Chicago: University of Chicago Press, 1970), 5-21.

6. *American Museum* 1, no. 1 (Jan. 1787): 44 (untitled article).

7. On the prevalence of alcoholism in the United States at this time, see W. J. Rorabaugh, *The Alcoholic Republic: An American Tradition* (New York: Oxford University Press, 1979). Women's drinking is considered in Christine Stansell, *City of Women: Sex and Class in New York, 1789-1860* (New York: Knopf, 1986), 80.

8. "The Prostitute: A Fragment," *American Museum* 1, no. 1 (Jan. 1787): 44-45. Emphasis in the original. Prostitution during this period is discussed briefly in Robert E. Riegel, "Changing American Attitudes toward Prostitution (1800-1920)," *Journal of the History of Ideas* 29 (Sept. 1968): 437-452, whose thesis that most commentators blamed the prostitute's depravity for her plight is not supported by the *American Museum*'s essay; and Ruth Rosen, *The Lost Sisterhood* (Baltimore: Johns Hopkins University Press, 1982).

9. "Nitidia," *American Museum* 1, no. 1 (Jan. 1787): 53-55, an extract from the *Columbian Magazine*. Hopkinson's mockery of women's devotion to housecleaning, "A Letter from a Gentleman in America, to His Friend in Europe, on White-Washing," first appeared in a newspaper, the *Pennsylvania Packet*, June 18,

1785, and was reprinted in the *American Museum* 1, no. 1 (Jan. 1787): 48-54. For the history of the *Columbian Magazine*, see William J. Free, *The Columbian Magazine and American Literary Nationalism* (The Hague: Mouton, 1968); Green, *Carey*, 7; and Lawrence J. Friedman, *Inventors of the Promised Land* (New York: Knopf, 1975), 6. For a contrasting interpretation of "Nitidia," which quotes a passage out of context to make her appear to champion a greater political role for women, see Susan Branson, "Politics and Gender: The Political Consciousness of Philadelphia Women in the 1790s" (Ph.D dissertation, Northern Illinois University, 1992), 40.

10. "Nitidia," 54.

11. Nancy F. Cott, "Passionlessness: An Interpretation of Victorian Sexual Ideology, 1790-1830," *Signs: A Journal of Women in Culture and Society* 4 (1978): 219-236. See also Jan Lewis, "The Republican Wife: Virtue and Seduction in the Early Republic," *William and Mary Quarterly* 44 (Oct. 1987): 689-721; and Marlene LeGates, "The Cult of Womanhood in Eighteenth-Century Thought," *Eighteenth-Century Studies* 10 (Fall 1976): 21-39, which (perhaps misleadingly) emphasize the treatment of women as sexual objects in eighteenth-century literature, with examples drawn mostly from French and English writers. A revisionist argument that the *philosophes*—Voltaire in particular—respected woman's intelligence and autonomy is Arthur Scherr, "Candide's Garden Revisited: Gender Equality in a Commoner's Paradise," *Eighteenth Century Life*, 17, n.s., no. 3 (Nov. 1993): 40-59.

12. "Nitidia," 54. Italics in original.

13. "Nitidia," 55. For the seriousness with which even enlightened women like Mercy Otis Warren and Judith Sargent Murray conceived of their housekeeping role, see Linda K. Kerber, *Women of the Republic: Intellect and Ideology in Revolutionary America* (Chapel Hill: University of North Carolina Press, 1980), 253, 256-258.

14. "Nitidia," 55. Women's complaints about male sloppiness, which extended to tobacco chewing and spitting, a practice which remained popular through the 1920s, are examined in Lois W. Banner, *American Beauty* (New York: Knopf, 1983), 228-229.

15. "Nitidia," 55. For various definitions of "slut," see *Oxford English Dictionary* (14 vols.; Oxford: Clarendon Press, 1961), 9: 251.

16. "Nitidia," 55.

17. Clifford Geertz, "Ideology as a Cultural System," in Geertz, *The Interpretation of Cultures: Selected Essays* (New York: Basic Books, 1973), 204-205, 209, 212-213. Studies of the ways in which blacks incorporated the white man's Christianity with traditional folk beliefs as instruments for forging an autonomous identity include: Eugene Genovese, *Roll, Jordan, Roll: The World the Slaves Made* (New York: Pantheon, 1974), 168-284; Albert J. Raboteau, *Slave Religion* (New York: Oxford University Press, 1978); and John W. Blassingame, *The Slave Community* (New York: Oxford University Press, 1979).

18. Francis Hopkinson included "Nitidia" in his *Miscellaneous Essays and Occasional Writings*, 3 vols. (Philadelphia: Thomas Dobson, 1792), 2: 146-168. The text of "Nitidia," along with the identification of Hopkinson as author, is in Linda

K. Kerber, "The Politicks of Housework," *Signs: Journal of Women in Culture and Society* 4, no. 2 (Winter 1978): 402-406. See also Kerber, *Women of the Republic*, 257-258.

19. "The pitiable case of an old bachelor," *American Museum*, 1, no. 1 (Jan. 1787): 56-57. Italics in original.

20. Norton, *Liberty's Daughters*, 51-60, 229-231; James, *Changing Ideas*, 47-48; Lee Virginia Chambers-Schiller, *Liberty, A Better Husband: Single Women in America: The Generations of 1780-1840* (New Haven: Yale University Press, 1984), discuss women's powerful position during the courtship stage of heterosexual relationships.

21. "The pitiable case of an old bachelor," *American Museum* 1, no. 1 (Jan. 1787): 57.

22. See, e.g., Joan Hoff Wilson, "Dancing Dogs of the Colonial Period: Women Scientists," *Early American Literature* 7 (Summer 1973): 225-235; Catherine Clinton, *The Other Civil War: American Women in the Nineteenth Century* (New York: Hill and Wang, 1984); Ruth Bloch, "The Gendered Meanings of Virtue in Revolutionary America," *Signs* 13 (Autumn 1987): 37-58; Mary Beth Norton, "The Evolution of White Women's Experience in Early America," *American Historical Review* 89 (June 1984): 593-618; James, *Changing Ideas*, 56-57.

23. "Comparison between the sexes," *American Museum* 1, no. 1 (Jan. 1787): 59.

24. "Comparison between the sexes," 59.

25. For Adams's ideas, see C. Bradley Thompson, *John Adams and the Spirit of Liberty* (Lawrence: University Press of Kansas, 1998), and Clinton Rossiter, "The Legacy of John Adams," *Yale Review* 46 (June 1957): 528-550. An article which argues that men manipulated their idealized stereotype of the selfless woman to justify their monopoly of political power is LeGates, "The Cult of Womanhood."

26. "Comparison between the sexes," 60.

27. See Frank L. Mott, *A History of American Magazines* (3 vols.; New York: Macmillan, 1930-1938); Lyon N. Richardson, *A History of Early American Magazines, 1741-1789* (New York: Thomas Nelson & Sons, 1931); Norton, *Liberty's Daughters*, 246-247; James, *Changing Ideas*, 102-107, 290; Bertha M. Stearns, "Early Philadelphia Magazines for Ladies," *Pennsylvania Magazine of History and Biography* 64 (Oct. 1940): 479-491. For later developments, see Ann Douglas, *The Feminization of American Culture* (New York: Knopf, 1977), and Mary Kelley, *Private Woman, Public Stage: Literary Domesticity in Nineteenth-Century America* (New York: Oxford University Press, 1984). Journals such as the short-lived Philadelphia *Lady's Magazine*, which lasted only from June 1792-May 1793, printed articles by men, similar to those appearing in the *American Museum*, informing women of their influence over the opposite sex. It is available on microfilm in the *American Periodicals Series*, 18th Century.

28. "The happy influence of female society," *American Museum* 1, no. 1 (Jan. 1787): 61-64.

29. "The happy influence of female society," 61.

30. "The happy influence of female society," 61. For a comparative study of

Europe and the United States with regard to feminism, see Donald Meyer, *Sex and Power: The Rise of Women in America, Russia, Sweden, and Italy* (Middletown, Conn.: Wesleyan University Press, 1987).

31. "The happy influence of female society," 62. See David Hume, *A Treatise of Human Nature*, ed. L. A. Selby Bigge (Oxford: Clarendon Press, 1978; originally published, London, 1739-1740).

32. "The happy influence of female society," 62. For earlier arguments that women, like Adam's mistress Eve, embodied seduction and the powers of evil, see Lonna H. Malmsheimer, "Daughters of Zion: New England Roots of American Feminism," *New England Quarterly* 50 (1977): 484-504, and Carol Karlsen, *The Devil in the Shape of a Woman* (New York: Norton, 1987). A recent extreme statement of this view, which asserts that men regarded women and even their own children as parasites, is Stansell, *City of Women*, 19-30.

33. "The happy influence of female society," 63. Recent discussions of women's reputation for possessing covert power over men during this period are Herman R. Lantz et al., "Pre-Industrial Patterns in the Colonial Family in America: A Content Analysis of Colonial Magazines," *American Sociological Review* 33, no. 3 (June 1968): 413-426, and Cott, "Passionlessness."

34. "The happy influence of female society," 64.

35. See Laurel Thatcher Ulrich, *Good Wives: Image and Reality in the Lives of Women in Northern New England, 1650-1750* (New York: Knopf, 1982), and Ulrich, "'Vertuous Women Found": New England Ministerial Literature, 1668-1735," *American Quarterly* 28, no. 1 (Spring 1976): 20-40; Malmsheimer, "Daughters of Zion."

36. "Family disagreements the frequent cause of immoral conduct," *American Museum* 1, no. 1 (Jan. 1787): 66. Though this article was far less sympathetic to children than similar essays would be today, its patriarchal perspective was soon overshadowed by more permissive attitudes toward childhood. See Jay Fliegelman, *Prodigals and Pilgrims: The American Revolution Against Patriarchal Authority, 1750-1800* (Cambridge: Cambridge University Press, 1982), and Bernard Wishy, *The Child and the Republic: The Dawn of Modern American Child Nurture* (Philadelphia: University of Pennsylvania Press, 1968). For early Puritan views on children's innate depravity, see Edmund S. Morgan, *The Puritan Family: Religious and Domestic Relations in Seventeenth-Century New England*, rev. ed. (New York: Harper and Row, 1966), 90, 92-97, 104, 138, 172.

37. "Family disagreements the frequent cause of immoral conduct," 65-66. On the Puritan/evangelical concept of "breaking the child's will," which persisted in varying forms from the 1600s to the 1800s (evolving from physical to psychological torture), see Philip J. Greven, *The Protestant Temperament* (New York: Knopf, 1977). An affectionate household environment proliferated on Southern plantations. See Daniel Blake Smith, *Inside the Great House: Planter Family Life in Eighteenth-Century Chesapeake Society* (Ithaca, N.Y.: Cornell University Press, 1980).

38. "Family disagreements the frequent cause of immoral conduct," 66.

39. "Family disagreements the frequent cause of immoral conduct," 66. For the

prevalence of similar views in the mid-eighteenth century South, see Jan Lewis, "Domestic Tranquillity and the Management of Emotion in Pre-Revolutionary Virginia," *William and Mary Quarterly*, 3d Ser., 39, no. 1 (Jan. 1982): 135-149. Elizabeth Pleck's sketchy study, *Domestic Tyranny: The Making of American Social Policy Against Family Violence from Colonial Times to the Present* (New York: Oxford University Press, 1987), concentrates on more recent trends in family violence.

40. "Family disagreements the frequent cause of immoral conduct," 66.

41. *Ibid.* During the eighteenth century, David Hume and Benjamin Franklin, among others, elucidated the negative connotations of the terms "ambition and avarice." Such character traits were considered inimical to the survival of the republic, wherein the public good must have priority over selfish personal gain. See, e.g., Gerald Stourzh, *Benjamin Franklin and American Foreign Policy* (Chicago: University of Chicago Press, 1954), 15-19, and Albert O. Hirschman, *The Passions and the Interests: Political Arguments for Capitalism Before its Triumph* (Princeton: Princeton University Press, 1977).

42. "Select Poetry: The happy pair," in *American Museum*, 1, no. 1 (January 1787): 74-75. The "advice literature" read by American women in the 1780s is well-surveyed in Mary Sumner Benson, *Women in Eighteenth Century America: A Study of Opinion and Social Usage* (New York: Columbia University Press, 1935). James, *Changing Ideas*, tends to concentrate on English and New England ministerial "prescriptive literature" concerning female character and deportment.

43. "Advice to the married," *ibid.*, 75-76.

44. "A Jealous Man," *American Museum* 1, no. 2 (Feb. 1787): 137.

45. Philadelphia farmer's almanacs, whose scope and arrangement were similar to the *American Museum*'s, printed stories about wife-beating and male sexual abuse of women into the 1820s. Joan M. Jensen, *Loosening the Bonds: Mid-Atlantic Farm Women, 1750-1850* (New Haven: Yale University Press, 1986), 117-118. For later pathological male sex stereotypes, see Estelle B. Freedman, "'Uncontrolled Desires': The Response to the Sexual Psychopath, 1920-1960," *Journal of American History* 74, no. 2 (June 1987): 83-106.

46. "Plan for the establishment of a fair of fairs, or market of matrimony," *American Museum* 1, no. 2 (Feb. 1787): 140-142. Conflicting demographic evidence exists as to whether the marriage rate was lower in New England than elsewhere in the country. Robert Higgs and H. Louis Stattler III, "Colonial New England Demography: A Sampling Approach," *William and Mary Quarterly*, 3d Ser., 27 (1970): 282-294, while John Demos's study, "Families in Colonial Bristol, R. I.: An Exercise in Historical Demography," *ibid.*, 25 (1968): 40-57, argues that marriages were generally postponed for financial reasons, as does Philip Greven's work on family patterns in Andover, Massachusetts, during the eighteenth century, *Four Generations* (Ithaca, N.Y.: Cornell University Press, 1966). "A husband, a lord and master, whom she should love, honor and obey, nature designed for every woman," Virginia's racial philosopher George Fitzhugh wrote in 1854. "If she be obedient she stands little danger of maltreatment." *Sociology for the South* (1854), quoted in

Scott, *Southern Lady*, 17.

47. "Plan for the establishment of a fair of fairs," 140. The well-known historical fact that New England's population was declining relative to the rest of the Union has been reemphasized by Daniel Scott Smith, "'All in Some Degree Related to Each Other': A Demographic and Comparative Resolution of the Anomaly of New England Kinship," *American Historical Review* 94 (1989): 45-46.

48. "Plan for the establishment of a fair of fairs," 141-142. Banner, *American Beauty*, 17, exaggeratedly writes, "American periodicals in the 1790s were filled with attacks on fashion."

49. "On the happiness of domestic life," *American Museum* 1, no. 2 (Feb. 1787): 156-158, quote at 158.

50. "On the happiness of domestic life," 158. This view became especially prevalent after 1830. See Barbara Welter, "The Cult of True Womanhood: 1820-1860," *American Quarterly* 18 (1966): 151-174.

51. Linda K. Kerber, "The Republican Mother: Women and the Enlightenment: An American Perspective," *American Quarterly* 28 (Summer 1976): 187-205; William D. Liddle, "Virtue and Liberty: An Inquiry into the Role of the Agrarian Myth in the Rhetoric of the American Revolutionary Era," *South Atlantic Quarterly* 77 (1978): 15-38.

52. "To the ladies: the distinction," *American Museum* 1, no. 3 (March 1787): 263.

53. "Lines, address'd to a coquette," *American Museum* 1, no. 3 (March 1787): 263. For the efforts by some writers in the 1790s to control what they perceived as the dangerous excesses of woman's passionate sexuality, see Patricia J. McAlexander, "The Creation of the American Eve," *Early American Literature* 9 (Winter 1975): 252-266.

54. "Account of a Buyer of Bargains," *American Museum* 1, no. 4 (April 1787): 307-308. On the importance of women's role as consumers in the Anglo-American world in colonial and more recent times, see *Of Consuming Interests: The Style of Life in the Eighteenth Century*, Cary Carson, Ronald Hoffman, and Peter J. Albert, eds., (Charlottesville: University Press of Virginia, 1994); T. H. Breen, "Baubles of Britain: The American and Consumer Revolutions of the Eighteenth Century," *Past and Present* 119 (May 1988): 73-104, reprinted in *Of Consuming Interests*; Breen, "Narrative of Commercial Life: Consumption, Ideology, and Community on the Eve of the American Revolution," *William and Mary Quarterly*, 3d Ser., 50, no. 3 (July 1993): 471-501; *The Culture of Consumption in America*, Richard W. Fox and T. J. Jackson Lears, eds. (New York: Pantheon, 1983); Jeanne Boydston, *Home and Work: Housework, Wages, and the Ideology of Labor in the Early Republic* (New York: Oxford University Press, 1990); Carole Shammas, *The Pre-Industrial Consumer in England and America* (Oxford: Clarendon Press, 1990); *Consumption and the World of Goods*, John Brewer and Roy Porter, eds. (London: Routledge, 1993); *The Birth of Consumer Society: The Commercialization of Eighteenth-Century England*, Neil McKendrick, John Brewer, and J. H. Plumb, eds. (Bloomington, Ind.: Indiana University Press, 1982); and William R. Leach, "Transformations in a Culture of Consumption: Women and Department Stores,

1890-1925," *Journal of American History* 71 (1984): 319-342.

55. "Account of a Swiss Captain," *American Museum* 1, no. 3 (April 1987): 309-311. On the American obsession with individual economic and concomitant moral and political independence and its evolution in the young republic, see two excellent essays: Richard L. Bushman, "This New Man: Dependence and Independence, 1776," and Rowland Berthoff, "Independence and Attachment, Virtue and Interest: From Republican Citizen to Free Enterpriser, 1787-1837," both in *Uprooted Americans: Essays to Honor Oscar Handlin*, Richard Bushman et al., eds. (Boston: Little, Brown, 1979), 79-96, 97-124.

56. "On Trifles," *American Museum* 1, no. 5, 2nd ed (May 1787): 444-450, quote at 446.

57. "On Trifles," 447-448. On the passive resistance of black slaves in the south, see, e.g., Kenneth M. Stampp, *The Peculiar Institution: Slavery in the Antebellum South* (New York: Knopf, 1956).

58. "On Trifles," 448-449.

59. An outstanding overview of the transition from a task-oriented to a time-oriented mentality in early modern Europe, with implications for burgeoning American industrialism, is E. P. Thompson, "Time, Work-Discipline, and Industrial Capitalism," *Past and Present* 38 (1967): 56-97.

60. See, e.g., Gregory H. Nobles, "Capitalism in the Countryside: The Transformation of Rural Society in the United States," *Radical History Review* 41 (April 1988): 163-176, and Nancy F. Cott, *The Bonds of Womanhood* (New Haven: Yale University Press, 1977).

61. "On Trifles," 450.

62. "Consequences of Extravagance," *American Museum* 1, no. 6 (June 1787): 549-552.

63. "Consequences of Extravagance," 552. In accordance with the thesis expounded by Lantz and Cott, a subordinate theme of the story is the covert power the wife exerted over the husband, thereby forcing him to accede to her demands.

64. Sylvia Strauss, *"Traitors to the Masculine Cause": The Men's Campaign for Women's Rights* (Westport, Conn.: Greenwood Press, 1982), 7. However, Strauss is primarily concerned with nineteenth-century Great Britain rather than the United States. For excellent discussions of how the optimistic libertarian spirit fostered by success in the American Revolution increased men's awareness of women's oppression and their desire to rectify it by means of increased educational opportunities, see Norton, *Liberty's Daughters*, 256-294; James, *Changing Ideas*, 65-83; Kerber, *Women of the Republic*, 189-231; and Selma R. Williams, *Demeter's Daughters: The Women Who Founded America, 1587-1787* (New York: Atheneum, 1976), 316-325. On middle-class Victorian male culture's assertion of an absolute right to property in women, see the astute analysis in Keith Thomas, "The Double Standard," *Journal of the History of Ideas* 20, no. 2 (April 1959): 195-216.

65. See Ruth Bloch, "The Gendered Meanings of Virtue in Revolutionary America," *Signs* 13 (Autumn 1987): 37-58; Lance Banning, "Some Second Thoughts on Virtue and the Course of Revolutionary Thinking," in *Conceptual Change and*

the Constitution, Terence Ball and J. G. A. Pocock, eds. (Lawrence: University Press of Kansas, 1988), 194-212; Norton, *Liberty's Daughters*, 243-244; Kerber, *Women of the Republic*, 11, 199-200, 229, 287. For a more negative view, see Joan R. Gundersen, "Independence, Citizenship, and the American Revolution," *Signs* 13 (Autumn 1987): 59-77, and Elaine F. Crane, "Dependence in the Era of Independence: The Role of Women in a Republican Society," in *The American Revolution: Its Character and Limits*, Jack P. Greene, ed. (New York: New York University Press, 1987), 253-275.

Chapter 4

Marriage, Manners, and Morals

At a time when American leaders looked to ancient republics like ascetic, self-disciplined Sparta and Rome for political models, perhaps one might expect that they would try to adopt dignified, modest examples in marital conduct and fashion as well.[1] Whatever the actual practice, the *American Museum* sought to inculcate such virtuous habits in its readers during the critical year 1787, when the United States Constitution was being hammered out at the Philadelphia Convention. In *Spirit of the Laws* (1748), a work that Americans highly regarded, Montesquieu taught that virtue was an essential personality trait for citizens in a republic. Contributors to Carey'magazine did their best to propagate this ideal in relations between men and women, as well as in their dress and personal habits.[2]

Foremost among the *American Museum*'s concerns was that American women eschew the debauched mode of dress prevalent in the corrupt Old World's decadent monarchies, from which the United States had recently asserted its independence. In November 1787, the author of an "Address to the ladies of America," deriding various fashions in hats and dresses which had been transferred to the United States from Europe, demonstrated that they originated primarily from the attempts of aristocratic (usually French) women to hide some physical or facial defect or convert it into an advantage, using their power in society and the *beau monde*. Employing the pseudonym "Frank Amity" to indicate his desire for American women's friendship, he advised his female readers to create their own styles, on a more sensible pattern than Europe's:

> How much more consistent with your dignity would it be, to assume a national distinction, invent your own fashions? Your country is independent of European power: and your modes of dress should be independent of a groupe of coquettes, milliners, and manufacturers, who, from motives of vanity on one hand, and avarice on the other, endeavour to enslave the fancy of the whole world.

As *American* women, members of a *republic* (if not yet full citizens), "Frank Amity" advised the ladies to wear simple garb and follow the dictates of frugality and virtue. He concluded with a poem counseling them to observe modesty and restraint in their relationships with the opposite sex as well:

> Be frugal then: the coyly-yielded kiss
> Charms most, and gives the most sincere delight.
> Cheapness offends: hence on the harlot's lip
> No rapture hangs, however fair she seem.
> Hail MODESTY! fair female honour, hail!
> Beauty's chief adornment, and beauty's self!
> For beauty must with virtue ever dwell,
> And thou art virtue! and without thy charm,
> Beauty is insolent and wit profane.[3]

While professing himself their "frank admirer," the author apparently preferred humble, self-effacing ladies to the more aggressive types who were frequently depicted in the *American Museum*'s short stories. In any case, taking a patriotic stance, he urged American women to distance themselves from the corruptions of their sisters across the Atlantic.

The question of American women's imitation of European fashions became a nationalist shibboleth at this time for several reasons. Not only did such emulation insult the new nation's republican ethos of virtue and frugality, it hindered domestic manufactures and, by encouraging the importation of luxuries from Europe, contributed to a serious trade deficit.

It seemed crucial that American women learn their duty to abstain from such ostentatious frippery, especially "bustlers" (bustles), a superfluous undergarment that accentuated the buttocks. "Bickerstaff," a contributor from Newport, Rhode Island, who had strong feelings about this matter, argued that American men preferred the natural beauty of the female face and form, not its ridiculous distortion by the fashions of the day, often borrowed from a decadent Europe. He declared himself pleased to discover that the ladies of London had recently abandoned their bustles, and "are again falling into the shapes which nature gave them—that broad hoops, bell-hoops, high heads, and low heads have all had their day; but the genuine figure is now restored." "Bickerstaff" insisted that the natural woman was the most attractive. He eagerly anticipated the time when "the fair of this town . . . no longer disguise their beautiful forms with hoops or *bustlers*, nor divert our attention from the symmetry of their features, and the carnation of their complexions, by enormous hats, bedizened with a profusion of ribans [ribbons] and feathers." If young ladies wanted to attract him, they need not go to much trouble.

More seriously, the author noted that the bustle on a woman's *derrière,* in addition to being unsightly, wasted huge amounts of wool that could be more productively and charitably utilized to clothe the poor and reduce the price of necessary clothing for all. Therefore it was both aesthetically and economically beneficial to eradicate the bustle from the American scene. As "Bickerstaff" poignantly explained:

> The sheep's wool that grows in this state, is, I believe, not sufficient for stockings for its inhabitants; what then must be the wretched situation, particularly of the poor of this town, the approaching winter, when the wool, which might cover the legs of hundreds, is diverted from that use, and manufactured into odious bustlers![4]

In Newport alone, the author asserted, the amount of wool consumed in bustle-making would provide stockings for six hundred people.

"Bickerstaff" confidently expected that his appeal to women's benevolence and vanity would convince them to forego their bustles. His optimism suggests that, unlike many later Victorians (including Sigmund Freud), at this juncture Americans thought women were compassionate. "Female softness and pity could not sustain the painful reflection" that the poor might suffer as a result of women's ostentation, he predicted. "The *bustler* must yield to the feelings of humanity." The cumbersome padding warped the "female form," increased the burden on the poor, and endangered women's health.[5]

Moreover, "Bickerstaff" regarded the bustle as a depraved excrescence of Europe's monarchies, specifically Germany and England. Recounting the garment's history, he traced the bustle back only as far as 1783. At that time the German "duchess of Bustledorfe," who was visiting London, caused quite a stir among "the ladies of the court," who were astounded by "the redundant protuberancy" of her buttocks. According to him, the ladies' "fondness of imitation," as well as the niceties of international diplomacy, resulted in the creation of "some habiliment, that would impart to them a jutting magnificence similar to that of the duchess." This was the origin of the "bustler" in England and of its introduction to the United States, which won its independence in the same year. American women's slavish imitation of British fashions aroused the writer's contempt. "Its [the "bustler's"] passage to, and its adoption in, America, will find an easy key in that strange cupidity for foreign fashions, for which the ladies of this country are so remarkable," he observed.[6]

"Bickerstaff" hoped that the recent decline of the bustle's popularity in London would precipitate its downfall in America. But he was also counting on his appeal to the sympathy of American women for "the restoration, or rather development, of the beautiful forms of the fair," and the alleviation of the needs of the laboring poor.[7] Thereby "Bickerstaff" linked his preferences in female fashion with a declaration in favor of republicanism and a humane concern for the lower classes, whose interests, he believed, had priority over the frivolous, "effeminate" luxury of bustles.

In Bickerstaff's case, as in most of the others we have examined from the pages of the *American Museum*, men did not perceive women as one-dimensional figures, embodying a uniform standard of behavior, either noble and "delicate" or vicious and deceitful. Rather, they were limned in the amoral, highly ambiguous role of consumers, capable, as consumers generally are, of much good as well as much bad.[8] Neither angels nor devils, they were regarded as rational beings to whom appeals to act rationally, in accord with the general good of society, might be expected to have some effect. They were independent, with wills of their own.

The existence of independent thought, even cantankerousness, in women whom historians have depicted as universally subjugated and suppressed, often emerges from the *American Museum*'s pages. One Susannah Trapes (probably a pseudonym), for instance, vigorously complained about the dirty mudholes and wagons blocking her path in the Philadelphia streets. One day, descending a small hill, she fell into one of these mudholes, and ruined her Sunday finery. Susannah protested that, as a taxpayer, she should be entitled to clean streets unblocked by wagons on market days. A politically astute woman, she may have been single or widowed. In any case, perhaps we may consider "Susannah Trapes" an unheralded precursor of the Women's Movement.[9]

As "Benvolio" discovered to his chagrin, a gentleman could not even rely on women to uphold his position on so uncontroversial an issue as the offensiveness of tobacco smoke. Subjected to fumes from cigars, the young man feared to antagonize the smokers by complaining, so he "artfully" observed "that the effects of this amusement might be disagreeable to the ladies; but one and all exclaimed, that they were accustomed to it, and did not by any means think it offensive; so that, deserted by the support which I had expected from *female delicacy*, I had no alternative but a precipitate retreat, to save me from intolerable sickness and disgrace."[10] The non-smoker can sympathize with the author, whose tribulations had not yet ended. A snuff-smoking visitor blew some smoke in his wife's face, after which "she was seized with a fit of sneezing, that tormented her for the rest of the day," "Benvolio" recalls. "At length, our guest retired, but not before he had deposited the relics of his exhausted quids [chewing tobacco or snuff] in every corner of the room."[11] Apparently, both men and women were ineffectual in deterring the smoker's onslaught. The story has a modern ring. More importantly, Benvolio reveals that women were perceived to possess sufficient willpower to reject men's pleas for cooperation. On the other hand, the (male?) smoker could be the enemy of both men and women.[12] This might supply a basis for comradeship.

Judging from the popularity of the "old bachelor," whose series, reprinted from the *Pennsylvania Magazine*, acclaimed the benefits of marriage (in a somewhat satirical vein), men had become more aware of the "fair sex's" positive traits. Irked at observing a happily married pair, the bachelor was envious because he had no wife of his own. "I had rather see it all fire and smoke and then the laugh would be on my side," he admitted. This ludicrous debauchee enjoyed observing arguments between husbands and wives. Now sixty-five years old, the bachelor regretted that he had never married and that now it was too late. "I tell you, I ought to be *hanged* for not being married *before*," he said. "But I ought to be *hung*, in chains, if I get married *now*." He favored a law "to make it a felony for any man to remain a bachelor after forty." This droll example of male depravity claimed to have fathered many illegitimate children, "some are black and some are white, and some are neither." But he regrets he does not know what became of them, nor did he interest himself in their education. This subversive denunciation of men's promiscuity, with its implications of *male* lack of self-control, ends on a note more serious than sardonic:

> Ever since I reformed, which is now two years [the "Old Bachelor" writes], I have pondered very seriously thereon [about his bastard brood]. I reason thus—to beget them was a *natural* crime; to disown them, a *proud* one; and to neglect them, a cruel one.[13]

The aging bachelor is ready to admit his loneliness. He concludes that a licentious, promiscuous existence is not so pleasant as one might think.

In his new identity as a sage, the "Old Bachelor" conveys accepted wisdom about the danger of marriages undertaken for "false motives," primarily unrestrained sexual desire or eagerness to acquire a wealthy spouse. Such pernicious stimuli can impel members of either sex, who "richly deserve" their inevitable unhappiness. As the bachelor pointed out, "As badly off as I am, I had rather be a solitary bachelor, than a miserable married man." Young people generally married under the influence of short-lived erotic drives, which were replaced by "mutual hatred and contempt," he remarks. They did not employ foresight; instead, "for a few hours of dalliance, I will not call it affection, the repose of all their future days are sacrificed; and those, who but just before seemed to live only for each other, now would almost cease to live, that the separation might be eternal."[14] This mordant depiction of young married people does not single out women for reproach as being more irresponsible or immature than their spouses. In other words, husbands and wives receive the same condemnation and are viewed as being similarly unable to control their impulses.

Those who married from a calculated desire for their spouses' wealth—fiscal rather than physical passion—were even more execrable than those who joined together out of sexual attraction: they "intermarry fortunes, not minds, or even bodies," the old bachelor declared. While this type of arrangement led to an "insipid" stability, it was a far cry from "happiness." Those who had money generally possessed "ease"—leisure, the necessary condition for happiness—but they lacked happiness itself. Young fortune-hunters, like those who married out of temporary, passionate impulse, were equally misguided about the meaning of happiness. "If, therefore, the rash who marry inconsiderately, perish in the storms, raised by their own passions," the bachelor argued, comparing two categories of individuals who lived by different, but equally invalid world-views, "these slumber away their days in a sluggish calm, and rather dream they live, than experience it by a series of actual sensible enjoyments." Those who married for money were in essence prostitutes no matter what their gender, "however softened by the letter of the law; and he or she who receives the golden equivalent of youth and beauty so wretchedly bestowed, can never enjoy what they so dearly purchased." Marriages undertaken for such corrupt reasons were bound to fail: These people would so quickly tire of each other, especially the youth who married an older individual for money, that they would soon abandon even "good manners," which were in those days considered essential to a good marriage. As the bachelor succinctly put it, he was not surprised "that those who either marry gold without love, or love without gold, should be miserable." These remarks applied to women as well as men.

Paradoxically, even people with competent incomes who married for love often ended up angry and disappointed. Spouses with the best intentions soon became bored, "indifferent," and eventually hostile: "As extacy abates, coolness succeeds, which often makes way for indifference, and that for neglect." Old couples grow insensitive to one another, careless of each other's feelings, and take each other for granted, the bachelor pointed out. For this, the man and woman are equally responsible. After a while, they "pursue separate pleasures" and seek new lovers, and "mutual infidelity makes way for mutual complaisance" and reciprocal deception. The old bachelor quizzically concurs with the Native Americans (Indians), who estimated that only one out of a hundred American marriages were happy; the best marriages were like those of the natives, whose men and women stayed together only so long as they loved and desired to please each other.[15] This was good advice, but inappropriate for the descendants of Puritans.

In any case, the "Old Bachelor" series, obviously popular since it was reprinted in several periodicals, astutely delineated men's views of women concerning the all-important marital relationship. In those days, many individuals regarded marriage as the quintessential, indeed the only viable, option for women. Others acclaimed "Liberty, a better husband."[16] For the author of the "Old Bachelor" series, however, men and women had similar reasons for and like inclinations toward marriage. He did not stress woman's urgency to find a mate. Perhaps historians have exaggerated the eighteenth-century woman's belief that she was hopelessly devoid of social identity unless she were some man's wife.

The relative weight of erotic, financial, and moral imperatives in marriage aroused much popular discussion. Comparing the respective pecuniary advantages of married and single life, "Philander" opts for the former. At the same time he defends women as frugal, responsible people who were more cautious in spending money than men. Warning that the onerous pursuit of "luxury" deterred early marriages, he insisted that married people should simultaneously be able to save for family emergencies and live in reasonable comfort. American families should avoid emulating European manners, especially in pursuit of "refinement in living," which threatened household frugality and fiscal viability. Moreover, "Philander" noted, excessive purchases of foreign goods undermined national economic and political independence. He thereby delineated the connection between the loving, cooperative, autonomous family and a strong, economically independent republic.

Unfortunately, "Philander" observed, the number of marriages was declining as a result of the obsession with "expensive and unnecessary articles" from abroad. Young men thought they had to be rich and able to afford luxuries before they could propose marriage. He hoped to disabuse them of this pernicious idea, which was rooted in an unflattering view of women as unduly attached to expensive things. "Philander" insisted that women were not all ruthless gold diggers intent on forcing their husbands into debt. As he tersely explained:

> The expence of a family is considerable, but so is the expense of a single life; and notwithstanding there are many ladies, who would help to squander away the hard-earned profits of industry, yet there are many, too, who would assist in preserving them, and in accumulating an estate.[17]

Contending that bachelors were greater spendthrifts than married men, "Philander" implied that women were in fact less wasteful and extravagant than either. This was an unusual position for a man to take, but he seemed to think that women properly embodied the republican ethos of industry and frugality so frequently stressed by American writers during the 1780s:

> A woman of any understanding will always contract her expences, within her husband's income, provided she knows what that income is. I have no doubt many men deceive their wives in this article, and when they fall in arrears, lay all the blame to their [wives'] extravagance. Such a conduct is equally mean and criminal.[18]

More avid in his support of the institution of marriage than the "old bachelor," "Philander" (whose name in the original Greek meant "loving one's husband") thought that men should marry for love (at approximately age twenty-five) and not worry about the expense of a family. Reminiscing that he had once doubted his ability to support a wife, he asserts, "in the fascination of love I ventured to try the experiment, and have yet no cause to repent of my rashness. Either I earn more money by more diligent attention to business, or I spend less in useless amusements, or my partner is a better economist, than I was when a bachelor," he explains. Obviously, the love he is advocating is cautious, thoughtful, mature and rational, not childishly spontaneous. Moreover, his wife participates as an equal partner in the marriage. Unlike the old bachelor, "Philander" is optimistic in his predictions and expectations of women and marriage. Money does not present a problem, and his wife is apparently responsible for the economic feasibility of the household. "Whatever may be the reason," he found "subsistence as easy" as when he was single; "and I flatter myself [I] have added to the sum of social felicity . . . . The merit of American ladies is universally acknowledged."[19] "Philander's" essay is another example of men's respect for women. He does not write about them condescendingly, but rather as equal, loving partners in a mutual relationship.

What makes the *American Museum* so useful as a barometer of male opinion on women, however, is its presentation of a variety of views, rather than serving as mouthpiece for a specific stance. "A.B.," a Philadelphia tradesman whose wife is a talkative, shrewish nuisance, has learned from experience that marriage is far from idyllic. He writes about a trip he, his wife, and their little daughter took to New York City to visit his spouse's wealthy cousin, a journey she had long wanted to make. In her anticipation, she kept him awake the night before the trip with her chatter. As "A.B." sarcastically recalls, "Thus passed the night away in delightful discourse—if that can properly be called a discourse wherein my wife said all that was said; my replies never amounting to more than the monosyllables yes or no, uttered between sleeping and waking." The rest of the story continues in this ironic tone, as he recounts the petty annoyances of his "notable wife," as he mockingly calls her, employing a complimentary term of the period.

Reluctantly leaving his "old negro wench" (possibly a slave or servant) in charge of the house, he embarked with his wife and daughter. The former scolded him for letting a cartman get ahead of him on the Bridge. Like many backseat drivers today, she complained that, "I had not the spirit of a louse—that I let everybody impose upon me." Halfway to New York, she noticed her daughter had left her new hat behind and demanded that her husband drive back to get it. Blaming *his* remissness, she insisted that "it was my place to see that every thing was put in the chaise [carriage] that ought to be—that there was no dependence upon me for any thing—that unless she looked after every thing herself, she was sure to find something neglected—and that she saw plainly, I undertook this journey with an ill will, merely because she had set her heart upon it." The wife's tirade bears some similarity to discussions that take place in modern families, and to the dialogue in "soap operas" and situation comedies today.

In contrast to the traditional depiction of eighteenth-century husbands as austere, patriarchal ogres, *this* husband tries to keep calm. "Silent patience was my only remedy," he admits, while his wife and daughter complained about everything—the travel, the food at a Trenton inn, etc. The author ludicrously recalls: "My wife found fault with every thing; ate a very hearty dinner—declaring all the time there was nothing fit to eat. Miss Jenny [his daughter] crying out with the tooth-ach, her mother making sad lamentations—all my fault." The husband remains passive despite his wife's screaming abuse: "I acknowledge every thing my wife says, for fear of discomposing her." When they finally arrive in New York City after several misadventures en route, his wife, the epitome of the negative attributes men imputed to women, wastefully "spent a great deal of money in purchasing a hundred useless articles, which we *could not possibly do without*," all the while insisting that other husbands treated their spouses much more generously.

To conclude this stereotypical farce, the author tells us that on their return to Philadelphia he discovered various disasters had afflicted his employees and his home. Of course his wife reproved him: her "usual ingenuity continued to throw the blame of all these misfortunes upon me. As this was a consolation to which I had been long accustomed in all untoward cases, I had recourse to my usual remedy, to wit, silence and patience."[20] "A.B.'s" tale is familiar to us as the standard comedy of the henpecked husband, but in the 1780s it had not yet been reduced to a hackneyed, formulaic plot. The author's serene stoicism is worthy of notice. It is a sincere statement of character, rather than a comic ploy. Again, we find that the woman is depicted as aggressive and self-willed. Although not especially reasonable or admirable in this case, she is definitely assertive and unintimidated by her husband. Perhaps this was the reality behind the stereotype of the passive, submissive, obedient colonial housewife.

An opposite perspective on husband and wife is conveyed in the article, "On Contentment." The author denounces a man whose obsession with earning a fortune took precedence over the happiness of his wife and children, who were satisfied with their small farm. He brought them to the city, became a merchant enslaved to his shop, and was never happy. In this instance, the wife is not interested in her husband's wealth. Instead, *he* is dedicated to the pursuit of riches and, though driven by his goal, is disillusioned when it is achieved.[21]

Indeed, writers and poets in the *American Museum* tended to stress male rather than female passion and irrationality. They also recognized that married women might feel desire for another man, and act on that desire. Both themes are encompassed by "The Injured Husband's Complaint," a powerfully emotional poem. The husband, whose wife has left him, experiences "anguish and despair." He asks the Heavens above to teach him to "hate The fair he must despise." Despite his torment, he will "tear her from his breast, and root her from his soul." She had callously betrayed him:

> Once, pure as winter's whitest snow,
> She gave her sacred vow!
> Once, pure as innocence: but oh!
> Just heav'n! what is she now?
> Then grant a wish, indulgent fate,
> On which my heart is set:
> Or, if I must not think to hate
> O let me but forget![22]

Men understood that women were not passionless beings. They might even stray from their wedding vows if they felt the tug of desire. Female reformers such as Judith Sargent Murray were more likely than male critics to denounce the exhibition of women's passion through such modes as Susanna Rowson's romantic novel, *Charlotte Temple.* They decried female novelists' romantic fiction for purveying unwarranted displays of women's emotion, passion, and sexuality, along with unduly explicit seduction scenes.[23]

On the other hand, men candidly blamed their sexual lust and callousness for the existence of prostitution, rather than ascribing it to female wickedness or hypersexuality, as later became common.[24] They failed to look beyond psychological factors to the social and economic determinants of prostitution. But they were more aware than later generations that prostitution is not a victimless crime. Rather simplistically, a poem, entitled "Seduction—An Elegy," analyzed an erstwhile virgin's turn to vice following her treacherous seduction by a young man. Now no man wants her. Ubiquitously subjected to the gossips of both sexes, she is doomed to prostitution:

> She, who so late in virtue's garden bloomed,
> The sweetest flower beneath the chearful sky,
> Is now to want or prostitution doomed,
> To hear the jest obscene, the lewd reply.

The poet implores God to punish the seducer during his lifetime, but to forgive him on Judgment Day:

> May heaven's vengeance still the wretch pursue,
> May infamy still fasten on his name,
> Who from fair honour's path the virgin drew,
> And gave her up to poverty and shame.

A companion piece, "The dying prostitute," depicts a pathetic harlot's thoughts during her final moments.

Carey's poets, usually anonymously, unabashedly attacked grim social and sexual evils. They looked upon the prostitute's predicament with sympathy rather than disdain, though their analysis seldom went beyond the refrain that male seducers and an unforgiving, straitlaced society were responsible for her bitter fate. The prostitute was the victim of depraved men and their abuse. Sadly, she had felt a genuine love for the brutes who debauched her and "repaid [her] by want and woe, disease and endless shame." Seldom paid by her clients, she endured a pauper's life, often lacking shelter or a place to sleep. She had once been young and beautiful, but a life of dissipation and illness had wasted her. She too was driven to her tragic fall by an insidious young seducer:

> Ah! say, insidious Damon! monster! where?

> What glory hast thou gained by my [the prostitute's]
> defeat?
> Art thou more blest, because that I'm less fair?
> Or bloom thy laurels o'er my winding sheet?[25]

The empathy for the prostitute these writers convey makes it difficult to believe that they are male, but during this period there were few female poets, and such a sordid topic would not be likely to attract them. Indeed, during this period *male* proto-feminist writers often adopted *female* pseudonyms. Though we may consider their analysis quaint and naive, at least they were willing to confront this serious social problem rather than irrationally blame it on the myth of irrepressible female sexuality.[26]

Lighter essays, tailored to the middle-class lifestyle, were more common entries. In February 1788 an adviser of "fine ladies" urged women readers to acquire as many suitors as possible, and use whatever deceitful tricks they knew to reap the privileges accruing to their gender. Social dissembling, raised to the level of a fine art, was the key to success, especially if one were physically unattractive. In the matter of sowing one's teeth, for instance, the author counseled:

> Are your teeth white? shew them upon all and no occasions: laugh at every speech, whether a joke or not; and *swear [u]pon honour, you can't help it.* Are your teeth black? then never, never laugh. If some rude unexpected story should provoke you, screw up your mouth as much as possible . . . . if all should fail, it will appear *good breeding.*

Satirically suggesting that a young lady display whatever physical charms she possesses to best advantage, the author insisted that a woman devote her life to catching a desirable husband, even at the risk of deceiving her female friends and competitors. Religious worship was not exempt from manipulation in the pursuit of so vital an objective. "To go to church every Sunday morning and evening, is very necessary," the author argued. "To old ladies and gentlemen it conveys good ideas; they will naturally suppose you ['fine ladies'] are praying for your sins, and those of your neighbours, when at the same time you may cast a coaxing eye to the first beau you can see; who, if he possesses any gallantry, will take the hint."[27] This caustic essay's intent was undoubtedly to depict bad breeding and female deceitfulness masquerading as "lady-like" behavior in a city grown alarmingly corrupt and overrefined. Its Rousseauist message was cushioned by wit and humor.

Another mordant article dealing with woman discusses the "Character of an Old Maid," caricaturing a popular stereotype. Bitterly castigating "one of the most cranky, ill-natured, maggotty, peevish, conceited, disagreeable, hypocritical, fretful, noisy, gibing, canting, censorious, out-of-the-way, never-to-be-pleased—good-for-nothing creatures," the author incanted, "God help her poor nieces!" The spinsterish "old maid" did not enjoy life, therefore she wanted to inhibit the pleasures of the people around her. Constantly nagging the youth under her care, she vents her own lack of fulfillment on them. Because she had never married or enjoyed a satisfying relationship with a man, she preaches hatred of them. Though she pretends to be religious and God-fearing, she hates all families that are happy and have carried out God's will by raising children. She clandestinely reads deplorable romantic novels and magazines, but tells her acquaintances that the Bible is her only literary fare. Her only purpose in life is to make young people miserable. Devoid of the "tender passion," she was ignorant of both giving and receiving love. "Indeed, an old maid's heart is, of all hearts, the most detestable," the author continued in unabated denunciation. "It contains neither sympathy, feeling, or any one thing appertaining to the *tender passion*—it is so full of *self*, that it can make no room for another; an old maid, therefore, can bear no other company, except such as herself—or, now and then, an old bachelor."[28] Both the bachelor and the spinster are useless to society and concerned only about themselves. Ignoring the young nation's need for increased population, they failed to marry and bear children and isolated themselves from their fellow citizens. At least by implication, this essay attacked male as well as female "old maids." As is often the case with satire, the parody disguised a more general public theme of expansionist republicanism: the new American community needed energetic, sociable, and reproductive inhabitants.[29]

In the process of deriding another stock stereotype, the author of an essay on the "Character of a Pedantic Schoolmaster" mocked male conceit, egotism and irrationality while pointing out the superior character of the autonomous, reasonable woman. Despite his bookishness and arbitrary demeanor, the male pedagogue in question is apparently very much attracted to women, who find him tiresome and reject his advances. But, like an "arrant *Don Quixote*," he pursues his lady in "gallant" fashion. He prefers relaxation rather than his teaching duties, and "is as happy, at the thoughts of holidays and vacations, as the youngest child; because he then is at liberty to make love." However, women are "disgusted with his ridiculous pedantry," and he fails to achieve his goal. Alarmed by his elaborate literary effusions, his would-be "mistress" concludes that he is insane, and "repels with equal violence his approaches, telling him that he is fitter for *bedlam* than a *school room.*" Following this repulse, the frustrated, prurient schoolmaster then attempts to seduce his female students, by giving them preferential treatment:

> If he has any of the *fair sex* under his tuition, they are sure to be his favourites, and the greatest proficients [the essay continues]; his boys then become a parcel of blockheads, and he tells *pretty miss*, she has more sense than twenty of them. He introduces *love* into her *lessons*, and flourishes amorous expressions into her *copy book*; but advancing to further liberties, he is detected and punished by the father or brother, as ignominiously as any of his pupils ever felt birch from himself.[30]

If women pedants, in later decades, could be charged with a vain display of bookishness,[31] the pedantic schoolmaster of the 1780s was equally guilty of a vain display of libido. The amorous schoolmaster differed in degree rather than kind from his more villainous counterparts, the seducer and the prostitute's client. Society disdained each of them, since, solely concerned with the satisfaction of their sexual drives, they showed disrespect for women as well as for the community, whose moral rules and republican well-being dictated the channeling of erotic desires into the productive (and reproductive) paths of marriage and family.

The view that marriage was essential for individual happiness as well as social harmony pervaded the literature of the time. A major theme of the *American Museum*'s entries, it was among the favorite motifs of Philip Freneau, the "poet laureate" of the American Revolution. His piece, "The sea-faring bachelor," chided the single man's lonely pursuits and advised him to settle down with a good wife. "Seek a bride," he implored the wandering sailor:

> In all your rounds 'tis wondrous strange
> No fair one tempts you to a change:
> Madness it is, you must agree,
> To lodge alone till forty three.

Old Plato own'd, no blessing here
Could equal love—if but sincere:
And writings, penn'd by heav'n, have shewn
That man can ne'er be blest alone.

In mawkish verse Freneau juxtaposed a lovely young girl, close to Nature and the land, and the restless, lonely seaman:

Myrtilia fair, in yonder grove,
Has so much beauty, so much love—
That on her lip, the meanest fly
Is happier far than you or I.

Though marriage was usually depicted as the ideal state, and women were viewed as rational, benign beings in most of the literature printed in Carey's magazine, another side occasionally appeared, as we have seen: the stubborn, demanding female who bullied her husband and controlled the household. While neither viewpoint showed contempt for women, despite some modern historians' arguments that the "Founding Fathers" enjoined them to servile, dependent, infantile behavior, one might still be surprised to read an anonymous eighteenth-century poet's claim that, "throughout their lives/All men are governed by their wives." Yet this poet, a young man who traveled through the country examining marital behavior, concluded:

Look where you will, in every stage
Of this degen'rate, wicked age,
Whether in high or lower life,
Each man is govern'd by his wife.[32]

Young American males at the beginning of the republic thus perceived at least two kinds of wives: the reasonable, mild-mannered type and the domineering termagant. But the assertive wife may have been forced to assume this character in order to compensate for an unduly passive husband. This was the opinion of the "Old Bachelor," whose articles frequently appeared in the *American Museum*. He imputed the wife's domination in some households to an excessively docile husband's abnegation of authority. In "Letter to the married man," reprinted in Carey's journal in March 1788, the bachelor's target is the subservient, "hen-pecked husband, and hens never triumph over any other than a dunghill cock; the want of dignity in the one, begets insult in the other." His acerbic wit at times conveys keen insights into relations between the sexes in marriage. "If he [the submissive husband] examines himself, he will find that what he calls patience, is fear," the "Bachelor" contends, "his humility, duplicity." The henpecked husband is merely trying to deceive himself; his good-natured disposition is really nothing but cowardice. The strong wife only fills the power vacuum left by a timid, ineffectual husband. "Women will naturally aspire to supremacy, when the proper head of a family does not fill out the character," he asserts. "Yet they are tempted more by the vacancy, than by any original desire to dispute precedency. A governing woman is never truly happy, nor a submitting husband perfectly reconciled." Seething discontent underlay a family scenario when the wife held the reins—"wore the pants," as a later generation might say. "It infallibly happens, that when a woman acts the man, the man acts the fool," the "Bachelor" mordantly concluded.[33]

Despite its superficially sexist tone, "Letter to the married man" actually conveys a message similar to most of the other essays in the *American Museum* on this topic: marriage, and relations between the genders generally, should be characterized by mutual respect and reciprocal obligation. After all, the domineering, insensitive wife who may emerge when the husband is unduly servile or apathetic no more facilitates the establishment of an optimal relationship than the severe, patriarchal husband. This is really the underlying point of the "Old Bachelor's" efforts.

While writers preached cooperation between the sexes, they also expressed a fear of effeminate, "unmanly" types of behavior. "Harry Hogarth" believed that men should avoid attendance at women's salons and parties. Not only were they a ridiculous waste of time, they were potentially emasculating as well, and distracted men from performing the world's "business," which was their solemn social obligation. "Of all the employments which are chosen to supply the want of real business, that of dancing attendance at tea-tables, and engaging in the learned debates of female coteries upon a feather or a fan, is the most ridiculous," he argued. Even men of literary talents, who prided themselves on their sensitivity, should keep their distance from these female cliques. "Hogarth" agreed that women stimulated a man's literary creativity and "sentiment"; still, they should be admired from afar rather than in their boudoirs:

> The society of ladies is certainly capable of communicating the most refined pleasure, and of elevating the passions to the noblest heights of

> sentiment [he wrote]; but female occupations and manners are as unbecoming a man, as the petticoat or the head-dress; and Mrs. Jolly [an allegorical figure], who engages in all the *manly* pleasures of the bottle, is not a more disgusting character, than Renaldo [a large, ungainly male allegorical character], who engages in all the little pleasures of the tea-cup.

According to "Hogarth," the man who wasted his time at women's teaparties and drawingrooms "counteract[ed] those qualifications which might render him an ornament of society," and abnegated his masculine role, which was to perform the essential business and political functions of his community.[34] Although his outlook was somewhat condescending toward women, it merely reflected existing social realities. Women lacked political rights, and in the cities, bourgeois women *could* lead indolent lives.[35]

At the opposite socioeconomic extreme, the author of an article on female convicts employed at forced labor in the Philadelphia workhouse praised the beneficial effects of linen production on these despised members of the "fair sex." Pointing out that the work supplied a skill to those who had formerly been "ignorant in every branch of that manufacture," he denied that women had any monopoly on vice or criminal "depravity." He merely lauded the virtues of compulsory employment, by which means "punishment is directed to its noblest end—the reformation of the offender; who having thus acquired a skill by which an honest livelihood may be obtained, will be under no temptation to return to the paths of vice; and may hereafter make atonement to society for those transgressions, which oftener proceed from the want of reputable resources, than from the mere depravity of the mind." Thus the author concluded that environment, not innate wickedness, precipitated crime among both men and women.[36] Unlike the prejudicial stance of Puritan ministers toward the daughters of Eve in the seventeenth century, this latter-day puritan regarded the moral potentialities of both genders as relatively equal.[37]

Indeed, men might envy and admire certain women's abilities that they lacked. Among them was female procreativity. The ubiquitous "Old Bachelor," once again lamenting his misspent life, professes a desire to reproduce, like an oyster, "without the expence of a female assistant." He admits the possibility that oysters have two genders, but he prefers to believe otherwise. (In fact, scientists have found that some species have separate genders; in others, the sex organs are united in one individual). A recent illness, which left him close to death, made him aware that no one cared whether he lived or died. That is why he now desires offspring, in order "to keep my name and memory alive in the world, and to talk of their father some ten or a dozen years after my decease." Moreover, the "Old Bachelor" is cognizant of his need for women.

Nevertheless, he remains dubious whether it is worse for a man to marry or to stay single. Concluding that "ninety nine times out of a hundred, it is passion, not reason, that points to matrimony," the Bachelor asserts that, once one reflects on "all the disasters, troubles, and inconveniences, which probably may, which certainly must, occur in the married state, he would never have courage to undertake the task." This had been his problem, he regretfully confesses; though he had been in love several times, he was too cautious to take the leap into marriage.[38] As if to confirm his regrets, a poem, "The Happy Man," which appeared in the same issue of the *American Museum*, states that a good wife and children are essential for man's gratification.[39]

If traditional concepts of woman's docility and servility to man held sway anywhere in the new republic, it was in its rural areas. Though apparently emanating from Philadelphia, a letter from a young man, born on the farm but familiar with urban mores, lent implicit approval to these beliefs. Purporting to advise his sister, who was in the process of "removing from the country to live in the city," he voiced the proverbial rural fear of townsmen's vice and dissipation. He warned his sister to resist the city's wickedness, which threatened to undermine "that sweet timidity, that charming delicacy, that enchanting bashfulness, that artless, blushing modesty," which comprised "the brightest ornaments of your sex." While she possessed these rustic virtues in ample measure, she might be tempted to renounce them in the company of "the gay and fashionable ladies of the present day," adopting instead "their manners . . . and free and forward airs." However, seductive women would be the least of her temptations.

Notorious for their untiring efforts to deceive feminine virtue, the bogus "gentlemen" of the city would eagerly take liberties with her modest chastity, "the first female charm, and the want of which the most brilliant accomplishments cannot compensate." The dutiful brother informed his sister of the paradox that, when women allow men to treat their bodies with contempt, men have a lower opinion of them afterwards. In addition, he advised her to discreetly leave the room when so-called "gentlemen" in "polite society" began to spew out lewd, "indelicate" talk.

While graphically describing how the city's "fashionable ladies" permitted men to fondle and kiss them without restraint, the brother hypocritically refused to blame the members of his gender for their outrageous behavior. He bluntly stated, "If they [promiscuous women] did but know how much they suffer in our opinion by such conduct, how cheap they render themselves, how they lessen our esteem, and how much we prefer your amiable diffidence, your blushing timidity, they would endeavour to be like you, if not from principle, at least from pride, and the desire of making conquests." Expediency as well as morality, therefore, suggested that a woman employ self-discipline in sexual matters. Somewhat unconvincingly, the author placed the onus for men's prurient behavior on women's failure to resist their advances. This was hardly fair to the "gentle sex."

According to the author, young men relished temporary, physical relationships with permissive women, but preferred wholesome ladies for their wives. Writing his sister, he upheld this sexual double standard:

> Believe me, my dear sister, I am well acquainted with the sentiments of our [male] sex, and can assure you, however desirous they may be, that their companions of an hour or of a day, should indulge them in every possible freedom, they wish to find very different manners in those whom they would choose for the companions of their lives.[40]

Should his sister pursue a promiscuous path, he warns, not only would she fail to find marital bliss, she was likely to wind up on the abysmal road to prostitution. She might even become the victim of libertines masquerading as wealthy aristocrats. "There are many who are called gentlemen, who have nothing but the name," he pointed out. He upbraided young women who were more interested in a man's ostensible wealth than in upholding their own dignity and modesty. "How mortifying it ought to be to an amiable girl, to be hugged and slavered over by an insolent brute, because he happens to be well dressed and has money in his pocket," he protested. In this burgeoning capitalist society, where the pursuit of individual wealth and ostentation was gaining respectability, proponents of a slowly vanishing hierarchical and traditional way of life fought against the corrosive symbols of the emerging order.[41] The threatened trivialization of sexual relationships was among their primary concerns.

In his effort to preserve his sister's contact with the old-fashioned morality of the farm, her brother suggested that she attend parties only when old and venerable people were present to restrain the lascivious elements. At the critical moments, she must resist any man's "first attempt" to maul her. As he carefully explained:

> That young lady, who, when a gentleman is sitting by her, will remove the hand that is pressing her knee, or otherwise improperly employed, and does it in such a manner as shews [*sic*] her disapprobation—or when a gentleman rudely attempts to clasp her in his arms, and ravish a kiss from her lovely lips, will with spirit put him from her, and assure him she does not approve such freedoms—will soon prevent their repetition.[42]

Hoping to assuage any fears that such decisive conduct would impede a young lady's marriage prospects, the author was sure that a decent man ("a man of sense") would understand and approve her rejection of improper advances. The young woman who preserved her innocence would inevitably obtain the love of the richest and worthiest man in the city, he predicted. Yet many of the city's women did not think in this way.

Unfortunately, the solicitous brother warned, the "polite, fashionable young ladies" of the town, despite their veneer of good breeding, had lost their virtue in their "rage for the admiration" of profligate, sophisticated men. Sly male sexual innuendoes, which, like "a canker worm which preys upon and blasts the fairest, loveliest flower of virgin modesty," should have aroused righteous women's fear and disgust, instead received their amused tolerance. In their younger days, even these depraved women had possessed sufficient virtue to deplore and denounce obscene suggestions. Gradually, habit and custom had reduced fashionable city women's morality to a shadow of its former integrity.

Perhaps these two versions of the eligible wife-to-be—the overrefined, sensuous urban woman, who surrendered her self-respect for money and popularity, and the simple, modest, chaste farming woman, who resisted men's attempts to corrupt her—were, in a sense, embryonic forms of the two types of wives delineated by the *American Museum*'s writers: the egregious shrew and the rational, mild-mannered spouse respectively. In the end, the latter would gain the city's richest man for her spouse while she withstood urban debaucheries. Virtue had its rewards.

This was all the more reason for young newcomers to the city to avoid sexual sophisticates who informed them that innocence was unfashionable. Though the author imputed blame to naive women who succumbed to men's blandishments, he despised callous male seducers whose only goal was to gratify "mere momentary pleasures, unmeaning gallantry, or . . . their vanity, and self-importance; [they] care nothing abut them [women], beyond the present hour, and are well pleased to take every liberty with which they can be indulged, as they are thereby freed from the restraint they must otherwise observe, and are furnished with a subject to boast of among their associates." Notwithstanding his maleness, the author expressed contempt for those who treated women as if they were not equals, merely manipulable sexual objects whose feelings were unimportant.

In any case, an intelligent man seeking a wife thought a woman's character was more important than her physique or sensuality. "Though you are beautiful, think not beauty alone sufficient to constitute your merit," the man lectured his sister. The city's cultural and educational institutions would foster her intellectual growth, increase her attractiveness to a worthy husband, and temper and strengthen her virtuous traits, provided she withstood the temptations of urban "Society."

The author espouses a favorable opinion of his sister and of women in general. He predicts that, once she learns poise and graceful self-confidence in conversation, she will be "the delight and admiration of our sex," provided she continues to "maintain that modest reserve in the whole of your conduct" which she had developed as a farm girl. Elaborating on this theme, he says, "Beauty of person may catch us [men] at first; but the beauties of the mind can alone secure any conquest worth making." Significantly, he perceives the woman's quest for a husband in terms of "conquest"—decidedly unromantic phraseology. Apparently he attributes aggressive motives to the woman during courtship rather than merely a passive waiting for male suitors, an attitude which contradicted traditional outlooks.[43]

In other respects the "Letter from a young gentleman to his sister" is traditional in tone. In fact, it is affectedly corny. The letter concludes with a litany of mawkish sentiment: While physical beauty decays over time, "the beauties of the mind"—knowledge and a virtuous character—"will survive all the ruins of sickness and age." In common with many of the articles we have examined, this one warns young women to resist preoccupation with the latest fashions. Unlike those others, however, it expounds a new note when it evokes the importance of theology, urging the young lady to embrace a moderate religion, "free from the rage of bigotry, the gloom of superstition, and the extravagancies of enthusiasm." The author ends by listing those feminine virtues which will win her a virtuous (and, hopefully, rich) husband in her urban quest. Modesty, cheerfulness, affability with reserve, candor: these were the main qualities of the desirable woman. Others were a familiarity with books without pedantry; and ease, grace, beauty, and "that softness, that gentleness, and that tenderness peculiar to your [female] sex." Finally, somewhat pedantically himself, the "brother" recommended several standard advice manuals popular with the English bourgeoisie and their American counterparts: Mrs. Hester Chapone's *Letters to her Niece* (1772), Rev. James Fordyce's *Sermons for Young Ladies* (1765), and Dr. John Gregory's *Legacy to his Daughters* (1774). Quite possibly, these volumes, epitomizing the prescriptive literature for daughters of London's mercantile aristocracy, formed the provenance for the conservative epistle "from a young gentleman to his sister," which we have examined at such length.[44]

Beginning with this July 1788 issue, we may perceive a degree of change in Carey's editorial policy relating to the desired personality traits and social position of women. He selects articles with a more conservative viewpoint, which tend to avoid anecdotal, slice-of-life depictions of woman's rationality, autonomy, and self-assertion in favor of more prescriptive literature delineating *how* the "fair sex" *should* conduct themselves. While it is impossible to pinpoint the causes for Carey's sudden shift, one reason suggests itself. Carey was an enthusiastic supporter of the new United States Constitution. He boasted of the patronage the *American Museum* received from patriots like George Washington, John Dickinson, Benjamin Rush, President Ezra Stiles of Yale, and other Federalist leaders; in July 1788 he printed their testimonials to the periodical as a preface to the fourth volume. It may have been more than coincidental that New Hampshire became the ninth state to ratify the Constitution, on June 21, 1788, thereby rendering the new mode of government operational within the states agreeing to it.[45]

Perhaps in his exuberance over the "Founding Fathers'" achievement and his desire to ensure that the new government took power in a stabilized society, Carey adverted to more deferential, "patriarchal" ways of thinking. The new government would have enough problems without worrying about recalcitrant women's opposition, he may have reasoned.[46]

If this were Carey's rationale, he unwittingly shared the opinions of

Judith Sargent Murray and other proto-feminists who objected to the unsettling effect the depiction of passionate women in the romantic novels of the period might have on the paternalistic bourgeois social order. "The Republic did not need emotional women who could easily be manipulated by men for their own gratification or who would lure men away from the path of virtue," Linda Kerber insightfully observes, describing the motives of these prudish female critics of the plethora of women's novels, epitomized by Jean-Jacques Rousseau's *Nouvelle Heloise* and Samuel Richardson's *Clarissa*. "Novels seemed to offer approbation for precisely the sort of behavior that political and didactic literature had labeled a danger to the republic." Carey must have agreed that it was serviceable to the new leaders to have as few distractions from the tasks of nation-building as possible. By invoking traditional standards of behavior and woman's "due subordination" to man, Carey was helping create an environment of harmony, consensus, and order in a situation where they would prove most useful.[47]

Notes

1. For American concern with the accomplishments and mistakes of ancient Greek and Roman republics and confederations, see, e.g., Charles F. Mullett, "Classical Influences on the American Revolution," *Classical Journal* 35 (1939): 92-104; Edwin A. Miles, "The Young American Nation and the Classical World," *Journal of the History of Ideas* 35, no. 2 (April-June 1974): 259-274; Edward M. Burns, "The Philosophy of History of the Founding Fathers," *The Historian* 16 (1954): 142-168; and Richard M. Gummere, "The Classical Ancestry of the United States Constitution," *American Quarterly* 14, no. 1 (Spring 1962): 3-18; and Carl J. Richard, *The Founders and the Classics: Greece, Rome, and the American Enlightenment* (Cambridge, Mass.: Harvard University Press, 1994).

2. According to Donald S. Lutz, Montesquieu was the writer most frequently cited by the American media from 1760-1805. Lutz, "The Relative Influence of European Writers on Late Eighteenth-Century American Political Thought," *American Political Science Review* 78, no. 1 (March 1984): 189-97. See also Paul M. Spurlin, *Montesquieu in America, 1760-1801* (Baton Rouge: Louisiana State University Press, 1940).

3. "Address to the Ladies of America," *American Museum, or Repository of Ancient and Modern Fugitive Pieces, Prose and Poetical*, 2, no. 5 (Nov. 1787): 481-482 (2nd ed., Philadelphia, 1789-1792). The second edition of the *American Museum* may be easily accessed, since it comprises reels four and five of the *Early American Periodical Series, Part I*, on microfilm.

4. "Bickerstaff," Newport, R. I., Oct. 25, 1787, "On the use of bustlers [bustles],"

American Museum 2, no. 5 (Nov. 1787): 482-483.

5. "On the use of bustlers," 483.

6. "On the use of bustlers," 484. On the prevalent influence of English fashions in the United States, see the discussion in James, *Changing Ideas*, 31-33, and Kerber, *Women of the Republic*, 44-45.

7. "On the use of bustlers," 485.

8. On the recognition of women's importance as consumers, see Ann Douglas, *The Feminization of American Culture* (New York: Knopf, 1977).

9. "Susannah Trapes's complaint of the badness of the police," Philadelphia, Oct. 20, 1787, *American Museum*, 2, no. 5, 2nd ed. (Nov. 1787): 484-485.

10. "Benvolio," "On the use of tobacco and snuff," *American Museum*, 2, no. 5, 2nd ed. (Nov. 1787): 487-488. My italics.

11. "On the use of tobacco and snuff," 488.

12. "On the use of tobacco and snuff," 488. Smoking's adverse consequences for health were even apparent in the 1780s, although its link with cancer and heart disease were not yet known. In any case, anticipating modern legislation, "Benvolio" proposed to outlaw the use of tobacco and snuff in public places. He argued that it was even more harmful than opium because, while the latter affected only the user, "our snuffing, chewing, and smoaking [*sic*], are a grievance to every man who nauseates [i.e., is nauseated by] the fumes of tobacco, to every housewife who has regard for her furniture, and to every nostril that is not rendered callous to this piquant weed." He urged the exportation of tobacco abroad instead of its domestic use.

13. "The Old Bachelor, No. I," from the *Pennsylvania Magazine*, in *American Museum* 2, no. 5 (Nov. 1787): 498-499.

14. "The Old Bachelor, No. IV," *American Museum* 3, no. 1 (Jan. 1788): 89-90.

15. "The Old Bachelor, No. IV," 90-91. Original punctuation and spelling have been retained, except where otherwise noted.

16. Historians who denounce colonial women's dependence on the "marriage market" include Kerber, *Women of the Republic*, 204-205; James, *Changing Ideas*, 41, 57; and Norton, *Liberty's Daughters*, 44-51. A favorable depiction of the lives of single women may be found in Chambers-Schiller, *Liberty, A Better Husband*.

17. "Philander," New York, Dec. 17, 1787, *American Museum* 3, no. 1 (Jan. 1787): 51.

18. "Philander," 51.

19. "Philander," 51.

20. "A.B.," "From the *Pennsylvania Magazine*: Consolation for the Old Bachelor," *American Museum* 3, no. 2 (Feb. 1788): 119-122. On the widespread use of the term, "notable housewife," see Norton, *Liberty's Daughters*, 4-5, 28, 34, 38-39, 269.

21. "On Contentment," *American Museum* 3, no. 2 (Feb. 1788): 142-143.

22. "The Injured Husband's Complaint," *American Museum* 2, no. 2 (Aug. 1787): 205.

23. See Linda K. Kerber, *Women of the Republic: Intellect and Ideology in*

Revolutionary America (Chapel Hill: University of North Carolina Press, 1980), 241-45; Jan Lewis, "The Republican Wife: Virtue and Seduction in the Early Republic," *William and Mary Quarterly,* 3rd Ser., 44, no. 4 (Oct. 1987): 689-721, and James, *Changing Ideas*, 48, 52, 112, 128, 134-138.

24. See, e.g., Christine Stansell, *City of Women: Sex and Class in New York, 1789-1860* (New York: Knopf, 1986), 172-192.

25. "Seduction—An elegy," *American Museum* 2, no. 2 (Aug. 1787): 205, and "The dying prostitute—an elegy," *American Museum* 2, no. 2 (Aug. 1787): 206. Similar motifs in stories and poetry about prostitution, including belief in the culpability of the male seducer, persisted after 1800 in Pennsylvania almanacs designed for the farm community. Joan M. Jensen, *Loosening the Bonds: Mid-Atlantic Farm Women, 1750-1850* (New Haven: Yale University Press, 1986), 117-118.

26. Strauss, "*Traitors to the Masculine Cause,*" 13, 37n. For analysis of the myth of irrepressible female sexuality in the eighteenth and nineteenth centuries, see Marlene LeGates, "The Cult of Womanhood in Eighteenth-Century Thought," *Eighteenth-Century Studies* 10, no. 1 (Fall 1976): 21-39, esp. 21-30; Charles Rosenberg and Carroll Smith-Rosenberg, "The Female Animal: Medical and Biological Views of Woman and Her Role in Nineteenth Century America," *Journal of American History* 60, no. 2 (Sept. 1973): 332-356; and Graham J. Barker-Benfield, *Horrors of the Half-Known Life: Male Attitudes toward Women and Sexuality in Nineteenth Century America* (New York: Harper and Row, 1976), 171-306.

27. "Instructions for fine ladies," *American Museum* 3, no. 2 (Feb. 1788): 143-144. For a detailed analysis of the so-called "advice literature" which this satire parodied, which concentrates particularly on the English luminaries Dr. John Gregory, Rev. James Fordyce, and Miss Hester Chapone, see James, *Changing Ideas*, 35-57, 125-126.

28. "Character of an Old Maid," *American Museum* 3, no. 2 (Feb. 1788): 146-147. Although James, *Changing Ideas*, 105, 131-133, 286-287, discusses the American media's debate over the merits and faults of the spinster, she ignores the *American Museum.*

29. See Richard B. Morris, *The Forging of the Union, 1781-1789* (New York: Harper and Row, 1987), chap. 1.

30. "Character of a Pedantic School-master," *American Museum* 3, no. 2 (Feb. 1788): 147. Italics in original.

31. See James, *Changing Ideas*, 183-186.

32. Philip Freneau, "The sea-faring bachelor," in "Select Poetry," *American Museum* 3, no. 2 (Feb. 1788): 185, and "The Grey Mare the Better Horse," *American Museum* 3, no. 2 (Feb. 1788): 187-189. According to one scholar, writing about a slightly later period, men employed a stereotype of women in order to more clearly discern their own identity. "Religiosity, like delicacy, submission, and intellectual inferiority, came to be associated with female nature and provided males with a clearer image from which to distinguish themselves." Sexual "purity," "untainted thought and conduct," were foremost in the male canon of female attributes.

Barbara J. Berg, *The Remembered Gate: Origins of American Feminism: The Woman and the City, 1800-1860* (New York: Oxford University Press, 1978), 79. According to Carroll Smith-Rosenberg, both eighteenth- and nineteenth-century women were expected to be "emotional, pious, passive and nurturant." Moreover, especially among the urban middle classes, "The American girl was taught at home, at school, and in the literature of the period, that aggression, independence, self-assertion, and curiosity were male traits, inappropriate for the weaker sex and her limited sphere. Dependent throughout her life, she was to reward her male protectors with affection and submission." Smith-Rosenberg, "The Hysterical Woman: Sex Roles and Role Conflict in 19th-Century America," *Social Research* 39 (1972): 656. Similarly, Ruth Bloch, discussing male views of women in the 1770s and 1780s, argues that "the chief female virtues were 'modesty,' 'tenderness,' 'delicacy,' and 'sensibility.'" Bloch, "Gendered Meanings of Virtue," *Signs*, 13, no. 1 (Autumn 1987): 51. However, my intensive analysis of articles appearing in the *American Museum* from 1787-1790 has discovered little evidence that women were depicted in such a condescending manner.

33. "The Old Bachelor, No. V: Letter to the Married Man," originally printed in the *Pennsylvania Magazine*, in *American Museum* 3, no. 3 (2nd ed., March 1788), reprinted 1789 [microfilm]): 267. Apparently the "Old Bachelor's" view of women was unduly optimistic. A leading British writer, Hannah More, who according to Janet W. James represented the majority of articulate female opinion, wrote in 1793: "To be unstable and capricious, I really think, is but too characteristic of our sex; and there is, perhaps, no animal so much indebted to subordination for its good behavior as woman." Quoted in James, *Changing Ideas*, 97-98. A Georgia planter's wife expressed similar sentiments in her diary in 1855, praising her husband, who possessed "just such a master's will as suits my woman's nature, for true to my sex I delight *in looking up* and love to feel my woman's weakness protected by man's superior strength." Diary of E. G. C. Thomas, quoted in Anne F. Scott, *The Southern Lady* (Chicago: University of Chicago Press, 1970), 96 (Italics in original). Thus it appears that some of the female plantation gentry advocated a greater degree of submissiveness to men than even the irascible "Old Bachelor" thought advisable.

34. "Harry Hogarth," "Remarks on the different ideas of mankind, respecting the acceptation of the term, 'business,'" in *American Museum* 3, no. 6 (June 1788; 2nd ed., Philadelphia, 1792): 508-509. The article's original dateline is Philadelphia, Aug. 27, 1787.

35. For discussion of the desultory lives of bourgeois women in the cities, see James, *Changing Ideas*, 127-128, 146-150. Norton, *Liberty's Daughters*, 20-26, has a more favorable view.

36. "Observations on the management of the female convicts in the work-house, Philadelphia," Philadelphia, Jan. 3, 1788, *American Museum* 3, no. 6 (June 1788; 2nd ed., 1792): 512. See the brief discussion of female convict labor in the Philadelphia workhouse in Michael Meranze, *Laboratories of Virtue: Punishment, Revolution, and Authority in Philadelphia, 1760-1835* (Chapel Hill: University of North

Carolina Press, 1996), 90-91.

37. See Lonna M. Malmsheimer, "Daughters of Zion: New England Roots of American Feminism," *New England Quarterly* 50, no. 3 (Sept. 1977): 484-488.

38. "The Old Bachelor, No. VI," from *Pennsylvania Magazine*, in *American Museum* 3, no. 6 (June 1788): 565-567.

39. "The Happy Man," in *American Museum* 3, no. 6 (June 1788): 587.

40. "Letter from a young gentleman to his sister, on her removing from the country to live in the city," in *American Museum* 4, no. 1 (July 1788): 17-20. For women's obsessional concern with the threat of seduction, see James, *Changing Ideas*, 134-138.

41. "Letter from a young gentleman to his sister," 18. On the growth of individualism in America during the late eighteenth century, see James A. Henretta, *The Evolution of American Society, 1763-1815* (Lexington, Mass.: D. C. Heath, 1973); Richard D. Brown, "The Emergence of Urban Society in Rural Massachusetts, 1760-1820," *Journal of American History* 61 (June 1974): 29-51; and J. E. Crowley, *This Sheba, Self: The Conceptualization of Economic Life in Eighteenth-Century America* (Baltimore: Johns Hopkins University Press, 1974).

42. "Letter from a young gentleman to his sister," 19.

43. "Letter from a young gentleman to his sister," 20. Nevertheless, Reverend James Fordyce, a popular author of British advice manuals whom the "brother" highly recommended, made some blunt observations on the reality of the war between the sexes. "Let us not dissemble truth," he declared. "The greater part of either sex study to prey upon one another. The world, in too many instances, is a theatre of war between men and women. Every stratagem is tried, and every advantage taken, on the side of both." As was the case in wars between nations, "a general truce is always short, and a national peace never secure." Fordyce, *Sermons to Young Women* (Philadelphia, 1787), 232-233, quoted in James, *Changing Ideas*, 49. The *American Museum* article mutedly echoes these ideas.

44. "Letter from a young gentlemen to his sister," 20. The views espoused by Gregory, Fordyce, and Chapone are summarized in James, *Changing Ideas*, 39-57, 125-126, 289-290, who argues that American women followed British models of behavior.

45. On New Hampshire's ratification of the Constitution, see Richard B. Morris, ed., *Encyclopedia of American History* (New York: Harper, 1953), 120.

46. Carey's nationalist sentiments are emphasized in several studies, e.g., Lawrence J. Friedman, *Inventors of the Promised Land* (New York: Knopf, 1975), 6; William J. Free, *The Columbian Magazine and American Literary Nationalism* (The Hague: Mouton, 1968); and Earl Bradsher, *Mathew Carey* (New York: Columbia University Press, 1912). For a competent survey of Carey's patriotic stance on the international relations of the United States, see Robert W. Sellen, "The *American Museum*, 1787-1792, as a Forum for Ideas of American Foreign Policy," *Pennsylvania Magazine of History and Biography* 93, no. 2 (April 1969); 179-189. James N. Green, author of a fine essay on Carey, views him as "the greatest publisher in America in the first two decades of the nineteenth century," and "a

central figure in the politics of his time," who "worked behind the scenes and through his publications to reconcile differences between parties or regional factions and to promote national unity and public welfare." James N. Green, *Mathew Carey, Publisher and Patriot* (Philadelphia: Library Company of Philadelphia, 1985), 1. Carey's quest for national unity during the War of 1812 is the theme of Edward C. Carter II, "Mathew Carey and 'The Olive Branch,' 1814-1818," *Pennsylvania Magazine of History and Biography* 89, no. 4 (Oct. 1965): 399-415.

47. Kerber, *Women of the Republic*, 245. For a feminist neo-Progressive interpretation of the way in which the provisions and symbolism of the Constitution of 1787 undermined the radical potential for the transformation of gender relations implicit in the Revolutionary movement of the 1770s to 1780s, see Dana D. Nelson, *National Manhood: Capitalist Citizenship and the Imagined Fraternity of White Men* (Durham, N.C.: Duke University Press, 1998). Carroll Smith-Rosenberg, "Dis-Covering the Subject of the 'Great Constitutional Discussion,' 1786-1789," *Journal of American History* 79, no. 3 (Dec. 1992): 854-873, is a more convoluted "post-structuralist" exegesis.

Chapter 5

Turn and Return: The *American Museum* Views "The Fair Sex," 1788-1792

Perhaps it was appropriate that Carey should choose July 1788, the eve of the new Constitution's implementation, to reprint a series of articles on marriage and relations between the sexes written by Reverend John Witherspoon (1723-1794) and first printed in Thomas Paine's *Pennsylvania Magazine* during the "times that tried men's souls," September and December 1775 and March 1776. As well as anyone, Witherspoon symbolized the new nationalism that existed in America. Renowned as president of Princeton College and a leading exponent of the Scottish school of "common sense" or "moral sense" philosophy, Witherspoon had a career in politics that was as impressive as his achievements in education. Though he advocated freedom of religion, by reconciling differences between contending factions in the Presbyterian Church he encouraged its rapid growth in the 1770s. As a delegate to the Second Continental Congress, he signed the Declaration of Independence in 1776 as well as the Articles of Confederation two years later, remaining in the national legislature until 1782. Shifting his support to the new Constitution, he was a member of the New Jersey state ratifying convention in 1788. Witherspoon's vital role in setting up the national organization of the Presbyterian Church as well as in the achievement of American national integration (he coined the term "Americanism" in an article in a Pennsylvania newspaper in 1781) reveal him to be a man of acute intellectual penetration who was attuned to the trends and currents of his time. This makes his statements on marriage and women, and their republication in 1788, especially interesting and important.[1]

At the outset we should note that Witherspoon's three essays were entitled, "Letters on marriage." Though this vital institution had been of prime concern to writers about women in the *American Museum* the preceding year, it had never so completely overshadowed their discussions of the female character as in Witherspoon's series. In a sense his work was seminal, since seldom had a figure of such intellectual, theological, and political reputation engaged in so lengthy a discourse on relations between men and women.[2]

Using the pseudonym of "Epaminondas," an ancient Greek general, Witherspoon reduced to system many current ideas about men and women, marriage and bachelorhood. Contending that both Divine Providence and social well-being equally dictated marriage, Witherspoon was confident that the "criminal" mockery and "feeble attacks" of wicked men would never undermine the innate, God-given, "instinctive propensity" of the sexes to unite in the holy matrimony that was essential to perpetuating the human race. Like other writers, "Epaminondas" argued that bachelors "deserve to be detested" for their aggressive defense of their refusal to procreate and their attacks on the sacred institution of marriage.

On the other hand, Witherspoon pointed out, those who sought to defend marriage by depicting it in an absurdly idealized, romanticized manner inadvertently injured their cause, since young newlyweds who took their message seriously were headed for rapid disillusionment. Instead, "Epaminondas" chose to stress marriage as one's duty toward the nation, based on the "absolute necessity of marriage for the service of the state, and the solid advantages that arise from it, to domestic comfort, in ordinary cases." This sobering view of marriage, with its frightening totalitarian implications, belittled women's role, physical attractiveness, and personality as motives for wedlock. In this sense, Witherspoon degraded them into mere baby-making machines.

At the same time, Witherspoon staunchly defended marriage on the realistic basis of "common sense." Opposing respected writers like Joseph Addison, whose *Spectator* essays had extolled women as perfect and beautiful ladies, "Epaminondas" deplored the emphasis on radiant female beauty, considering it an invalid and misleading reason for marriage.

Detesting the ostensible prurience of authors whose writings "in favour of the female sex" consisted of exaggerating "the charms of the outward form," Witherspoon remarks, "This is the case in all romances—a class of writings to which the world is very little indebted." Pointing out that men already tended to regard women too much as sexual objects, Witherspoon feared the "romantic" obsession with physical beauty would result in consigning all homely women to the lives of old maids.

Experience had taught "Epaminondas" that a woman's physical beauty bore little relation to conjugal happiness. Husbands soon realize that a woman's beauty can often add to the frustrations of a bad marriage, while good personal qualities could redeem a rocky one. "For example," Witherspoon argued, "if a woman is active and industrious in her family, it will make a husband bear with more patience a little anxiety of countenance, or fretfulness of temper, though in themselves disagreeable." This was a realistic perspective. Witherspoon was keenly aware that the wife, as an equal partner in the marital relationship with an independent mind and personality, contributed equally with the husband to its success or failure.[3]

Like other "moral sense" philosophers (Francis Hutcheson, Adam Smith, Lord Kames), Witherspoon emphasized that sexual attraction is "natural" and that a "generous devotedness of heart . . . is often to be seen on one, and sometimes on both sides" in a marriage. These natural affections, sexual and benevolent tendencies, "under the restraint of reason, and government of prudence, may be greatly subservient [*sic*] to the future happiness of life," Witherspoon declared; they were far more crucial to marital enjoyment than the partner's physical beauty.

Even a sage of Witherspoon's Witherspoon's stature was aware that the exaggerated rhetoric about the lover's beauty depicted in romantic poetry and fiction conveyed an impression of passive perfection that was not true of real women. For example, deriding bloated poetic imagery about "flames, darts, arrows, and lightning from a female eye," he ironically pointed out, "some wives have lightning in their eyes sufficient to terrify a husband, as well as the [young unmarried] maids have to consume a lover." Even an intellectual man of the cloth like Witherspoon refused to lend credence to the illusory view that women were passive, frail, subservient creatures.[4]

Stressing the moderate benefits and "comforts" marriage had to offer, as well as its necessity for the propagation of the human race, Witherspoon admitted that conjugality was neither as blissful as the romances nor as painful as the bachelors portrayed it. His view was grounded on a realistic, "common sense" evaluation of the relationship. "The proposition . . . I mean to establish," he explained, "is that there is much less unhappiness in the matrimonial state than is often apprehended, and indeed as much real comfort as there is any ground to expect." Generally, especially when people approached old age, there was "much more satisfaction and chearfulness [*sic*] in the married than in the single" condition, he maintained.[5]

According to "Epaminondas," unmarried individuals grew irascible and "peevish" in old age. "The prospect of continuing single to the end of life, narrows the mind, and closes the heart," he observed. Men and women needed each other. Even wealthy, miserly bachelors usually became happier and more generous after marriage, especially toward their wives and children. For Witherspoon, marriage and childbirth were "the first of earthly blessings." In his view, raising a family stabilized and solidified a marriage which may originally have been entered into merely from passion. The beneficial effect which raising children had upon a marriage was even "greater in the lower than in the higher ranks," he concluded.

Witherspoon admitted that marriages went on more smoothly in prosperous families. He recommended that both husband and wife attempt to contribute to the household's economic support. In the woman's case, this entailed a talent for "good family management, which is seen at every meal, and felt every hour in the husband's purse." Since wives did most of the household's shopping, it was advisable for them to possess business acumen. Unfortunately, a wife's myriad responsibilities might reduce a wife's degree of elegance, stateliness, and physical beauty. But Witherspoon thought it was worth the price if she ably fulfilled her duties.

Contending that women were intellectually equal to men, a somewhat radical stance for the 1770s and 1780s, Witherspoon thought an intelligent wife facilitated a successful marriage. Perhaps unrealistically, he suggested that the marriage partners jointly agree to grant "superiority" in family decision making to the spouse with greater "understanding." This would ensure "domestic peace." Moreover,

Witherspoon insisted, "It is of little consequence whether the superiority be on the side of the man or the woman, provided the ground of it be manifest."[6] Applauding husbands who obeyed their wives in those instances where the latter were more rational and intelligent, he denied that they were henpecked. "Should not a man comply with reason, when offered by his wife, as well as any body else?" he pointed out. "Or ought he to be against reason because his wife is for it?" An exponent of reason, Witherspoon had contempt only for those husbands who obeyed their wives out of fear, not out of respect for their opinions. Perhaps he knew some "battered husbands," as a later generation would call them! He respected spouses who listened to their wives when the latter possessed greater reasoning power. "I, therefore, take the liberty of rescuing from the number of the henpeckt [*sic*], those who ask the advice, and follow the direction of their wives in most cases, because they are really better than any they could give themselves;" he magisterially explained, "reserving those only under the old denomination [henpecked husband], who through fear, are subject, not to reason, but to passion and ill humor."[7]

Witherspoon was ready to concede supreme authority in the family to the wife, if she earned it by superior "common sense." He found that women were more likely than men to combine reason with "just and amiable conduct." Witherspoon considers women more emotionally self-controlled than men, as well as more intelligent in matters of interpersonal relations. He had reached these conclusions as a result of personal observation. "I have known many women of judgment and prudence, who carried it with the highest respect and decency to weak and capricious husbands," he noted, "but not many men of distinguished abilities, who did not betray, if not contempt, at least great indifference, towards weak and trifling wives."[8]

In light of Witherspoon's highly favorable comments on women, as well as his towering reputation in the intellectual, theological, and political spheres of early America, it is disappointing that most scholars have glossed over, distorted, or entirely ignored his "Letters on Marriage." Perhaps this is because his writings fail to verify hackneyed ideas about male brutality and patriarchalism during the Revolutionary period.[9]

Witherspoon's views on family education, published in the same issue of the *American Museum* that contained his first letter on marriage, were also enlightened. Contrary to Mary Beth Norton, a historian who says that fathers in the Revolutionary period demanded sole authority

over their children's education, Witherspoon insisted "that husband and wife ought to be entirely one upon this subject, not only agreed as to the end, but as to the means to be used, and the plan to be followed, in order to attain it." He thought wives should have as much power over children as the father. As in household decision making generally, he urged recourse to reason and cooperation by both partners. "Certainly husband and wife ought to conspire and co-operate in every thing relating to the education of their children," he argued. "And if their opinions happen, in any particular, to be different, they ought to examine and settle the matter privately, by themselves, that not the least opposition may appear either to children or servants." Obviously he was addressing the needs of middle-class readers,
since the poor did not have to worry about curious servants. Parents who presented a united front posed the force of a "double authority" and a "double example" to impressionable children, whose "religious education" this Presbyterian divine thought should be particularly stressed.[10] Like most of the essayists we have examined, he saw woman's role in the family as equal in importance to the man's, and respected her right to individual autonomy and her own opinion.

The author of an "Address to the ministers of the gospel of every denomination in the United States" revealed that his moral prudery was not incompatible with advocacy of female influence. After denouncing liquor consumption along with "frequent elections" and freedom of the press as equally pernicious to his idea of a conservative republic and "the cause of liberty," acclaimed women as the anchor of family stability and order. Unlike earlier writers, he ignored female attraction to luxury and the gossipy salons, which others had depicted as antipodal to male seriousness and attention to business. On the contrary, this erstwhile cleric denounced male attendance at sex-segregated clubs, taverns, and cockfights, partly because of the absence of women's benign supervision. He advised men to stay at home under women's pristine influence:

> It is in private families, only, that society is innocent, or improving. Here manners are usually kept within the bounds of decency by the company of females, who generally compose a part of all private families; and manners, it is well-known, have an influence upon morals.[11]

Most writers agreed that women were a stabilizing influence on men. At the same time, they took for granted that men would remain the most powerful forces in society. When Witherspoon, in the second of his letters on marriage, expounded the rule that individuals should marry someone of equal socioeconomic rank, he added that when a man married a woman far below him in status, he committed a graver error than a woman who did so. As he explained, since more opportunities for social advancement were open to a man, a poor man who married a wealthy woman would soon find new doors for professional and educational advancement open to him that did not exist before. By "rank," Witherspoon meant educational attainments even more than wealth. As he put it, similar social backgrounds and cultural preferences ("education, taste, and habits of life") were essential preconditions for a happy relationship between the sexes. Witherspoon was convinced that if the partners had equal educational levels, the spouse with greater wealth would be extremely generous and the marriage would work. He assumed that people from similar social classes are likely to have the same interests and therefore get along better together than in cases where greater economic and cultural disparities exist.

Nevertheless, spouses with similar education and respectable social status held high standards of expectation of their mates. According to "Epaminondas," they were likely to divorce more for slight differences relating to tastes and amusements than members of the lower classes, because they put greater weight on issues of "delicacy" and "expect[ed] a sweetness and compliance in matters that would not be minded by the vulgar." He did not distinguish between the sexes on this issue. As usual, his advice was meant primarily for the middle and upper classes. Reflecting on the increased incidence of divorce since the liberalization of state laws after the Revolution, Witherspoon observed, "I have known a gentleman of rank and his lady part for life, by a difference arising from a thing said at supper, that was not so much as observed to be an impropriety by three-fourths of the company."[12] Therefore, a knowledge of decorum and proper etiquette was essential.

"Epaminondas" once again used the discussion of marriage as a springboard for praising the superiority of woman's character. "There is more of real virtue and commanding principle in the female sex than in the male," he observed, "which makes them, upon the whole, act a better part in the married relation."[13] On the other hand, he admitted that the middle-class man's more thorough formal education might teach him the importance of reason and self-control through outlets that were foreclosed to most women: "The advantages which men have in point of knowledge, from the usual course of education, may perhaps balance the superiority of women, in point of virtue; for none surely can deny, that matrimonial discord may arise from ignorance and folly as well as vice." Thus, while imputing "vice" to the male character, he merely *implied* that women, deprived by society of an adequate education, might be liable to "ignorance and folly."

Regretting that men had greater access to social mobility than women, Witherspoon observed that, even when a man rose to a higher occupational level, it was difficult for his originally lower-class wife to play a high-class role, since to a great degree she was kept isolated from her husband's new business and social milieu. Witherspoon quoted one upwardly mobile London tradesman who discovered that "all the money in Great Britain would not make his wife and his daughters *ladies*." But Witherspoon blames society, rather than women, for the latter's failure to fit gracefully into a new social status.

Analyzing the motives for marriage when individuals came from divergent economic strata, "Epaminondas" contended that rich women (usually widows) married poor men out of benevolence, while a wealthy man generally espoused a lower-class woman from feelings of sexual passion or attraction to her beauty. According to Witherspoon, his reading of Addison's *Spectator* confirmed his "impartial" observation, "that women are not half so much governed, in their love attachments, by beauty, or outward form, as men." In this matter, as in many others, Witherspoon found, women showed greater discretion, prudence, and kindness than men. He believed a talented, articulate man, even if physically unappealing, would be able to find a "very lovely woman" for his wife. Even though not very rich, members of the "learned professions" were especially attractive to women, since they were dignified and intelligent. But a rich man is invariably more concerned with physical rather than intellectual traits, especially when he marries a woman of lower social status, and his devotion fades as she grows old. "Now as beauty is much more fading than life," Witherspoon bluntly asserted, "and fades sooner in a husband's eyes than any other, in a little time nothing will remain but what tends to create uneasiness and disgust."[14] Therefore Witherspoon opposed marriages undertaken merely to gratify male lust, particularly when he was far wealthier than his wife.

He believed that such marriages were bound to be unhappy.

Witherspoon persisted in extolling feminine qualities, to which he found men's much inferior. He admired women's "graces and elegance of manners," the "outward form" of which was far more "beautiful" than the male's. Because men expect politeness and good manners from women, they become angry when their wives lack them. Ironically, women are less concerned about "refinement" in their husbands, at least in Witherspoon's opinion. Indeed, wives are amused when their spouses are awkward, boorish, and uneducated; it gives them a feeling of superiority. This was a universal female characteristic, "even down to the lowest rank." Ostensibly, Witherspoon did not think this condescension was a negative female quality. Perhaps he felt such an attitude was better for the husband, although the latter can never "take pleasure in a wife more awkward or more slovenly than himself." It appeared that woman's proper place, in both wealthy and working-class homes, was to be neat, orderly, and nagging. "A tradesman or country farmer's wife will sometimes abuse and scold her husband for want of order or cleanliness," "Epaminondas" argued, "and there is no mark of inward malice or ill humor in that scolding, because she is sensible it is her proper province to be accurate in that manner."[15] In this profoundly perceptive essay, "Epaminondas" detected that women regarded their display of grace and elegance as an essential aspect of their character, but considered its absence in men venial. Men concurred in this assessment. Curiously, a refined, upper-class woman found a relationship with a lower-class, boorish man more tolerable than would be the case if their statuses were reversed.

Witherspoon's final letter on marriage, which appeared in the *American Museum* in September 1788, applied his "common sense" philosophy and its stress on practical reason, synthesizing his earlier statements. He praised "good nature" and "good sense," especially the latter, as the most important traits for an optimal marriage. This included within its rubric the powers of "rational love" and "esteem" (respect for the other). But some "men of sense" maliciously employed their wit and insight for the psychological oppression of their wives. "There are many instances in which men make use of their sense itself, their judgment, penetration, and knowledge of human life, to make their wives exquisitely unhappy," Witherspoon wrote, with a modern psychologist's insight. He warned young married people not to expect the "refined delicacy" of the courtship and honeymoon periods to pervade the married state. Using an upper-class family of his acquaintance as an example, Witherspoon observed that proper, dignified behavior might merely disguise a married couple's lack of love and real feeling. Unlike some other *American Museum* essayists examined earlier, "Epaminondas" refused to regard stiffly formal, polite conduct in a marriage as an adequate substitute for love between husband and wife. [16]

Reiterating his view that sincerity, common sense, and similar educational backgrounds and personal interests were decisive factors in a successful marriage, Witherspoon placed etiquette in an ancillary role. "It is not the fine qualities of both or either party that will insure happiness," he contended, "but that the one be suitable to the other." Agreeing with many other commentators that it was essential that the conjugal partners' traits be *complementary*, he expounded the ideal of reciprocity rather than wifely subjection to the husband. If the mates' "temper and manner" were suited to one another, the benign husband would patiently bear his wife's complaints.[17]

As we have observed, Witherspoon ardently defends the conduct of women in society, and urges that they acquire the dominant role in marriage if their reasoning abilities justify it. Though initially he justifies marriage primarily for its patriotic utility in augmenting the nation's population, he does not intend his position to be derogatory to woman's character or abilities.

Likewise, Witherspoon entrusts the husband with the praise or blame for the outcome of the original marriage choice. The man's power of initiative confers on him the burden of starting a relationship with the woman. "He has a great advantage on his side, that the right of selection belongs to him," Witherspoon points out. "He may ask any woman he pleases, after the most mature deliberation, and need ask no other; whereas a woman must make the best choice she can, of those only who do or probably will ask her." In this respect things do not seem to have changed much over the last two hundred years. Then as now, the social opprobrium a woman incurs if she broaches the subject of marriage to a prospective mate to a large extent exonerates her from an unfortunate choice. Witherspoon quantified the degree of blame accruing to each gender: since the man had most power to select the wife, he should bear three-fourths of the odium for a "calamitous" marriage, while the wife, who had merely the option of refusing his proposal, bore one-fourth the onus! "Epaminondas" concluded his letters with the sage warning that it was folly for those who could not even relate well to each other during a "courtship" (the eighteenth-century equivalent of "dating"), when "refined delicacy" and romantic passion were at their zenith, to think they would suddenly get along better once they were married.[18] This advice has perennial validity.

Witherspoon's "Letters on Marriage" is the most important statement of male views on women to appear during the 1780s. We have noted his reiterated praise of women as more rational and benign than men, and his insistence on according them equality in the household, although he ignores the question of political and educational equality of opportunity. Nevertheless, he denounces the inferior education prescribed for women, even if he offers no adequate remedy.[19]

"Atticus," another writer in the August 1788 *American Museum*, sympathized with the plight of impoverished widows whose husbands, expecting them to remarry soon after their deaths, failed to provide adequately for them in their wills. Among his proposals to alleviate this injustice were that mothers have control of the children's inheritance; otherwise the latter, taking advantage of their fiscal independence, would disobey maternal commands. "Atticus" wrote objectively. Although sympathetic to women, he was, perhaps more than Witherspoon, aware of their fallibility. For instance, he objected to the widow's receiving all of the husband's estate, something which in any case rarely occurred. "This may be a deviation from reason in the other extreme, and necessary to be guarded against," he warned husbands who might leave their widows all their property, "because the temptation is thereby made strong for fortune-hunters, whom women, otherwise rational, are not always wise enough to withstand."[20] Like "Epaminondas," "Atticus" thought women were on the whole reasonable beings. But he realistically pointed out that they had foibles as well as their husbands.

Consistent with his view of female rationality, "Atticus" recommended that mothers be relied on to supervise their offspring's education after their fathers died. He suggested that the widow control her children's inheritance till her death, so that the frightful possibility of her surviving on a "scanty sustenance" or being forced to rely on her children's good will or sympathy would be obviated. This solicitous author trusted in widows' "discretion" and "prudence."[21] Like most of the essays which appeared in the *American Museum*, this one, entitled "Strictures on various follies and vices," was sympathetic, even favorable, to women's abilities and needs.

Second in importance only to Witherspoon's "Letters on Marriage" and of greater length, "The Visitant" series, which first appeared in

Philadelphia as early as 1768, was reprinted in the *American Museum* in August, September, October, and December 1788 and January 1789. The author was primarily concerned to defend women's proverbial traits, as well as their intellectual potential, from pejorative male imputations and prejudices. In the first article in a series which comprised eight parts by 1789, he praised female refinement, contending that women were essential companions of men. "I am happiest in small companies; and those I think are best, when they are composed of near an equal number of both sexes," he asserted, confuting the views of those who said men best conducted their "business" when isolated from the flippant company of the opposite sex. "The conversation has then an agreeable mixture of sense and delicacy," he continued. "Nothing offends me so much as *double entendres*, especially when ladies are present." A man of genteel temperament, he protested vulgar male behavior and innuendoes in the presence of women who were baffled and embarrassed by facetious remarks with sexual overtones. He denounced men who, "inhumanly sporting themselves at the expence of others," sought to "confuse" the ladies by means of suggestive comments. He had too much respect for women's company to follow their example. "I prefer the conversation of a fine woman to that of a philosopher," he confidently proclaimed.[22]

Readily defending his preference for women over philosophy, "The Visitant" anticipated "Epaminondas" in praising the superior common sense of the "fair sex." He denied that women were frivolous or infantile, saying that he derived "great improvement, as well as pleasure" from their society. He professed "veneration" for women, a result of much time spent observing their "foibles and many excellencies." Reiterating his preference for the company of fine women to philosophers, he argued that "reason justifies the choice." Woman's conversation was based on her "common observation," while the philosopher's discourse emanated from his reading and deductive logic; "hence your fair companion will entertain you with more plain, agreeable and just reflections than the profound philosopher," he counseled.

An advocate of "simplicity" rather than "finery" in a lady's dress, "The Visitant" was more interested in her mental attributes than her physical beauty. "I must inform my fair reader," he said, "that I *admire* the beauties of her person, though I am *enslaved* by the virtues of her mind." In his opinion, female conversation was characterized by "wit, sense, and delicacy." He thought of "delicacy," that refined affection that was concerned about the welfare of others rather than their humiliation, as an especially commendable female trait. Thus the "vein of satire" was very unwomanly, for it "can flow from no other source than that of ill-nature."[23]

Denouncing male prejudices and "injurious aspersions" on the female character, "The Visitant" abhorred the traditional misogynistic view, propounded even by the well-educated, "that women have little minds, that they are naturally vain, and disposed to be pleased with trifles!" Those who insisted that women's mental cultivation "is of less importance than the external accomplishments of person and behaviour" forced female education to take a superficial path, then complained of its result—relatively ignorant women. Objecting to those shoddy male-imposed standards of "female merit," he pointed out that they hindered women from fulfilling their intellectual potential:

> The mind accustomed to apply to trifling objects, in a short time becomes vain and trifling itself. Nothing pleases but what gratifies its vanity; and men are naturally led to ascribe to a lady such foibles as her education is calculated to encourage—*foibles which do not belong to the female mind, but owe their rise and growth to an improper education* [my italics].[24]

Like other male proto-feminists, this author asserted that conventional attributions of female childishness and lack of intellectual depth were based on male imputations and injunctions that women adopt *their* trite standards. "Every sensible woman must discover that the fashionable idea of an accomplished lady, is a satire upon the sex," he said, "and that it is her interest to confute, by her behaviour, the charges generally alleged against them in consequence of it." Though she might attract hostile attention to herself and incur male wrath for being "sentimental, learned, and bookish," by reading she would improve her innate "good sense" and expand her knowledge. Eventually the scholarly woman would gain "universal respect." She should continue to avoid men who were "Fop[s] and debauchee[s]," scoundrels who would never genuinely admire her worth.

Some men were so hostile that they misrepresented all of woman's actions in an unfavorable light, "The Visitant" warned. After impugning female charm and amiability as sluttish "forwardness," these commentators denounced women's "reserve" as "affectation." "If she behaves with an innocent freedom to one of our sex no doubt she has a design upon him," these mean-spirited individuals believed. "If she resents any impropriety in his behaviour—she is immediately noted as a coquette." "The Visitant" had nothing but contempt for these bitter, irrational men, who claimed that all women were bad-tempered, irritable, and envious of those who were more attractive. Such critics thereby evinced an "unmanly spirit," he asserted. They should be combated by "every man of honour and virtue" who was dedicated to helping "the weaker party."[25] More than mere chivalry, "The Visitant" was defending the right of women all over the world, who had hitherto been in a subordinate legal, political, and economic condition, to equal opportunity with men. He urged men to join them in demanding this right.

Insisting that he spends more time with women than most of his comrades, "The Visitant" finds that ladies can intelligently discuss literature as well as fashion. While he admitted he "generally judge[d] upon the charitable side" as far as women were concerned, he eschewed flattering them, believing they were not deceived by it. He maintained the validity of his generous opinion of women's integrity and ability, a viewpoint he upheld throughout the series, originally written in 1768.[26]

In a more detailed analysis of heterosexual relations, "The Visitant" described two types of men—the fop, who merely wants to attract attention to himself, and the "polite man," who is genuinely concerned with developing more intimate emotional relations with the women he meets. Depicting relations between the sexes as an affair of mutual communion, "The Visitant" tempered condescension with sincerity in denouncing the fop's hypocritical, self-serving conduct toward women. "The delicacy, the timidity, the beauty of the fair sex, require that they should be respected, protected, caressed," he argued. "They were designed an [*sic*] help-meet for man; and every principle of honour demands that they should not be losers by those, for whom they were made." Undoubtedly a degree of sexual chauvinism is present in "The Visitant's" assertion that women were created solely as "help-meets" for men, but he used the Book of Genesis, a respected source in those times, to back him up. In any case, "The Visitant" soon abandoned this line of argument, returning to his defense of women against offensive male imputations. "They should be treated with all imaginable tenderness by those, to whom something would still be wanting in creation without this, last-best gift of heaven," he contends. Despite his solicitous tone, "The Visitant's" remark that woman was God's gift to man conveys the implication that she may be more like a gifthorse than man's intellectual equal. His opinion here is somewhat inconsistent. While he believes in woman's right to self-improvement, he retains the paternalistic accents, albeit in muted form.

More concerned at this point with describing differing styles of male conduct toward the ladies than with defending their rights, "The Visitant" explains that the polite man appreciates a woman's beauty and "can make love to her, without expressing himself in a strain of adoration." An honest, rough-and-ready individual, not fulsome or excessive, the polite man disdains to flatter a woman by calling her "angel," and tells her what he sincerely feels. On the other hand, the fop can attract to himself only the "vain coquette," while the "sensible" woman thinks he is foolish. The fop is egotistical and insincere: he desires the woman's praise, her good opinion, rather than her love. Nor is he very intelligent or interested in people for what they are:

> The fop, indeed, will not make any remarks on her [a woman's] character; for he wants [i.e., lacks] discernment: but as he flattered her only to be thought well-bred, and to do himself honour—not her, he will leave her, when he has finished his compliments; and will, perhaps, take the first opportunity of gratifying the ill-nature usually found in little minds, by saying as many spiteful things of her, as he can invent.[27]

Shallow, callous, and volatile, the fop lacked even a *sexual* attraction to the woman. He exploited her solely as an ego object, a means of exalting his social role and prestige. On the other hand, the honest ("polite")man is impelled by a genuine desire for both sexual and intellectual camaraderie with the woman, and "The Visitant" wishes him well. Confident that the "polite" man will pursue a golden mean between the two extremes of blunt candor and disingenuous blandishment, he asserts: "This mean should be observed, and when it is observed, it will be applauded."[28]

Proceeding with his philosophical investigation of sexual relationships, "The Visitant," anticipating feminist historian Nancy Cott's hypothesis on female "passionlessness" by some two hundred years, delivered a few common–sense observations on how the "violence of our desires is proportioned . . . to the difficulties we must surmount in gratifying them."

Personal experience verifies his opinion that passion is inflamed by the overcoming of opposition to its satisfaction, but "what is easily obtained is little valued." The author applies this reasoning to heterosexual passion:

> Why does the artful mistress disappoint the impatient ardour of her lover, by affected delays of his happiness? She knows that those delays inflame his passion. Why is the ardour of the lover so soon lost in the indifference of the husband? Perhaps the conduct of the wife becomes too much the reverse of that, which the mistress observed.

In effect, "The Visitant" was recommending that women comply less readily with male sexual demands. By thus asserting their autonomy in the consequential realm of sexuality, they would increase their power in family and society. Once again, we see male authors with feminist inclinations, taking a woman-centered stance at a time when historians tell us they unanimously propounded ideas of woman's inferiority and subjection.[29] Moreover, rather than depicting women as mothers and homemakers, which Mary Summer Benson and Linda Kerber contend was the gist of periodical literature about them in the late eighteenth century, the *American Museum* chose to print (or reprint) essays which centered on their role as sociable and sexual beings.[30]

Carey continued to print "The Visitant's" "Remarks on the fair sex" during 1788. The series's aim was to analyze the roots of "the unfavorable sentiments, which are generally entertained of the fair sex" by men. "The Visitant" argued that, ironically, women's eagerness to please men was partly to blame, leading them to "not always make a proper distinction between admiration and esteem." He hoped women would prefer to earn men's "esteem" rather than their admiration. "Esteem" meant roughly what the word "respect" signifies today.

Insisting that woman is an "intelligent creature," "The Visitant" lamented that her efforts to attract admiration are not usually based on her wisdom. As a result a man developed little respect or "esteem" for her, though he was amply impressed by her physical attributes. "Should a man allow more admiration to these inferior qualities, than is due to them, yet still he may have less esteem for the woman than she merits," he warned. As the old adage puts it, one should not judge a book by its cover! Pursuing this theme, "The Visitant," while chiding men for their inordinate physical attraction to women, urged the "fair sex" to be less interested in "the art of pleasing" men than in evincing their intelligence. "For, whenever it comes to be a prevailing fault among the ladies, that they appear to pride themselves most upon accomplishments, which have very little connexion with the virtues of the mind—men are naturally led to imagine, that such accomplishments are the most important of female excellencies," he warned, "and hence they entertain sentiments of the sex, which tend to undervalue them." Ostensibly it was only by refusing to conform to male sexual fantasies about them and manifesting their intellects instead, that women could earn "esteem" and gain the respect of others.[31] Ironically, by resisting male efforts to mold them into a sexual stereotype of soft, seductive femininity, women would enhance men's opinion of them, earn a more respectable social status, and increase their eligibility as lifetime mates for bourgeois husbands.[32]

Unfortunately, though their conceit was encouraged by men who flirted with elaborately dressed, made-up women, "The Visitant" pointed out that only vain females were obsessed with their physical charms. "Vanity consists in valuing ourselves upon accomplishments, which are of little importance," he philosophized. "We look upon those who are addicted to vanity, as persons of narrow mind; and hence it is, that this vice is the object of our contempt as well as our aversion." Only foolish men value a woman on the basis of her graceful walk, pretty face, or talents as a dancer rather than her intellect. In "The Visitant's" opinion, the adoption of such criteria disgraced the members of both sexes: "Now it is for those very qualities, upon which the vain part of the fair sex value themselves, that their company is so much courted by the silly part of ours; and with these a fine woman sometimes signifies very little more, than an agreeable trifler, or a pretty fool."[33]

Denouncing immoral men's manipulation of woman's vanity, "The Visitant" insisted that the most important qualities, those which would earn "esteem" for the "fair sex," are "good sense, virtue, and delicacy." When young women seek to be agreeable to lewd young men by excusing their vices (such as drunkenness), they are merely encouraging men to feel less respect for them. "The Visitant" asserted: "If he had any opinion of her moral principles, he would, at least, have been ashamed of what he had done." With the insight of a natural psychologist, he pointed out that women should try to inspire men with shame for their bad actions instead of tolerating their behavior, which had adverse repercussions for both genders' self-esteem. The pretentious fop invariably evinces little concern for "the woman's understanding, to whom he pays his court; he thinks the excellencies, which will recommend him to her, are those, for which he is chiefly indebted to his taylor [*sic*], and his dancing master; and looks upon it as the utmost reach of her capacity, to admire him for these excellencies." This eighteenth-century equivalent of the modern playboy thought women lacked intelligence and were deceived by external appearances and flashiness.

With a keen grasp of the paradoxes of human nature, "The Visitant" noted that the "flatterer" actually held a low opinion of the woman he praised, since he assumed she would succumb to his blandishments: "The flatterer cannot but undervalue the woman he flatters; he must not only suppose her vain of her charms, before she can relish his flattery; but so blind, that she cannot distinguish truth from falsehood." On the other hand, a woman might play a decisive role in turning a man toward the path of virtue. In order to earn the respect ("esteem") of "a sensible and virtuous woman," he pointed out, a man must try to emulate *her* character. "If a man esteems a lady for her good sense, her modesty, and her virtue, he will recommend himself to her by such qualities, as will appear most amiable to one of that character."[34]

As in most other aspects of heterosexual relations, in this case each party's behavior ideally was governed by conditions of mutuality and reciprocal communion. Coming as they did from a male, "The Visitant's" prescriptive norms should have been reassuring to women who did not want to gain men's "admiration" by erotic outfits and seductive behavior, but preferred to earn their "esteem" by intelligence and sincerity.

Ironically, the "esteemed" woman was far more admirable than the "admired" one, "The Visitant" reiterated. "If a lady would acquire esteem," he advised, "she should cultivate those virtues which render the female mind amiable, and give importance to the sex; but if she would be admired only, let her exert all her skill to put on her best face, and take every opportunity of shewing [*sic*] it to advantage." While a woman could acquire "admiration" by means of expensive clothing and makeup, the "esteemed" woman is indifferent to such baubles, and concerned instead with "those virtues, which are the glory of a woman." These traits—intellect and personality, common sense and dignity—were crucial charms for republican inhabitants to possess.

Usually, women who sought admiration rather than respect ("esteem") from men were led into silly and "ridiculous follies." They generally consorted with immature, worthless people of both genders. "A young lady, for instance, is engaged to a set of company, where she expects to meet with a circle of her own sex, as trifling as herself, and a number of ours, more trifling still," "The Visitant" charged.. The vain woman spends hours trying to make herself pretty; she considers this the means to "the admiration due to her transcendent charms." The sensuous woman "supposes herself followed by the eyes and hearts of every one near her," he notes. "Now and then, perhaps, she gives a shy glance, to observe whether it is really so."[35] But her shallow personality will only repel men of intelligence and integrity searching for permanent relationships based on more than physical attraction.

Women who pride themselves on their physical beauty alone are apt to suffer disappointment, "The Visitant" warns, especially if they flaunt their sexuality:

> A lady should consider, that the world is apt to undervalue her beauty, in proportion as she seems to over-rate it:—we begin to ask ourselves, if the woman is really as handsome, as she thinks herself; nay, 'tis ten to one, that we begin to search narrowly for her blemishes, and place them in opposition to her boasted excellencies.[36]

Again proving himself an adroit student of human nature, both male and female, "The Visitant" notes that soon the lady, finding she is not admired as much as she wishes or expects, becomes disgusted. To "preserve her good nature and peace of mind," therefore, she should be "moderate in her expectations."

Although he had earlier pointed out that most men attached too much importance to a woman's physical attractiveness, while the decent man thought her intelligence and demeanor critical, "The Visitant," perhaps feigning amnesia as a means to make "the fair sex" assume more responsibility for their actions, professed ignorance of the reasons for women's "excessive love of admiration." Avowing his "profound respect" for women, he proposed that they try to arouse male esteem, not admiration. An expert on woman's efforts to attract male attention to her varied physical attributes—"In the street I can discover whether it is her face, her gait, or her shape, she would have you most admire"—he even claims he can discern whether a woman is speaking in order to show the whiteness of her teeth or because she really has something worthwhile to say! The implication is that, if he can see behind a woman's facile, shallow facade, other men will, too. Arrogating to himself "the character of a public monitor to the fair sex, by acquainting them with the foibles to which they are liable," he sympathetically explains he is only criticizing egotistic ladies out of a desire that they change their habits and "become more amiable in the eyes of the world."[37]

Apparently "The Visitant's" literary efforts gained a favorable response. He printed a poem from grateful female readers who applauded his call to liberate women from their deplorable status as men's sexual playthings and raise their level of intellectual distinction:

> No keen reproach from satire's pen we
> fear,
> Of little minds, or painted toys to
> hear,
> You, sir, with better sense, will justly
> fix,
> Our faults on education, not our
> sex,
> Will shew [*sic*] the source, which makes
> the female mind
> So oft appear but puerile and blind.
> How many would surmount stern custom's laws,
> And prove the want of genius not the cause;
> But that the odium of a bookish fair,
> Or female pedant, or 'they quit their sphere,'
> Damps all their views, and they must drag the chain,
> And sigh for sweet instruction's page in vain.
> But we commit our injured cause to
> you,—
> Point out the medium which we should pursue;
> So may each scene of soft domestic peace
> Heighten your joys, and animate your bliss.[38]

The theme of complementary, companionate reciprocity between man and woman continually pervaded the pages of the *American Museum* through the end of 1788. When the "Old Bachelor" resurfaced in the August volume, it was to compose his last will and testament, believing he would soon leave the "vain and forlorn estate of celibacy" for the warm, affectionate sociability of marriage. For him, wedlock had become a panacea that would cure his loneliness and remove undesirable personality traits like "bashfulness, irresolution, doubts, fears, obstinacy." He was enthusiastic about his impending marriage and recommended that all his bachelor friends follow his example.[39]

In a similar vein, Witherspoon's "Letter on education" stressed the mutuality between husband and wife, mother and father, in the process of disciplining the young child. Each parent should be in charge of different aspects of training the infant. In the matter of restraining him from seizing for himself whatever objects he desires, the father ought to be the one who exercised authority over the child, since there were many instances in the course of a day when the mother was required to discipline this baby, who is hypothetically under a year old. As Witherspoon explained, "It is also better that it should be by the father than the mother or any female attendant, because they [the women] will be necessarily obliged in many cases to do things displeasing to the child, as in dressing, washing, &c., which spoil the operation [of discipline]." The writer displayed keen insight into child psychology and its relation to authority. The parents should present a united front in dealing with a refractory child. "Neither is it necessary that they ['female attendants'] should interpose, for when once a full authority is established in one person, it can easily be communicated to others, as far as is proper," he pointed out. Witherspoon warned that the mother should never disagree with the father's conduct toward the child or appear to take the latter's side: "The mother or nurse should never presume to condole with the child, or show any signs of displeasure at his being crossed; but, on the contrary, give every mark of approbation, and of their own submission to the same person."[40]

Notwithstanding his monitory tone, Witherspoon does not really recommend that the father possess absolute power over the child. He is referring only to those instances in which the infant unwittingly "steals" objects that do not belong to him. One is left with the impression that he advocates shared authority between the parents, rather than unitary control. The mother's role is not slighted. As is usually the case with articles in the *American Museum*—which was to a great extent a microcosm of middle-class opinion in late eighteenth-century America—women were accorded recognition as relative equals of men, despite laws and mores which dictated otherwise.

However, beginning in 1789 there was a subtle change in the viewpoint of the essays appearing in Carey's magazine. Although women were still often eulogized and treated with a semblance of respect, the message tended more to inculcate passivity, docility, and obedience to men rather than incite a striving for autonomy and individuality by the "fair sex." Some writers strongly implied that women were childish, immature, and intellectually inferior to men, though they simultaneously suggested they had the ability to deftly manipulate them. Carefully regulated educational and religious training and male-prescribed limitations on female dress and ornamentation were other means by which these essays sought to enforce woman's docility and cooperation with male-dictated values and norms.

Among the first pieces to manifest the *American Museum*'s changed attitude was "The Visitant's" essay, "Remarks on the Dress of the Ladies." Though this series had earlier espoused the merits of better education for women and praised female characteristics, "The Visitant" now laid greater emphasis on female dress—external matters—rather than more vital issues like women's intelligence and personality. He said that a lady friend had advised him that, in addition to encouraging women to improve their minds, he should try to appreciate women's "love of dress," which they "generously" attend to for "the sake of the men." His female friend admitted that women used the arts of dress to beguile men, "and endeavor to accomplish in this manner, what we [i.e., women] are not suffered to accomplish" by actively participating in the political arena.[41]

"The Visitant" pondered these remarks. He agreed that a "fine lady" always exerts a "secret influence." Moreover, both "impartial reason" and passion acknowledged apparel's importance for a woman.

Never one to act the prude, "The Visitant" believed that clothing should display female physical charms. As the novelist and poet should depict nature in her most charming light, women ought to dress in accord with an analogous theory. In a similar manner to the effusive, inventive poet's enhancement of language, a woman was justified in ornately adorning her body. Women should dress elegantly because it matched their beauty, "The Visitant" asserted. "If the dress should be suited to the subject, who will deny that the dress of the ladies should be elegant?" he argued. "They have the masterpiece of nature to adorn: its ornament deserves their attention." While his previous contributions had urged that women be granted greater opportunity to improve their minds, he now viewed them primarily as physical objects for men's delight.

Woman's sexual attractiveness was all the more important, "The Visitant" insisted, because it was a major support of the socially beneficial institution of marriage. Provocative clothing attracted men to women, often resulting in marriage, while the woman who failed to take pains with her physical appearance aroused only nausea. "If any one doubts the tendency of an handsome dress to excite agreeable emotions," he cogently pointed out, "let him reflect on the disgust, with which he beholds a slattern."[42]

Penurious fathers and husbands might be alarmed by "The Visitant's" proposal that women purchase expensive, ostentatious clothing—a recommendation that violated the Protestant republican ethos of "frugality" while abetting female tendencies to "profusion." Like satirist Bernard Mandeville in *The Fable of the Bees*, "The Visitant" took issue with men who impugned the luxurious whims of the much-maligned "giddy sex,"as they were sometimes derisively labeled. Turning the tables on his critics, he remarked, "In my opinion, what they murmur at, as a grievance, should be regarded by them as an instance of their good fortune." He pointed out that, as long as the wife was not trying to seduce other men, all her beautifying efforts were directed toward attracting and keeping her husband happy and faithful. Her elaborate and ostentatious costumes were actually *flattering* to the husband, he assured his fellows. "She has heard of the inconstancy of man: she knows it may be a difficult task to preserve your affection, which, however, she is solicitous, above all things, to preserve," he sympathetically argued, informing his male readers: "Her fond passion represents you possessed of every accomplishment." Strange as it may at first appear, the woman's extravagance was designed to please and compliment the male, whom the woman idealized. She is "anxious to appear lovely in his eyes." "You are her greatest ornament," "The Visitant" told the husband. "Her proudest wish is to be yours." Thus the woman's painstaking efforts at her toilette were directed, not to enhancing her own pleasure in her appearance or displaying traits *she* admired, but to satisfying and attracting man.

From "The Visitant's" perspective, the wife's ornate dress revealed her love for husband, and he should enjoy rather than condemn it. Indeed, "The Visitant" argued, the husband should worry if his wife is *not* extravagant. Frugal behavior would signify her indifference to his opinion of her appearance and a stolid reaction to his physical desire for her. On the other hand, "The Visitant" deplored those "inconsiderate wives" who sought, "by their unbounded extravagance," to reduce their husbands and children to "misery and ruin." He found such instances extremely rare. The opposite case was far more alarming and indicated an unhappy marriage: "When I have seen a married woman neglect to dress in a manner suitable to her age, and to the rank and fortune of her husband, I have always considered this circumstance as a melancholy symptom of an aversion, or, at least, of an indifference, subsisting between them."[43] The equivalency between the satisfaction of elaborate wifely tastes and the presence of a happy connubial relationship, as depicted in "The Visitant's" essay, suggests the existence of a burgeoning consumerism, for which the United States has since become famous (or infamous), as early as the late eighteenth century, represented—then as now—by women.[44]

Pursuing his theme that male wishes ought to (and often did) determine women's modes of dress, "The Visitant" regretted that hard-pressed fathers sometimes were burdened by wasteful, frivolous daughters whose purpose in bedizening themselves was more often the pursuit of irresponsible flirtations than the quest for a suitable husband. He concluded by stating that beautiful dress actually complemented a woman's "beauties of the mind." He assured his readers that male disapproval would soon drive from the market any repulsive pieces of female apparel.

In his conviction that men's opinions dictated female modes of dress, "The Visitant" showed little cognizance of woman's autonomy or ability to think for herself. On the other hand, he thought that a man should prize woman's intelligence and character above her physical attractiveness. As he put it, "The winning graces of the mind should never be sacrificed to the less powerful attractions of the person or dress; especially as these attractions derive all their influence from those graces."[45] This theme was more muted than it had been in "The Visitant's" previous articles, an alteration which suggests that Mathew Carey had decided to revise his editorial policy to accommodate the opinion that a woman's proper sphere was in subordination to man.

Manifesting an orthodox attitude respecting the prevailing social distinctions in society, "The Visitant" insisted that traditional class barriers to extravagant purchases by lower-class women were essential to social order. Public opinion censures rather than praises the poor young woman who dresses in a "splendor" she cannot afford, since more attention is bestowed on "her imprudence and vain ambition" than her "taste and elegance," which would have been applauded were she wealthier. "The Visitant's" earlier support of increased rights for women had apparently not resulted in a more democratic social outlook than that of his aristocratic contemporaries.

Though he insisted that women take care that their mode of dress pleased male admirers, "The Visitant" urged that they attire themselves modestly, in keeping with a sedate, intelligent persona. He had contempt for the conceited woman, who was obsessed with her physical appearance and its role in securing male attention. Since dress is merely an "inferior embellishment" to the beauty of the female mind, "the less her dress is the object of her attention, the more it becomes the object of ours." For him the ideal is a "dignified" yet ornately dressed woman, who at least *seems* to be modest: "We praise a lady who dresses with skill, yet seems wholly insensible to the effects of her ingenuity." He praised elegance but not gaudiness. "The fair sex [must] distinguish between elegance and superfluous finery in dress," he concluded. While chintzy costume was out of the question, refined opulence rather than flamboyance was the optimal women's dress.[46]

Despite occasional disclaimers, "The Visitant" had ostensibly abandoned his interest in women's intellectual advancement for more superficial aspects of the feminine lifestyle. Above all, he made clear that woman's primary purpose was to please man, a stance which had been largely absent from his earlier essays. The recourse to this traditional, conservative viewpoint that a woman was not entitled to a life, identity, or opinions independent of her man became increasingly common in the *American Museum* in 1789.

For instance, Carey reprinted an article written by a Massachusetts pundit, "The Worcester Speculator," who invoked the traditional stereotype of woman as weak, "tender" and passive, with a natural "inward sense of propriety." The author fondly began by praising "female delicacy," by which he surprisingly meant "their advancement in mental and moral, as well as in external perfection." He insisted that they deserved the right "to share in that happiness which such perfection will insure to themselves and to the rest of the world." Like other commentators, the "speculator" argued that woman's attention and influence had caused man to restrain his "appetites and passions" and converted him into an intelligent being. Women were also a source of pleasure for the male. Considering all the benefits man derived from her, the author pointed out, "it ill becomes him, who is born of woman, to speak degradingly of the sex."

Indeed, woman's influence might presage world reformation, "The Worcester Speculator"asserted. The philanthropist and "friend of mankind" would never condemn her, since he "knows the influence which woman has upon man, and the hand she has, or might have, in promoting the virtue and happiness of families, of larger communities, and of the world." Certainly the writer seemed to perceive woman's role in society as crucial.[47]

Unfortunately, "The Worcester Speculator" soon shifted his emphasis to a discussion of woman's physical attributes rather than her power to change society. The Creator had formed the female body "with a delicate hand," he observed, and the ideal woman was a tender and passive being. In lyrical tones, he exulted:

> The slender texture of their bodies, the softness of their features, the tunefulness of their voices, the general placidness of their tempers, and tenderness of their hearts, together with a similar niceness in their intellectual powers, denote a characteristic delicacy.

The men who ran the society should accordingly form woman's education, sentiments, vocations, and deportment to correspond with this ideal. "Education and culture" ought to fortify natural female sensitivity, that "inward sense of propriety, which regulates and beautifies the whole conduct; an unsullied and inflexible virtue and sweetness of temper beaming forth in everything that is spoken, and in every thing that is done." Woman's deliberate cultivation of her allegedly innate refinement and elegance would enable her to better perform her primary role as man's inoffensive, compliant companion.

In view of the author's membership in Worcester's Puritan/Congregationalist community, it was not surprising that he emphasized the priority of religious occupations in a female paragon's life. This was a viewpoint which had been absent from previous issues of Carey's magazine. All agree that virtue is good and vice is bad, "The Worcester Speculator" admitted. Therefore, rather than cooking, sewing, and painting, woman should spend her time in the "refined exercises of virtue, of devotion, and religion." The most significant contribution that woman could make to social and familial well-being, thereby fulfilling her debt to "human nature," was the unstinting pursuit of spiritual rectitude and knowledge. The male gender would also benefit if women spent more time in church: "A course of conduct formed upon such maxims, will exalt the [female] character, add a lustre to all their other charms, and secure their hearts from seduction, their lives from blemish, and their bosoms from remorse."[48] As they had done since the time of John Wheelwright, Anne Hutchinson, and Cotton Mather, proponents of religious revival sought to enlist women in their cause.[49] It seemed a worthwhile outlet for women's (optimally) passive devotions.

Perhaps it was appropriate, therefore, that the *American Museum* published an extended series of essays, entitled, "Letters to a Young Lady," by Reverend John Bennet, the Anglican vicar of St. Mary's Parish in Manchester, England. Bennet's letters were not very original. At many points they hardly did more than reiterate the views of his more famous predecessors, Reverends Gregory and Fordyce. Nevertheless, by publishing Bennet's work in the *American Museum*, Carey facilitated its wide circulation throughout the United States. In propagating Bennet's conservative views on women's dress, manners, and education, Carey further evinced his changing attitudes.

In his "Letters," Bennet reiterated such clichés as the view that, for women at least, cleanliness was next to godliness, and intellectual pursuits should take a backseat to the pursuit of heavenly salvation. He exceeded "The Visitant" in his conviction that female attire must serve as one more aspect of woman's subjection to man.

Bennet applauded female piety as an easily available means for women to achieve self-esteem, even if they lacked access to "those intellectual endowments, which procure a greater share of fame and admiration." Though Bennet argued that female parishioners' moderate employment of reason and curiosity in the search for knowledge would fortify their virtue and religious convictions, he warned that some women became obsessed with intellectual pursuits. They strove to become like men, and forgot the importance of neat and clean personal habits. On the other hand, he admitted that in refined social circles ignorant women were despised, creating quite a quandary for "a judicious woman," who wished "to avoid the imputation of pedantry" as well as the stigma of stupidity. For these well-meaning souls Bennet thought he had the answer.

The woman of "good sense," Bennet argued, must pursue a middle-of-the-road course, a happy medium between pedantry and illiteracy. She should avoid serious matters that might "bring wrinkles," though she ought to strive to add an intellectual "polish" to her "manners." "Cultivate, then, such studies, as lie within the region of sentiment and taste," he condescendingly suggested. "Let your knowledge be feminine as well as your person." He insisted on restricting women to the realms of artistic imagination and prohibiting them from mathematical and metaphysical speculation:

> The prominent excellencies of your [women's] minds are taste and imagination; and your knowledge should be of a kind, which assimilates with these faculties: Politics, philosophy, mathematics, or metaphysics are not your province. Machiavel[li], Newton, Euclid,

> Malebranche, or Locke, would lie with a very ill grace in your closets. They would render you unworthy indeed. They would damp the vivacity, and destroy that disengaged ease and softness, which are the very essence of your graces.[50]

Inveighing against "unwomanly" learning, Bennet implied that women's understandings could not transcend the superficial and ornamental. They could not compete with men in the domain of rational insight. "While men, with solid judgment . . . and a superior vigour, are to combine ideas to discriminate, and examine a subject to the bottom, you [women] are to give it all its brilliancy and all its charms," he advised. "They build the house; you are to fancy and to ornament the ceiling [*sic*]."[51] Although Bennet was an English curate, Carey's printing of his essays reveals that he thought their purport was relevant to the new republic's gender relationships as well. Bennet's message did not flatter female abilities: men were more profound thinkers than women, who were frilly and whose minds were suited only to extrinsic matters.

Discussing ladies' apparel, Bennet stressed "neatness" while confessing that women were better judges of dress than men. He warned women who eschewed tidy habits that their husbands might "seek that satisfaction abroad, which they found not at home" by pursuing extramarital affairs. (There were many roads by which an inattentive wife might precipitate her spouse's infidelity: an unmade bed and an unmassaged male ego were two of them). Since a woman's main purpose in life was to get and keep a husband, Bennet reminded his readers, she should not smugly believe that, once she was married, she no longer need maintain a cleanly appearance. "If they conceived some efforts necessary to gain the prize" of a husband, Bennet argued, "more, I am sure, are required to preserve it." In the marriage game, only the fittest survived. This is especially true because man's affection diminished after marriage, Bennet warns, while woman's increased. Thus, his remarks tended to relegate the wife to a passive, humble, and insecure status vis-à-vis the husband, who to some extent assumed once again the feudal role of lord and master.[52]

Elaborating on the theme that, for women, like children, cleanliness was sacrosanct, Bennet warned that even servants showed diminished respect and deference for a slovenly mistress. He pithily stated, "Neatness is the natural garb of a well-ordered mind, and has a near alliance with purity of heart." Objecting as well to extravagant dress and coiffures, he advocated instead "an elegant simplicity." He especially deplored women's attempts to mimic male attire and hair styles, including the donning of female riding habits, which he considered scandalous. Conversely, he regarded such "feminine" accouterments as cosmetics, wigs, false eyelashes, and other artificial contrivances as malicious female efforts to "deceive sensible men" into marriage. A woman who painted her face insulted the Almighty's creation. "Let the fairness of your complexion be only that of nature, and let your rouge be the crimson blush of health, arising from temperance, regularity, exercise, and air," he effusively advised the ladies.[53]

In the following letter, Bennet, rather surprisingly in light of his earlier praise of feminine purity, advised women on how best to deceive the opposite sex. His tone was less disparaging of women than before. Writing "On dress and ornament," he admitted that, unlike a man, who would be considered intolerably effeminate if he employed artificial contrivances to enhance his looks, a woman might properly add some ornamentation to her costume. At the same time, Bennet was sure, the discerning woman will "endeavour to convince every beholder, that she . . . does not wish to seduce by her appearance, but only to please; that she has cultivated her mind, much more than her person." Ostensibly Reverend Bennet had arrived at the conclusion that men appreciated intelligence more than beauty, and that it was by touting the former that a woman would succeed in her goal of attracting a husband.

Evincing his pleasure that women were adopting more conservative modes of dress, Bennet counseled, virtually plagiarizing Dr. John Gregory's famous work, *A Father's Legacy to His Daughters* (London, 1774): "Bosoms should throb unseen . . . . Wherever delicacy throws its modest drapery, imagination always lends inexpressible charms."[54] On the other hand, he admitted, the Quakers' "plain" attire was excessively drab and uninspiring.

Betraying his conviction that women were incapable of pursuing autonomous adult social roles, Bennet preferred that young ladies dress like children. "I very much admire the sashes, which of late, have been so fashionable among ladies," he asserted. "They give me the idea of a childish simplicity, innocence and ease. These, and flowing ringlets, are on the system of nature. And nature will always please." On the other hand, he considered it inappropriate for older, married women to dress in this fashion. In any case, he pointed out, the body is only a "temporary receptacle for an immortal mind." He advised the Christian matron to donate to the poor the money she saved by abstaining from expensive baubles and costumes.[55] While Bennet regarded the young woman as little more than a child, he conceived that elder members of the same gender need only fulfill the duties of Christian charity—itself a somewhat passive avocation—to successfully perform the limited responsibilities he assigned them. Though they focused on the question of appropriate women's attire, Bennet and other commentators on fashion at this time strove less to judge issues of style than to instill in women the values of passivity and subordination to men.

"A letter to a very good-natured lady who is married to a very ill-natured man," printed in the *American Museum* in October 1789, eulogized the elegance of female passivity in the face of male provocation. The author, bearing the pseudonym "Z," writes to his cousin, who has experienced some "rufflings" (disagreements) with her husband, that he regretted that a woman of "so much goodness" should suffer so. But he encouraged her to maintain a calm and affable demeanor despite these altercations, "for I know the steadiness of your mind, and the prudence you have in alleviating every thing that would disturb a less-settled temper; and make [*sic*] some wives out into violences, that would render them ridiculous, as well as wretched." Professing a hope to spare his beloved cousin from such "wretched" and "ridiculous" actions, he expounded what he considered the basic principles of married life.

Like earlier sympathetic male writers in the *American Museum*, "Z" thought marital reciprocity and affection were essential. The partners "can never be happy in themselves, unless they are well with their consorts." As he felicitously explained, husband and wife were so closely connected, like two halves of one individual, "that the one cannot be happy, if the other is miserable." Spouses who could not relate harmoniously found it necessary to leave each other's company, "or else you must sit jarring together, like a couple of bad instruments that are always out of tune."

Unlike other advocates of conjugal cooperation, "Z" recommended that the wife assume a posture of passive obedience if that were necessary to attain an agreeable household. She should submit rather than assert her point of view in family disputes. "The most necessary thing then for a married woman, to make her self happy, is to endeavour to please her consort," he asserted. "And one comfort is, that the very endeavouring to please, goes a great way towards obtaining its end." In the writer's view, since women get pleasure by pleasing their spouses, his even-tempered cousin should calmly and cheerfully fulfill her husband's wishes. Apparently reciprocity had become a very one-sided affair.

Unabashedly advising that the wife fawn and cringe before the husband, the author tersely affirmed, "Complacency [*sic*] naturally begets kindness, as a disobliging way does aversion." Not only should the wife avoid saying or doing things to anger the husband, he urged, "but one should be apt to say and do every thing that is likely to be agreeable to him." He assured her that such slavish servility and obsequiousness were guaranteed to create harmonious marriages. "A woman that thoroughly considers this, and puts it honestly in practice, can scarce ever fail to make both herself and her husband happy," he said. The wife would find it easy to mollify her spouse since they "are so thoroughly acquainted with one another's tempers and inclinations," the result of years of courtship and marriage. He noted that women deliberated carefully before undertaking "the most important step in their whole lives." They would not marry until they had gained an intimate knowledge of the man's personality, and the ability to "see into the whole character of a man; how far he is apt to submit, and how far to domineer." In contrast to previous writers, who had slyly suggested that women use their intimate knowledge to gain covert power over men, "Z" advised that the wife employ her skill in "open[ing] all the more hidden folds of his heart" solely to gain more precise knowledge of his psyche, the better to please him![56]

Painfully aware that married couples often argued over trivial matters, "Z" concluded, not that these issues were silly and unimportant, but that they acquired significance from their threat of alienating the husband. Since "married people disagree ten times oftener about trifles, than about things of weight," a wife would find that the best way to gain victory "often" in a marriage, would be to "yield sometimes" to her husband. Somewhat cynically assuming that women spent all their time calculating how best to catch a husband, he advised wives: "Yielding to a married woman, is as useful as fleeing is to an unmarried one; for both of these methods most naturally obtain what they seem to avoid." Arguing that servility was natural to woman, he went so far as to state that her "vanity," the universal "passion," might paradoxically be sated by magnanimous submission to her husband's will.

At the same time that he advocated their stoic subservience, "Z" subtly pointed out that married women in American society had little choice but to capitulate to their spouses. "For to get the better of oneself, is at least as glorious, as to get the better of any other person whatever," he explained to his cousin, advising her to comply with her husband's demands. "And you would, beside, have the inward satisfaction of considering, that in all such cases, you do not yield out of cowardice, but prudence, and that you enjoyed the superiority of knowing what you ought to do, much better than the obstinate man, who seems outwardly to have carried his point, where you have really carried your's [*sic*]."[57] By fulfilling her sacred duty—obeying her husband—she overcame her own selfish will, thereby proving she was more virtuous than the male gender, more willing to sacrifice for the well-being of family and community.[58]

Commending woman's cultivation of Stoic virtues of self-discipline and self-denial, "Z" advises his cousin that the conscious act of pleasing her husband would gradually become a satisfying habit. At the same time he warns that this "scheme of pleasing," as he calls it, should not be undertaken as part of "a life of artifice and dissimulation," but rather from sincere conviction. Thus the wife, like the child or the slave in patriarchal societies, must subject herself to her husband like an automaton or a doll without a will of her own. He assured her that eventually she would like it!

The wife's voluntary subjugation to her husband was guaranteed to "introduce or increase a real mutual love and good will between" them, "Z" asserted. He delivers this message "for the world": all wives should strive to become their husbands' playthings. In the future, he hoped, his cousin would utilize his advice to gain "the serenity of mind, which all the world thinks to be in you," but which had actually consisted merely of social *politesse* and dissembling. He predicted that "all those virtues and excellencies which I know to be in you" would achieve fruition through a policy of submissive cooperation with her husband, "unruffled by any disturbances, and cleared from every little cloud that may hang over" their conjugal relationship.[59] By 1789, the traditional view that female "virtue" was synonymous with passive submission to the male had reasserted itself. This writer in the *American Museum* surely would have agreed with the ancient Greek scholar Plutarch that "the wife ought not to have any feelings of her own but join with her husband in his moods whether serious, playful, thoughtful, or joking."[60]

In a similar vein, "An Affecting and true history" praised a young woman's unstinting devotion to love. Her obsession with the safety and security of her betrothed results in her needless death. The theme of the story, that romantic love can arouse loyalty, and that marriage based on such love is preferable to marriage arising from economic self-interest, adhered to the emerging literary trends of the age. According to the author, women were inherently dependent on the men they loved. A woman in love, filled with "the tender passion," had lost her reasoning powers. Her thoughts were completely preoccupied with her lover: "She sees, she is alive only to the pain of being torn from the object that was far dearer to her than herself. And these are the feelings—this the conduct of genuine love."[61] Woman's destiny—a fate she irresistibly accepted—was to live vicariously through her love for man. To judge from the articles appearing in the *American Museum*, after 1789 the ideal woman was increasingly characterized by unwavering devotion to the male mate and a selflessness devoid of aggression, autonomy, or individuation.

Moreover, after 1789 writers in the *American Museum* resented and ridiculed the idea of female self-assertion. A short story printed in October

1789, "The school for husbands and wives," concerns a husband involved in an erotic affair with an exotic courtesan and sex goddess. At one point in the story, his wife, whose identity is not known to the mistress, asks her the secrets of lovemaking. The implication of the story is that wives *should* serve as eager sexual objects for their husbands; otherwise men will stray, searching for more compliant and sensuous lovers.[62]

"The matrimonial creed," a satire on marriage, argued that the wife had too much power in the family, in light of her natural inferiority to her husband. The creed states in part, "that there were two rational beings created, both equal, and yet one superior to the other; and the inferior shall bear rule over the superior, which faith, except every one keep whole, and undefiled, without doubt, he shall be scolded at everlastingly." The final phrase ("*he* shall be scolded at everlastingly") resolves the conundrum of which gender is superior to the other. The satire contends that the wife holds all of the real power in the family, and that the patriarchal ideal of male rule is at variance with the reality. For example:

> The man is superior to the woman, and the woman is inferior to the man; yet both are equal, and the woman shall govern the man. The man was not created for the woman, but the woman for the man; yet the man shall be the slave of the woman, and the woman the tyrant of the man.[63]

This misogynistic, sarcastic "matrimonial creed" is not an isolated instance of men's resentment of what they perceived as women's arrogation of power in the household. Although wryly humorous, an anecdote "On Appearing what we neither are, nor wish to be," indicates that, at least to an extent, conflict had replaced cooperation between the sexes. The protagonist, Doctor D., is obsessed with "his favourite subject . . . that implicit obedience in a wife, and the strictest subordination to her husband constitute all his ideas of domestic happiness." Though he incessantly boasts "that he is absolute master in his own family," he seldom invites his friends to his house to witness his exercise of power. "Having dined there lately," the narrator recalls, "I perceived his reason" for such unsociableness, "for during the repast, while he was constantly engaged in asserting his authority, his wife was as anxious to dispute it: and the comforts of conviviality were banished by this domestic contention, which gradually increased, till the lady left the table." The Doctor's house assuredly was no peaceable kingdom, as his relief at his wife's departure attested. "I could discover that he dreaded she would return to the combat," the narrator concludes, "and that the suspension of hostilities would end with my visit."[64] Rather than harmony and subordination, relations between husband and wife were now characterized by hostility and mutual recrimination.

After about 1790, we find that the theme of heterosexual discord, which had been present though generally subdued in favor of the motif of reciprocity and mutual accord, becomes dominant in articles in the *American Museum* focusing on male/female, which invariably were husband-and-wife relations. Male writers became increasingly disturbed by the existence of female assertiveness and seemed to prefer its suppression. They enjoyed making fun of the stereotypical "aggressive" woman, but their derision badly masked their anxiety.[65]

As a means of safeguarding man's self-ascribed attributes of power and assertiveness from female encroachment, male writers in Carey's magazine drew a rigid dichotomy between proper "masculine" and "feminine" behavior. The anonymous author of an article "On Beauty" in the September 1790 *American Museum* argued that, if a physically attractive woman lacks an upright character, her mere corporeal beauty "is rather a disgrace than an ornament to the person possessed of it." Since "virtue" is the most essential feature of the human being, a lascivious woman is undesirable even though she is beautiful and well-educated. "In short, the most celebrated lady in the land, that has lost her innocence, will appear no less unamiable in the eyes of a man of sense, than the meanest oyster-wench along the wharves," the writer, precursor of a mode of thought which has come to be called "Victorian," argued. "Amiability"—a shorthand term for agreeableness—was an indispensable trait for the virtuous woman. It was taken for granted that promiscuous women and lower-class fish-wives, as social outcasts for their respective moral and economic derelictions from the middle-class norm of respectability, were without it.

"Modesty" is another quality without which female beauty is a "dis-grace," the essay pointed out. The author defines modesty as "withal a certain graceful bashfulness, which is the peculiar ornament and characteristic of the fair sex." On the other hand, boldness and courage in a man are "commendable," but they denote "an impertinent assurance and haughtiness" in a woman. The female who drew attention to herself, negating the passive essence of her being by "masculine," aggressive,

even self-assertive conduct, degraded herself in society:

> The more feminine softness and beauty one has in her countenance, the more insufferable is her masculine behaviour: her good qualities (if she have any) will be generally unobserved, seldom approved of, and never commended; and though in all other respects she may be completely amiable, yet, for want of a becoming modesty, she will appear completely disagreeable.[66]

Thus, the woman who acted in a "masculine" manner, who was forthright and outspoken rather than demure and coy, negated her femininity even if she were "amiable" in all other respects. "Modesty" and "amiability" were equally indispensable for the "virtuous" woman.

Another crucial female quality with priority over beauty, the author explained, was "good-sense." One can only feel pity for an "insipid" beauty, devoid of intelligence: "To be pleased with the beauty of a fool, is a mark of the greatest folly." Of course, although the writer adopted the perspective of the male suitor looking for the proper wife, he seldom made this clear, treating his standards as if they were absolute.

Nearly synonymous with "good-sense" was "good-nature." Another vital womanly characteristic, it bestows a "graceful," "engaging sweetness" upon the "handsome face," in contrast to the hideous scowl of the angry woman:

> On the other hand, the frowns of ill-nature disgrace the finest countenance: not even the wrinkles of old age can make it so homely and deformed. A scold, though ever so handsome, is universally hated and avoided: the very sight of her is odious, and her company intolerable.

What was desirable in women was graciousness and passivity. Modesty, virtue, good nature, and good sense would make them pleasing to the men around them. At the same time, by holding up the standard of docile innocence as a model, men suggested that it was the ideal rather than the reality of everyday life; perhaps their wives and sweethearts did not often display this optimal behavior.

Finally, exhibiting an aristocratic, or least *haute-bourgeois* frame of reference, the author insisted that his paragon of female beauty possess "good breeding. As a precious stone, when unpolished, appears rough; so beauty, without good breeding, is awkward and unpleasing." "Genteel behaviour" was equally important in enabling a truly beautiful woman to be "agreeable: virtue, modesty, good-sense, and good-nature will signify but little without it." Almost as an afterthought, the author noted that a physically attractive woman cannot be "completely agreeable" unless she has adorned her beauty with "a good education" and "polite behaviour." So tepid an endorsement of women's education was a far cry from the *American Museum*'s earlier vigorous defense of female acumen and mental capacity, and its proposals to expand them through greater educational opportunities.[67]

Readers of a more humble socioeconomic status found essays and poetry addressed to their situation expounding a similar theme. They were told that women's destiny was to soothe their husbands and provide tranquilizing joy in their lives after the bitterness of the work-a-day world. Though they were not considered sexual objects, women in this context were still regarded largely as auxiliary to the male need for peace and fulfillment rather than as autonomous beings. A poem published in the *American Museum* in December 1788, when the new government was about to commence operations, expounded this concept of "qualifications, required in a wife." Arguing that a husband does not need to marry a beautiful, wealthy woman or a titled aristocrat, the author explained that all he desired from his mate was that she cheer him up, and "soften the painful reflexions [*sic*] of woe, or banish distress from our hearts." He longed for

> the temper unclouded and gay,
> The countenance ever serene;
> To chear [*sic*] with sweet converse, as youth wears away;
> And dissipate anger and spleen;
> Whose smiles may endear and enliven the hours,
> Retirement shall oft set apart;
> Whose virtues may sooth, when disquietude sours,
> And tenderness cherish the heart.

The poet emphasizes domestic, family-oriented virtues. He professes the values of a simple man who wants a good, simple woman for a companion. While his attitudes are ostensibly neither evil nor chauvinistic (to use a more modern term), his wish for a benevolent companion who will "share" with him rather than dominate or be dominated, conceals an underlying selfishness that regards the wife as somewhat less than an equal. As he puts it, his wife's purpose, to "consume" his sorrow, is the price she pays for being allowed to "share with me, life's little store":

> For fortune, be honour her portion assign'd;
> For beauty, bright health's rosy bloom:
> Let justice and candour ennoble her mind,
> And chearfulness sorrow consume:
> Thus form'd, would she share, with me, life's little store,
> It's [*sic*] mixture of pleasure and smart,
> She'd ever continue, 'till both were no more,
> The constant delight of my heart.[68]

Far from expressing a wish for a "Republican Mother," male writers in the *American Museum* seem to have developed an infantile preoccupation in yearning for a "maternal wife" who would comfort them in their sorrows and act the part of the benevolent, surrogate mother. In their desire to escape from the burdens of work and a competitive, urbanizing, capitalist market society, men writing about the ideal woman in the *American Museum* were beginning to sound like whining children themselves.[69]

Perhaps this outlook explains these writers' increasing tendency to demarcate boundaries between proper "male" and "female" behavior, and to warn each gender against violating the rules. Thus Reverend John Bennet's "Letters to a Young Lady" denounced those women who became obsessed with pursuing the "male" domain of knowledge and intellect to such an extent that they forgot the importance of being neat and clean (prototypical "female" traits). When he urged women to adopt "an elegant simplicity," with hairstyles consisting of "natural, easy ringlets," his primary concern was that ladies eschew mannish coiffures and clothing. As he put it, "The nearer you approach to the masculine in your apparel, the further you will recede from the appropriate graces and softness of your sex." Recurring for support to Joseph Addison's famed *Spectator* magazine, Bennet was especially critical of ladies who wore "riding habits," which he thought were disgustingly unfeminine, "wholly unsex her, and give her the unpleasing air of an Amazon, or a virago." Such an "absurd" female attire was comparable to men dressed in women's "muffs." On this issue Bennet scolded women unsparingly, even irrationally:

> You [ladies] immediately despise the ridiculousness of the one; we daily feel the unnaturalness of the other. We forget that you are women in such a garb, and we forget to love.

The woman who experimented with masculine behaviors risked losing man's love. This was the punishment for attempting to transgress divinely appointed sexual boundaries.[70]

The marrow of the question was men's fear that women (and perhaps other men) sought to deceive them about their sexual attributes and attractiveness and—this was the greatest fear—about their sexual identity itself. Although Bennet did not state it explicitly, men feared that their own dependent urges and wishes for maternal nurturance in the hostile new capitalist world might render them "effeminate," emasculated beings, unsuited for the "manly" existence of republican citizens. Addressing his "young lady" friend, Bennet projected this masculine fear onto women. Appalled at the lengths to which women would go to attract a man—applying odoriferous perfumes, wigs and artificial hair and even teeth—Bennet regretted that men encouraged these deceptions. "Blush, my dear girl, at such unseemly practices," he pleaded. "Be content to be, what God and nature intended you: appear in your true colours; abhor any thing like deceit in your appearance, as well as your character." The male feared that the woman intended to trick him into thinking that she was more attractive—more sexual, more of a woman—than in fact she was: "What must all sensible men think of a woman, who has a room filled with a thousand preparations and mixtures to deceive him?" The logical conclusion to this train of thought was that this "woman" was not a woman at all—"she" was a *man*.

That such anxieties preoccupied Bennet becomes evident from his attack on male sexual deviants who degenerately employed "effeminate artifices" for unnamed purposes. It is not clear whether he was describing transvestites, homosexuals, or merely "effeminate" males who liked to use perfume and wear elaborate outfits. But he felt unmitigated disgust for these sexually nondescript or androgynous beings. "They have already the scorn and ridicule of one sex, and the stern contempt and indignation of the other," he observed. "They are poor, amphibious animals, that the best naturalists know not under what class to arrange."[71] It was crucial that "young ladies" make no attempt to deceive male suitors regarding any aspect of their sexuality. To act otherwise offended both God and man. *That* was the primary reason for masculine objections to women's "painting" their faces with makeup. Not only did it insult God's Creation, it hastened the approach of wrinkles and "destroyed constitutions"—a term that the author may have unconsciously applied to the new, written United States Constitution and its precursors on the state level as well as to women's physical health.

Most importantly, such deception comprised an attempt to obscure the woman's physical reality. "Let the fairness of your complexion be only that of nature," Bennet advised the lady, "and let your rouge be the crimson blush of health, arising from temperance, regularity, exercise, and air."[72] It was a responsible male citizen's duty to forestall any female attempts to disguise their true physical features in order to entrap unsuspecting potential mates. After all, a hoodwinked man was the antithesis of the *masculine*, virile man, the type who was qualified for self-government in the young republic.

At this time, the *American Museum*'s poets were likewise engaged in an earnest attempt to delineate proper boundaries between gender characteristics. The August 1791 issue contained a mellifluous piece of verse, "A poetical essay on the comparative merit of the two sexes," effusive in its praise of noble, self-sacrificing woman. The poet concluded that woman's passive traits—meekness, endurance of suffering, and submissiveness to God—paradoxically rendered her the superior gender. His attempt to define the sexes combined elements of the old Medieval view of woman as man's chattel with late eighteenth-century ideas of intergender reciprocity and egalitarian relationship. However, the poet's idea of reciprocity is that the "meek" and "modest" woman should look to the strong, virile man for protection, and (unless *he* were effeminate) he would not fail to fulfill her needs.[73]

Commencing his verse with the creation of Adam and Eve, the poet first lists man's proper characteristics—valor, power, vigor, "a mind with noble resolution steel'd." The virile man's role is to defend the "pure innocence" of "the injur'd fair"—women in distress. The author derided prissy, excessively fashionable men, "ye macaronies of the age," who, "but for your dress, bespeak the weaker sex." They refused to defend either female "virtue" or their country's honor. The writer is sure that most American men are virile, responsible, and "industrious," dedicated to providing for the well-being of their progeny. Like Reverend Bennet, this author seeks to discriminate between the small, effeminate minority of men and the virile, virtuous majority who are good husbands and fathers and zealous soldiers of the new republic.

Even the toughest man eagerly served woman, whose "virtuous modesty," "winning grace," and "soft attracting charm" are designed to make "the proudest of the human race [man] stoop at its shrine." But a woman's beauty was less impressive and far less enduring than her modesty. As the poet explained:

> But 'tis the pride, the glory of the sex,
> By just reserve and winning modesty,
> To raise a solid monument of worth.
> What though some females, bred around the court,
> Have swerved from Chastity and left
> her paths,
> Yet still it beams with lustre in the fair.

Enumerating other valuable feminine traits like "economy and frugal management," and especially "serenity and calm of mind," the poet argued that these characteristics evinced women's superiority to men. Paradoxically, in a society that put a premium on aggressive, "manly" qualities, the author asserted that women's meekness and resignation to fate were the sources of their preeminence. Although men were noted for bravery and physical strength, they would do well to try to emulate women's moral courage, endurance of pain, and compassion for others' suffering:

> But what should humble man, and make him own,
> Superior wisdom to adorn the fair,
> Is that serenity and calm of mind,
> That silent composure, that submission meek
> Which always marks them in the adverse hour.

Despite women's "soft" and "delicate" nature, the author observes, "they bear affliction with heroic strength,"

> While man oft' shrinks beneath th' oppressive weight.

Women probably acquired their reputation for stolidly facing pain as a result of male admiration for their bearing the agonies of childbirth. This was perhaps one of the roots of their "benevolent" disposition, their "compassion, tenderness, and charity." These traits are closest to those of that "Almighty Power, whose name is love." The poet thinks women are "heaven's most perfect work" because they "feel for another's sufferings as their own," and instinctively sympathize with and try to assist the unfortunate. "The generous fair's" compassion for suffering leads her to act to assuage pain, and her efforts "turn the tears of grief to tears of joy." She is obviously indispensable to society, even more so than her mate. But the poem emphasizes that the sexes act harmoniously

> To raise the social passions into life,
> And fit them for a state of perfect bliss.[74]

The assessment of male attitudes toward women uncovered by reading the *American Museum* for the period from 1787 to 1792 turns out to be surprisingly positive. At the outset (1787 to 1788), except for a few satires of women spendthrifts, the pervasive theme is the idea that women, though naturally kind and good as individuals, are corrupted by the men who dominate the society. Writers expressed the view that, had men not deprived women of educational freedom, they would have been equally adept and capable in the sciences. Some writers also argued that woman's intuition was a better moral guide than male reason.

Women were less selfish and egotistical than men, more involved with and concerned about the welfare of others. Moreover, a woman's presence had a salutary effect on a man's personality. The company of women made men behave in a more refined and civilized manner. A few commentators even argued that men owed their reasoning ability to the example of women rather than to their education. Most of these views were expressed in the context of short stories or essays about marriage. In marital relationships and the affairs of everyday life, authors constantly recommended "reciprocal love" between spouses or, failing that, mutual courtesy and respect.[75]

Some thinkers, influenced by the Scottish "common sense" or "moral sense" school of philosophy that was popular in the United States in the late eighteenth century, held an especially high opinion of women's talents and intelligence, which they expressed in articles that appeared in the *American Museum*. Foremost among them was John Witherspoon, who believed that women were more rational and self-controlled than men. This seems to be the trend of most *American Museum* pieces, including the final poem pertinent to the topic in the "Appendix" to the

August 1791 issue.[76]

Male writers in the *American Museum* invariably respected women's intuition and "common sense" and believed they were qualified for household management and a central, conciliating role in the family. The most discerning male commentators depicted women as more tolerant of the foibles of others. As Witherspoon had characterized them in his "Letters on Marriage," they were more kind, good-natured, and socially enlightened than men. Other authors considered women bulwarks of social stability and familial self-regulation and order.

Few of the men writing in the *American Museum* held a completely negative attitude toward women, contrary to the stereotypes of some historians. Most men, except for those who wryly emphasized women's consumerism and alleged extravagant shopping habits, praised them as essentially rational beings. Indeed, many male writers concluded that women were more reasonable and possessed a greater degree of intuitive "common sense" than men. Men revered women's charity, benevolence and common sense in essays appearing throughout the magazine's run.

It seems likely that the stress on women's religiosity and mode of attire in later volumes of the *American Museum* reflected women's own increasing interest in the church, which culminated in the Second Great Awakening at the end of the eighteenth century, and their growing preoccupation with fashion, which was an index of the burgeoning wealth of the American middle class as a result of greater foreign trade in the 1790s.[77] Therefore, it would seem unwarranted to presume that the *American Museum* underwent an antifeminist shift in its editorial stance after 1789.

On the other hand, perhaps men, overwhelmed by the rapid changes produced in an emerging capitalist/democratic society, needed to reassert their masculinity by juxtaposing it against the feminine identity and insisting that the differences between them were sacrosanct and unbridgeable.[78] Some male authors seemingly equated women and children. They warned them against mimicking male fashions and hairstyles. But only a minority voiced this fear. Most writers appeared eager and willing that women achieve a reputable station (though one that was inferior to the male) in a democratic society and showed respect for their abilities, integrity, and potential for growth.

The few negative essays, which appeared mostly after 1789, indicate that male writers perceived a divergence between the old-fashioned, traditional male "ideal" (that women should be passive and helpful to their husbands and to men in general) and the reality—that women were autonomous and at times defiant in their relationships with men. Several ironic essays subtly, often humorously combined the motifs of woman's rising assertiveness as wife and consumer and the husband's "unmanly" submissiveness. Indeed, the final article on gender relations that Carey published, in the "thirteenth volume" of the *American Museum* (1799), conveyed this viewpoint. A Massachusetts farmer and his spouse visit Boston to do some shopping, and he is forced to sell two of his three cows to pay for a muff his wife insists she must have. He acquiesces to the purchase (on ninety days' credit), primarily because he does not want to quarrel with his wife in public.[79] Although the number of favorable essays far outweighed pejorative ones, the *American Museum*'s writers expressed both points of view.

Notes

1. Unfortunately, no satisfactory modern biography of Witherspoon exists. But see Varnum L. Collins, *President Witherspoon, 1723-1794*, 2 vols. (Princeton: Princeton University Press, 1925), and Morris, *Encyclopedia of American History*, 733. It is perhaps worthy of mention that, a few years before his death, Witherspoon married a woman young enough to be his granddaughter, which caused a great deal of gossip at the College of New Jersey.

2. The most thorough discussion of Witherspoon's "Letters on Marriage" is Edward S. Fody, "John Witherspoon: Advisor to the Lovelorn," New Jersey Historical Society, *Proceedings* 84 (Oct. 1965): 239-249. See also Mary Summer Benson, *Women in Eighteenth-Century America: A Study of Opinion and Social Usage* (New York: Columbia University Press, 1935; reprinted New York: AMS Press, 1976), 169-170.

3. "Letters on marriage. Ascribed to the Rev. John Witherspoon, president of Princeton College: Letter I," *American Museum* IV, no. 1 (July 1988): 21-25; signed with the pseudonym "Epaminondas." The quoted passages are at 22. For the Founders' generally negative opinion of bachelors, whom they considered dependent, immature, and childlike, and therefore unworthy of exercising political rights, see Mark E. Kann, "The Bachelor and Other Disorderly Men During the American Founding," *Journal of Men's Studies* 6, no. 1 (Fall 1997), 1-27.

4. "Letters on marriage," 23. Gladys Bryson, *Man and Society: The Scottish Inquiry of the Eighteenth Century* (Princeton: Princeton University Press, 1945), is a standard survey of the "common sense" philosophers who heavily influenced Witherspoon. For an example of Witherspoon's wide-ranging political influence, see James Conniff, "The Enlightenment and American Political Thought: A Study of the Origins of Madison's *Federalist Number 10*," *Political*

Theory 8 (August 1980): 381-402.

5. "Letters on marriage," 24.

6. "Letters on marriage," 24. Fody, "Witherspoon: Advisor to the Lovelorn," a valuable contribution, stresses that the "Letters" reveal the "utilitarian side of Witherspoon's character" (242), and contrasts his down-to-earth, common-sense views with the traditional, elitist concept of a male-dominated family hierarchy espoused by the Puritans (246). Fody notes that, under "Enlightenment influence," Witherspoon favored ideas of sexual equality and marital reciprocity.

7. "Letters on marriage," 24-25.

8. "Letters on marriage," 25.

9. Both Kerber, *Women of the Republic*, and Norton, *Liberty's Daughters*, the most thorough studies of women during the Revolutionary period, based largely on family correspondence, diaries, and legal documents, avoid discussing Witherspoon's "Letters." More surprisingly, Janet W. James, *Changing Ideas About Women in the United States*, though primarily concerned with contemporary literature and attitudes toward women, ignores Witherspoon's essays. A recent literary, "deconstructionist" example of feminist scholars' tendency to interpret the formation of the U.S. Constitution (particularly the creation of the office of President) and the politics of the early national period as Protestant white male conspiracies against women, blacks, and ethnic minorities is Dana D. Nelson, *National Manhood: Capitalist Citizenship and the Imagined Fraternity of White Men* (Durham, N.C.: Duke University Press, 1998).

10. Witherspoon, "A series of letters on education: Letter I," *American Museum* 4, no. 1 (July 1788): 25. Norton, *Liberty's Daughters*, 94-100, admits that familial practice often diverged from strict patriarchal theory. In his second "Letter on education," *American Museum* 4, no. 2 (Aug. 1788): 111, Witherspoon suggests that father, mother, and "female attendant" or "nurse" divide between them the responsibility for the infant's discipline.

11. "Address to the ministers of the gospel of every denomination in the United States," *American Museum* 4, no. 1 (July 1788): 30-34, quote at 32.

12. "Letters on Marriage Ascribed to the Reverend John Witherspoon: Letter II," *American Museum* 4, no. 2 (Aug. 1788): 105-108, quote at 105. On the liberalization of divorce laws in Pennsylvania after the Revolution, see Thomas R. Meehan, "'Not Made Out of Levity': Evolution of Divorce in Early Pennsylvania," *Pennsylvania Magazine of History and Biography* 92, no. 4 (Oct. 1968), 441-464.

13. "Letters on Marriage: Letter II," 107.

14. "Letters on Marriage: Letter II," 107-108.

15. "Letters on Marriage: Letter II," 108. See also Fody, "Witherspoon," 247.

16. "Letters on Marriage. Ascribed to the Rev. John Witherspoon," Letter III, *American Museum* 4, no. 3 (Sept. 1788): 213-214. For an earlier panegyric to marital propriety, see "Family disagreements the frequent cause of immoral conduct," *American Museum* 1, no. 1 (January 1787): 66.

17. "Letters on Marriage: Letter III," 215-216.

18. "Letters on Marriage: Letter III," 217.

19. *American Museum* 4, no. 4 (Oct. 1788), 315-316, continued to print excerpts from Witherspoon's "Letters on Marriage," e.g., "Queries and answers thereto, respecting marriage. The former by an anonymous writer. The latter by the rev. dr. John Witherspoon, or 'Epaminondas.'"

20. "Atticus—No. I, Strictures on various follies and vices," *American Museum* 4, no. 1 (Aug. 1788): 113.

21. "Atticus—No. I," 113. On legal impediments to a widow's acquisition of some portion of her deceased husband's estate during the Revolutionary War era, see Kerber, *Women of the Republic*, 141-147, who points out that state legislation and judicial decisions eroded their rights; Joan R. Gundersen and Gwen Victor Gampel, "Married Women's Legal Status in Eighteenth-Century New York and Virginia," *William and Mary Quarterly*, 3d Ser., 39 (Jan. 1982): 114-134; Marylyn Salmon, "Equality or Submersion: *Feme Covert* Status in Early Pennsylvania," in *Women of America: A History*, Carol Berkin and Mary Beth Norton, eds. (Boston: Little, Brown, 1979), 96-99; Norton, *Liberty's Daughters*, 132-136, 149-150; Elaine Forman Crane, "Dependence in the Era of Independence: The Role of Women in a Republican Society," in *The American Revolution: Its Character and Limits*, Jack P. Greene ed. (New York: New York University Press, 1987), 259-266.

22. "The Visitant, No. 1," *American Museum* IV, no. 2 (August 1788): 116-117.

23. "The Visitant, No. 3, "Remarks on the fair sex," *American Museum* 4, no. 2 (Aug. 1788): 119-121, quote at 119. According to the date cited in the *American Museum*, "The Visitant" series was first published at Philadelphia, Feb. 15, 1768. Apparently it had withstood the test of time.

24. "Remarks on the fair sex," 119. My italics.

25. "Remarks on the fair sex," 120-121.

26. "Remarks on the fair sex," 121.

27. "The Visitant," *American Museum* 4, no. 3 (Sept. 1788): 220-223, originally published, Philadelphia, Feb. 22, 1768. The relevant quotes are on 221-222.

28. "The Visitant," 222.

29. "The Visitant, No. 5," "On the wants and desires of mankind," *American Museum* 4, no. 4 (Oct. 1788): 319. Nancy F. Cott's excellent article, "Passionlessness: An Interpretation of Victorian Sexual Ideology, 1790-1850," may be most easily found in *A Heritage of Her Own: Toward a New Social History of American Women*, Nancy F. Cott and Elizabeth H. Pleck, eds. (New York: Simon and Schuster, 1979), 162-181. It originally appeared in *Signs*: *A Journal of Women in Culture and Society*, 4, no. 2 (Winter 1978): 219-236.

30. "On the wants and desires of mankind" originally appeared in Philadelphia, Feb. 29, 1768. Mary Summer Benson, *Women in Eighteenth-Century America*, concentrates more on women's educational and cultural activities and the opinions of British and Continental thinkers than on American attitudes, male or female, while Kerber's studies, e.g., "The Republican Mother: Women and the Enlightenment, an American Perspective," *American Quarterly* 28 (Summer 1976):

187-205, depict women as functioning within the circumscribed role assigned them by a white male patriotic political culture. I found the maternal emphasis far less prevalent than Kerber assumes, at least judging from my examination of the *American Museum*. Nor do I find convincing Benson's assertion that "American writers in this decade [the 1780s] said more of women's education at school and of their later duties in the home" than of gender relationships. *Women in Eighteenth-Century America*, 168-169.

31. "Remarks on the Fair Sex, No. VII," by "The Visitant," *American Museum* 4, no. 6 (Dec. 1788): 489.

32. Helen Waite Papashvily, *All the Happy Endings* (New York: Harper, 1956) suggests that women authors wrote sentimental novels during the nineteenth century as a means by which to assert their independence and autonomy from men and at the same time prove their intellectual competence. Mary Kelley's detailed prosopographical study, *Private Woman, Public Stage: Literary Domesticity in Nineteenth Century America* (New York: Oxford University Press, 1984), depicts the anguish of female novelists as they violated orthodox conventions and struck out on their own in the literary sphere.

33. "Remarks on the fair sex," *American Museum* 4, no. 6 (Dec. 1788): 490.

34. "Remarks on the fair sex," 490.

35. "Remarks on the fair sex," 491.

36. "Remarks on the fair sex," 491.

37. "Remarks on the fair sex," 491. The adjective, "amiable," was widely used during this period to describe men, women, and even political institutions. Its meaning was apparently similar to that which it holds today, with its connotations of agreeableness and willingness to compromise. Albeit in an ironic context, a Federalist newspaper, describing its Democratic-Republican opponents, employed the term in this vein: "They censure, fear and hate our constitution, or, as they will acknowledge, several very important parts of it, and almost all its administration: its entire overthrow so far from dangerous, much less fatal, is only a new shuffling of the pack of cards, a new chance for the people to chuse [*sic*] a form of government, more pure, free and amiable." North Carolina *Minerva*, Jan. 7, 1797, quoting the Philadelphia *Gazette of the United States*.

38. Poem from "a circle of ladies," *American Museum* 4, no. 6 (December 1788): 491.

39. "The old bachelor, No. VII ("His Will")," *American Museum* 4, no. 2 (Aug. 1788): 125, an essay originally published in 1765. Nonetheless, in a sobering vein, "Aspasia" (who identified herself as a woman) cautioned the "Old Bachelor" that marriage was not always a pleasant idyll, especially when one's mate was a harridan. *American Museum* 4, no. 6 (Dec. 1788): 565-566.

40. [Reverend John Witherspoon], "Letter on education," *American Museum* 4, no. 2 (Aug. 1788): 111. See also above, note 9.

41. "The Visitant, No. 8," "Remarks on the Dress of the Ladies," *American Museum* 5, no. 1 (Jan. 1789): 65-68, quote on 66.

42. "The Visitant, No. 8," 66. "The Visitant's" position starkly contrasted with

earlier articles that recommended simple republican garb for women, rather than gaudy British and French imports. More in keeping with the ethos of republican simplicity, sketched at length in such monographs as Drew McCoy's book, *The Elusive Republic: Political Economy in Jeffersonian America* (Chapel Hill: University of North Carolina Press, 1980), were statements like those of "a well-meaning plain citizen," who suggested that the "rich and affluent," who served as role models for the "middle classes" should organize an "economical association" to abstain from the purchase of European luxuries and instead live frugally "in their dress, conduct, and whole domestic oeconomy [*sic*]." He warned that only such firm action would preserve "republican government," since the people's impoverishment was increasing by their purchase of "needless superfluities, imported from Europe in such abundance." *American Museum*, 4, no. 2 (Aug. 1788): 125 ("Philadelphia, July 6, 1787"). In an especially powerful philippic, "A Republican," writing from Boston in July 1788, denounced Americans who bought British goods and thereby weakened the domestic economy, once again courting slavery and humiliation from the former mother country. In his opinion, popular susceptibility to British fashions, the "taudry [*sic*] badges of our infamous servility," "disgraceful specimens of our pusillanimity," was tantamount to slave-like behavior on the part of free citizens; the British had successfully fettered the ex-colonists in "commercial bonds." *American Museum* 4, no. 4 (Oct. 1788): 331. Clearly, "The Visitant" did not adhere to such forthright, indignantly patriotic opinions.

43. "The Visitant, No. 8," 67. Crowley, *This Sheba, Self*, 14-15, 47, and McCoy, *Elusive Republic*, 25-27, summarize the significance of Mandeville's gospel of "private vices, public benefits," expounded in his famous poem, *The Fable of the Bees*
(1714).

44. The best study of the evolving relationship between women and the consumer mentality, though it regrettably commences with the nineteenth century and ignores the 1780s, is Ann Douglas, *The Feminization of American Culture* (New York: Knopf, 1977).

45. "The Visitant, No. 8," 67-68.

46. "The Visitant, No. 8," 68.

47. "The Worcester Speculator, No. I: Remarks on female delicacy," Worcester, Mass., July 1788, in *American Museum, or Universal Magazine* [the title of Carey's journal after 1789], 5, no. 1 (Jan. 1789): 68-69, quote at 68. For earlier articles in the *American Museum* defending woman's salutary influence on world affairs, see "The happy influence of female society," *American Museum*, 1, no. 1 (Jan. 1787): 61-64.

48. "The Worcester Speculator," 69. James, *Changing Ideas*, 24-30, 45-46, 162-163, 171-172, emphasizes the importance of religion in the lives of middle-class American women. See also Lonna H. Malmsheimer, "Daughters of Zion: New England Roots of American Feminism," *New England Quarterly* 50 (1977): 484-504, and Gerald F. Moran and Maris A. Vinovskis, "The Puritan Family and Religion:

A Critical Reappraisal," *William and Mary Quarterly*, 3d Ser., 39 (Jan. 1982): 29-63.

49. Among recent studies which note the preponderant role of women, who comprised the majority of church members in the eighteenth century, in colonial religion are: Cedric Cowing, "Sex and Preaching in the Great Awakening," *American Quarterly* 20 (Fall 1968): 624-644; Richard D. Shiels, "The Feminization of American Congregationalism, 1730-1835," *American Quarterly* 33 (Spring 1981): 46-62, and Patricia U. Bonomi, *Under the Cope of Heaven: Religion, Society, and Politics in Colonial America* (New York: Oxford University Press, 1986), 106-115. A provocative discussion of Anne Hutchinson's controversial religious activities in the 1630s, which views her as a prototypical feminist, is Lyle W. Koehler's detailed study of Antinomianism, "The Case of the American Jezebels," *William and Mary Quarterly*, 3d Ser., 31 (Jan. 1974): 55-78. For later developments, see Barbara Welter, "The Feminization of American Religion: 1800-1860," in *Clio's Consciousness Raised: New Perspectives on the History of Women*, Mary S. Hartman and Lois W. Banner, eds. (New York: Harper Torchbooks, 1973), 137-155.

50. Rev. John Bennet, "Letters to a Young Lady," *American Museum* 10 (Aug. 1791): 74-75. Bennet's *Letters* were reprinted as late as 1818. See Norton, *Liberty's Daughters*, 264, and James, *Changing Ideas,* 132, 135-136.

51. "Letters to a Young Lady," 75.

52. Rev. John Bennet, "Letters to a Young Lady: Letter X, on Dress," *American Museum* 11 (March 1792): 93-95, quote at 93.

53. "Letters to a Young Lady: Letter X," 93, 94.

54. Rev. John Bennet, "Letter XI: On Dress and Ornament," *American Museum* 11 (March 1792): 95. Dr. John Gregory's virtually identical statement, which Bennet may have consciously or unconsciously plagiarized, was: "A fine woman shows her charms to most advantage, when she seems most to conceal them. The finest bosom in nature is not so fine as what imagination forms." Gregory, *A Father's Legacy to His Daughters* (London, 1774; reprinted New York, 1775), 22-23.

55. Bennet, "Letter XI," 95-96. Noting the later popularity of female piety, Barbara Welter tersely concludes: "The attributes of True Womanhood, by which a woman judged herself and was judged by her husband, her neighbors and society, could be divided into four cardinal virtues—piety, purity, submissiveness, and domesticity." Welter, "The Cult of True Womanhood, 1820-1860," *American Quarterly* 6, no. 2 (Summer 1966): 152. Religious devotion was one more means by which the middle-class Victorian woman conformed to the male image of her as a passive, resigned being.

56. "A letter to a very good-natured lady who is married to a very ill-natured man," *American Museum*, 6, no. 4 (Oct. 1789): 315-316, quote at 315. Later variations on the theme of wifely obedience included injunctions to more egoistic female behavior. A study of Philadelphia farmers' almanacs of the 1820s cites stories of wife-beating coupled with "didactic advice [that] carries hints of female

assertiveness along with general advice to be submissive." Joan M. Jensen, *Loosening the Bonds: Mid-Atlantic Farm Women, 1750-1850* (New Haven: Yale University Press, 1986), 117, 119. A recent analysis of a leading mid-nineteenth century woman's magazine argues that, contrary to previous scholarly assumptions, it promoted women's autonomy and independence rather than advise passivity and obsession with the latest fashions. Laura McCall, "'The Reign of Brute Force is Now Over': A Content Analysis of *Godey's Lady's Book*, 1830-1860," *Journal of the Early Republic* 9, no. 3 (Summer 1989): 217-236. The first editor of *Godey's* was male.

57. "Letter to a very good-natured lady," 316. In several quantitative studies, sociologist Herman R. Lantz and his associates have concluded that the periodical literature of the late eighteenth century suggests that women rather than men actually dominated the household and exerted hidden control over social and sexual relationships. Lantz et al., "Pre-Industrial Patterns in the Colonial Family in America: A Content Analysis of Colonial Magazines," *American Sociological Review* 33, no. 3 (June 1968): 413-426; Lantz et al., "The Preindustrial Family in America: A Further Examination of Early Magazines," *American Journal of Sociology* 79, no. 3 (Nov. 1973): 566-588; Lantz et al., "The American Family in the Preindustrial Period: From Base Lines in History to Change, *American Sociological Review* 40, no. 1 (Feb. 1975): 21-36.

58. Woman's emerging role as a symbol of self-sacrifice for the benefit of the whole family/community, transcending self-centered, aggressive "male" ambition, is stressed in Mary Beth Norton, "The Evolution of White Women's Experience in Early America," *American Historical Review* 89, no. 3 (June 1984): 617-619, and Ruth Bloch, "The Gendered Meanings of Virtue in Revolutionary America," *Signs* 13, no. 1 (Autumn 1987): 49-57.

59. "A letter to a very good-natured lady who is married to a very ill-natured man," *American Museum* 6, no. 4 (Oct. 1789): 316.

60. Plutarch, *Advice to the Bride and Groom*, quoted in William Blake Tyrell, *Amazons: A Study in Athenian Mythmaking* (Baltimore: Johns Hopkins University Press, 1984), 53.

61. "An Affecting and true history," *American Museum* 6, no. 4 (Oct. 1789): 316.

62. "The school for husbands and wives," *American Museum* 6, no. 4 (Oct. 1789): 312-314.

63. "The matrimonial creed," *American Museum* 6, no. 4 (Oct. 1789): 314-315.

64. "On Appearing what we neither are, nor wish to be," *American Museum* 9, no. 1 (Jan. 1791): 30.

65. For a contrasting view, emphasizing writers' sympathy for the wife of the unfaithful husband and the seducer's victim, as portrayed by various media in the 1780s and 1790s, see Jan Lewis, "The Republican Wife: Virtue and Seduction in the Early Republic," *William and Mary Quarterly*, 3d Ser., 44, no. 4 (Oct. 1987): 689-721. Though Lewis's article is useful, she fails to make use of the *American Museum*, a notable defect in light of the popularity and prestige of Carey's

magazine.

66. "On Beauty," *American Museum* 8 (Sept. 1790): 128-129. Marlene LeGates, "The Cult of True Womanhood in Eighteenth-Century Thought," *Eighteenth-Century Studies* 10, no. 1 (Fall 1976): 31, 37-39, discusses the correlation drawn in the Enlightenment between poverty and "unladylike" behavior on the one hand, and vice on the other.

67. "On Beauty," 129.

68. "Qualifications, required in a wife—addressed to a young lady," *American Museum* 4, no. 6 (Dec. 1788): 578.

69. On the social and emotional dislocations produced by individual failures to adjust to the emergent competitive capitalist order of the late eighteenth century, see David J. Rothman, *The Discovery of the Asylum: Social Order and Disorder in the New Republic* (Boston: Little, Brown, 1971), and Michael Paul Rogin, *Fathers and Children: Andrew Jackson and the Subjugation of the American Indian* (New York: Knopf, 1975).

70. "Letter X: On Dress," *American Museum* 11 (March 1792): 94.

71. "Letter X: On Dress," 94.

72. "Letter X: On Dress," 94.

73. "A Poetical Essay on the Comparative Merit of the Sexes," *American Museum* 10, no. 2 (Aug. 1791) Appendix, 8-10. Males, clergy and laity alike, upheld the belief that men would always protect women when they were passive and dependent. "It being not possible that man should yield up his strength . . . or his own personal ease more chearfully [*sic*], than when he designs them to protect the dependent and lovely. For a female, therefore, to realize her dependence is to build her strong tower: For when she is defenseless, then she is invincible"—since she can count on the protection of the stronger male. Reverend Amos Chase, *On Female Excellence: Or a Discourse . . . Occasioned by the Death of his Wife* (Litchfield, Conn., 1792), 12, quoted in Malmsheimer, "Daughters of Zion," 501.

74. "A Poetical Essay on the Comparative Merit of the Sexes," 9-10.

75. For a general discussion of the growth of "romantic love" in Western society after 1750, see Edward Shorter, *The Making of the Modern Family* (New York: Basic Books, 1975), 120-167; Jay Fliegelman, *Prodigals and Pilgrims: The American Revolution Against Patriarchal Authority, 1750-1800* (Cambridge: Cambridge University Press, 1982), 123-154; and Bloch, "Gendered Meanings of Virtue," 46-47. Bloch comments (46n.): "In this period there was still far more literature on courtship, marriage, and the social utility of female education than on motherhood *per se*." My research confirms her hypothesis on this point.

76. For the role of Scottish "moral sense" philosophy, evangelical Protestantism, and sentimental fiction in improving the status of women by viewing the emotions ("female") in a positive light, see Bloch, "Gendered Meanings of Virtue," 50-51, and Rosemarie Zagarri, "Morals, Manners, and the Republican Mother," *American Quarterly*, 44, no. 2 (June 1992): 205-215.

77. On the growth in *per capita* productivity and income in the 1790s, see Dou-

glass C. North, *The Economic Growth of the United States, 1790-1860* (Englewood Cliffs, N.J.: Prentice-Hall, 1961), and George Rogers Taylor, "American Economic Growth Before 1860: An Exploratory Essay," *Journal of Economic History* 24, no. 4 (Dec. 1964): 427-444.

78. This thesis has been suggested most recently for this period, in a different context, by Toby L. Ditz, "Shipwrecked; or, Masculinity Imperiled: Mercantile Representations of Failure and the Gendered Self in Eighteenth-Century Philadelphia," *Journal of American History* 81, no. 1 (June 1994): 51-80.

79. "The Countryman and his Wife, with her new Muff and Tippet," *American Museum, or, Annual Register of Fugitive Pieces, Ancient and Modern for the Year 1798* (Philadelphia: Mathew Carey, 1799), 89-91. The author assures women that he is not "A Hater of Your Sex."

Chapter 6

Conclusion

How did other major magazines of the period from 1787 to 1792 handle issues of gender relationships and male attitudes toward "the fair sex" in their essays, short stories, poetry, and other pieces? It is impossible to investigate this question fully here. However, a few random citations from the *Massachusetts Magazine* and the *Columbian Magazine*, which according to Frank Luther Mott, the foremost historian of American journalism, shared with the *American Museum* the distinction of being the most important and reputable eighteenth-century periodicals, suggest that Carey held somewhat more liberal views on the subject of women's abilities and right to equal social treatment. (During this period, magazines generally eschewed the idea of women's suffrage or political equality). Our conclusion will examine these magazines, as well as the *Lady's Magazine*, which, though short-lived and not as well-known as the others, was chosen because it claimed to cater to women's interests.[1]

As we have already seen, the *Columbian Magazine*, which lasted from September 1786 to December 1792, was conceived by a five-man partnership consisting of Carey; John Trenchard, an engraver; Charles Cist; William Spotswood; and Thomas Seddon. After 1790 the *Columbian Magazine* changed its name to *The Universal Asylum, and Columbian Magazine*. Renowned for political articles and news items like its report on the proceedings of the Pennsylvania state ratifying convention that approved the United States Constitution in 1788, the

Columbian Magazine also printed significant papers on agriculture and the mechanic arts, such as John Fitch's description of his invention, the steamboat, in 1787.

The *Columbian Magazine* included a large number of fictional pieces—"moral novels" and short stories, many of which had Near Eastern and Turkish locales. It published much British verse, rather than American, as well as travel literature like William Byrd's description of Virginia's Dismal Swamp. Of greater retrospective than contemporary significance were early essays by Charles Brockden Brown, who later gained a reputation as one of America's greatest (and protofeminist) novelists. After 1789, the *Columbian Magazine* devoted an inordinate amount of space to articles on historical topics, especially the American Revolution. Dr. Benjamin Rush wrote many articles on scientific and educational questions for the magazine after 1790, when it changed its title to the *Universal Asylum*. It developed into a predecessor of the specialized historical magazines which flourished in the late 1800s and are still popular today. Even in the 1790s, this policy earned the *Columbian Magazine* many devotees. Although its popularity increased, it finally ceased publication at the end of 1792, largely because of the hardships imposed by that year's Post Office Act. Nevertheless, the high caliber of its articles, its elaborate portraits, copperplates, and other illustrations, and the quality of its news reporting made the *Columbian Magazine* one of the handsomest, most well-produced, and popular late eighteenth century magazines.[2]

According to Lawrence J. Friedman, the *Columbian Magazine* espoused the cause of what he calls "True American Womanhood": women were essentially male pawns, whose identity consisted of certain decorative, moral, and sentimental qualities that were only fantasies in the male mind, which a woman could not display "at her own discretion—only when men called upon her or needed her to compensate for their coarse, masculine qualities."[3] Is Friedman's charge that the *Columbian Magazine*'s view of women was sexist and showed a desire to keep them in a subordinate position valid? Our sample of three articles (from 1787, 1788, and 1790) suggests that there is some basis for his accusation.

The *Columbian Magazine*'s essays manifest a spectrum of opinion similar to the *American Museum*'s most conservative selections. Its editors seemed to fear assertive women who sought to monopolize household management. In June 1787 a piece by "Benedict" appeared, titled "How to Prolong the Happiness of the Marriage Union," warning that the omnicompetent "*notable housewife*" was "the most mutinous wife in the world." "Benedict" resented her overzealousness in taking charge of household affairs and her boasts of her husband's dependence upon her. "Avoid therefore, if you prize your ease, this *notable woman*, the busy trifler," he advised. He preferred a humble, ripened woman for his wife. "I would not be misunderstood to recommend a careless, extravagant woman, or be thought to include in this character the prudent affectionate wife, who is frugal without sordidness, discreet without ostentation, and anxious for your welfare without impatience," he explained.[4]

One might expect "Benedict" to disapprove of scholarly women as threats to his masculinity, and indeed he does object to "female pedants." He would *never* marry one of those "Lesbias and Cleomines" who try to prove that they are more well-read and better bred than their husbands! In contrast with the "notable housewife," this female "*wit*" is unconcerned about her physical appearance and the performance of her household duties. She expresses "no soft endearments, no fondly agreeableness" toward her hardworking husband, "just returned from business." Though the "*female wit*" is ignorant of the real world outside the covers of books, "Benedict" argues, she "is perpetually advising, and always fond and forward to convince you of the inferiority of your understanding." In addition, "Benedict" thought that beautiful women, even those with a reputation for "good sense," made bad wives: they were apt to cause their husbands trouble and heartache with their air of superiority and proclivity for marital infidelity.[5]

Like the conservative, sexist group of writers in the *American Museum*, "Benedict" prefers a passive, submissive woman as the optimal wife, even though some people might deride her as a "fool." He was unconcerned about other women's opinion of her. "That woman who is unjustly censured by her own sex for a deficiency of good sense, seems to be the best disposed to give comfort in the married state," he observed. "She is said to want spirit, to be a tame, helpless, dispassionate [i.e., lacking in sexual passion for her husband] creature, that she is a sad manager and would quickly undo her husband." On the contrary, "Benedict" thought that passive, compliant wives were not only better housekeepers, but also more affectionate than aggressive ones. "Who would not be contented under the imputation of having married a fool, when blessed with such a woman, to bring pleasure and comfort to his arms in all his vacant hours?" he rhetorically inquired.[6]

In return for his wife's obedience and kindness, "Benedict"expects that the husband will behave with good manners and "decency." This includes keeping to himself his business problems and any insults he has suffered in the workplace and not burdening his wife with them, since "Benedict" assumed that women are naturally unable to keep secrets. "Benedict" also advises against "loving her with passion," even though it is desirable for a wife to be affectionate toward her husband. If a husband "imprudently" manifested inordinate sexual desire for his spouse, "Benedict" warned, she would become arrogant, "obstinate" and uncontrollable, take advantage of the lustful husband's obsessive dependence, and "eventually all the seeds of affection will be eradicated, or your happiness totally destroyed."[7] This was a cynical essay, insofar as the woman's sexual and personal freedoms were strictly limited to the satisfaction of the husband's needs and desires.

Judging from a second essay appearing in the *Columbian Magazine*, the periodical tended to favor the publication of sexist materials. "Rules and Maxims for Promoting Matrimonial Happiness," which appeared in January 1790, initially seems to espouse a moderate position in support of mutuality and fairness in gender relationships. But it soon becomes clear that the author demands a wife who is servile to her husband. He cannot conceive of a woman possessing an identity independent of that of "wife," which he regards as her only legitimate social role and proper "place." "The likeliest way, either to obtain a good husband, or to keep one so, is to be good yourself," he advises. Though his remarks are ostensibly addressed to women, he is merely advocating traditional masculine ideals of female behavior. He advised men to avoid "tyrannical" women, and urged women to behave in a manner designed to placate and soothe their husbands: "Avoid, both before and after marriage, all thoughts of nagging your husband." A wife should be sure she never deceives or annoys her husband, "but treats him always, before hand, with sincerity, and afterwards, with affection and respect." Women should be patient with men, remembering they were "not angels." The writer tends to be didactic, addressing his female readers in a tone more appropriate for children than adults.

But what at first appears to be a plea for reciprocity and mutual forbearance quickly degenerates into a statement of slightly veiled contempt for women. The author thinks that women should always try to appear happy, even if they do not really feel that way, so that their husbands will not worry about them. "Resolve, every morning, to be chearful and good natured that day," he insisted, "and if any accident should happen to break that resolution, suffer it not to put you out of temper with every thing besides,—and especially with your husband." Surely a "chearful" wife was better for a husband's peace of mind and success in the business world than a scolding one.[8]

Combining themes of religious devotion that were again becoming popular in the 1790s with more secular messages on optimal marital relationships, the writer demanded the wife's obedience to her husband, recommending that she implore God's help toward being a good wife. To signify her obedience, she should always wear her wedding ring for protection against "improper thoughts." She must express her "conjugal love" with "decency and delicacy," not with "the designing fondness of a harlot." He advised the wife to be frugal for the household's sake. Hinting that a woman's life only possessed meaning when she lived for and through her husband, he urged her frequently to conduct a "serious examination [of] how you have behaved as a wife." His final message reminded the woman/wife that her only chance for "happiness" rested in the satisfaction she gave her husband. For this reason, she should avoid all arguments or disagreements with him. As he put it:

> Dispute not with him, be the occasion what it will; but much rather deny yourself the trivial satisfaction of having your own will, or gaining the better of an argument, than risque a quarrel, or create a heart-burning, which it is impossible to know the end of.
>
> Be assured, a woman's power, as well as happiness, has no other foundation but her husband's esteem and love; which, consequently, it is her undoubted interest by all means possible to preserve and increase.[9]

Another selection from the *Columbian Magazine,* a curious tale entitled "Chariessa: or, a Pattern for the Sex," reveals the ambivalence which plagued middle-class white American males regarding women's role in the new republic. If a woman were virtuous and charitable, was it essential that she marry and procreate in order to be regarded as having fulfilled her social function in the new nation? The tale of Chariessa hints that an unmarried spinster might be equally useful and socially conscientious. With her "pure and generous mind," Chariessa, then, is the well-nigh impossibly virtuous, altruistic spinster daughter of a benevolent father who bequeathed her a substantial estate equal to that of her "boisterous and jocular landed squire"older brother and petulant, hypochondriacal sister. These two prodigal, nefarious individuals eagerly await the death of this frail flower so that they may inherit and squander her wealth. Naively generous, Chariessa spends all her time helping her siblings, nieces and nephews, bestowing charity on the poor and largess to her neighbors. She forgives the foibles of her miserly, conniving brother, "Squire Trackum," who despite his inherited wealth, "never passed ten minutes in the company of any man, without considering how he might devise some degree of pecuniary or interested advantage from his acquaintance." Nonetheless, Chariessa is extremely devoted to her brother's beautiful, kindly, "prudent" wife and children.[10]

Persevering despite the asperity of her brother and sister and the envy of several malicious neighbors, the "universally beloved" Chariessa is so preoccupied in assisting her ungrateful brother and sister that she never marries. "Chariessa's" author laments her celibate state, but more significantly, he applauds her grasping the freedom to decide what kind of life will make her happy. While regretting that her failure to marry (which was in part the result of schemes concocted by an evil brother to prevent her from meeting respectable eligible bachelors) deprived worthy men of a virtuous wife, the author feels that, so long as "Chariessa" was content, her spinster's life style was justified:

> We cannot therefore avoid declaring, that notwithstanding the idea of an old maid may, in some cases be ridiculed, yet in many instances, more felicity is to be found in the single than in the connubial state;—though that is the most permanent human bliss, where unity of hearts and sentiments prevail.—Indeed, we may sum up all conditions of life with this axiom, that to be good is to be happy; and that, by a line of virtuous conduct sooner or later, a sure reward succeeds.[11]

Aside from acknowledging woman's right to an autonomous unmarried life in the persona of Chariessa, whom the story's subtitle labels "a Pattern for the Sex," the narrative glorifies the socially egalitarian inheritance legislation passed during the Revolutionary War period, which gave women fee simple ownership of an equal share of parental estates.[12] The story begins by noting that Chariessa's father had received a very "scanty patrimony" from his opulent, would-be aristocrat father, who "was infected with that ridiculous, or rather detestable, family pride, by which many persons are tempted to leave their younger children in absolute indigence, from the vain and absurd prospect of aggrandizing an eldest son; a project which was suggested to the old gentleman . . . by his discovery of a genealogical table, which unluckily enabled him to trace his progenitors to the reign of Edward the Fourth." Smarting from the sense of deprivation "arising from an unjust distribution of property," Chariessa's father bestowed an equal portion of his fortune among all his children, including his youngest daughter— Chariessa.[13]

As a result of her father's egalitarian social views, Chariessa gained an income, permitting her to survive without a husband, on whom she would otherwise have had to rely for support. The *Columbian Magazine* thereby reminds its readers that there were instances when the American Revolution's democratic social philosophy, eschewing European aristocratic, patriarchal traditions, benefitted women as well as men. At the same time, the writer regrets that, "had not avarice and artifice prevailed," Chariessa, with her "virtuous and exalted mind," "might with equal honor have rendered some generous man happy—who would have been sensible of her worth, and held her in esteem."[14]

Although "Chariessa's" tone is more sexually egalitarian and libertarian than the other two *Columbian Magazine* selections we have examined, by comparison with the *American Museum* the Columbian Magazine's essays more consistently depicted woman's proper position as being subservient to the male.

The *Massachusetts Magazine* was among the most popular monthly periodicals. Begun in January 1789 by Isaiah Thomas, who published it till December 1793, this Boston journal survived until December 1796. With its diverse array of articles—fiction, biography, original music, poetry, history, mathematics, lists of births and deaths, plays, essays, proceedings of Congress—as well as engravings, it was one of the first magazines to give prominence to fictional short stories. The *Massachusetts Magazine* also contained "foreign and domestic intelligence," although, being a monthly, the news it carried was invariably outdated. Its final issue (December 1796) printed George Washington's Farewell Address of September 1796.[15]

Most of the "contributions" appearing in the *Massachusetts*

Magazine had been previously published in other British and American books, periodicals, and pamphlets. At the close of 1793, its new publishers, Ezra W. Weld, William Greenough, and engraver Samuel Hill, made a special plea for women's patronage, promising to satisfy their tastes, "delicacy" and fancy.[16] We might therefore expect the essays and articles to flatter would-be female patronesses, extolling their keen spirits, independent thinking, and potential for intellectual equality with men.

However, the *Massachusetts Magazine*'s selections, like those appearing in the *Columbian Magazine*, exhort women to a dependent and servile behavior in their relations with the opposite sex. The June 1794 issue, for example, published after the new, "protofeminist" editors had taken charge, prints a selection from Mr Griffith's Essays, Addressed to *Young Married Women,* titled, "On Conjugal Affinities." The essay's deceptively bland title conceals its true message: that the wife should appease her husband, and try to anticipate his thoughts and desires. It was essential that a wife do everything possible to ensure her husband's tranquillity. "By a proper attention to your husband, you will easily discover the bent of his genius and circumstances," he points out. "To that turn all your thoughts, and let your words and actions solely tend to that great point." By inspiring his "gratitude," her "kindness" would redound to her benefit. "The kindness of your attention will awaken his, and gratitude will strengthen his affection, imperceptibly even to himself." Since "gratitude" was customarily considered the feeling that children should express toward good parents, there is a hint here of the male infantilization that appeared in the *American Museum*'s later essays, in which husbands seemed to be clamoring for a benevolent mother to take care of them. Moreover, in common with some of the *American Museum*'s writers, Mr. Griffith recommended that if, from the outset of the marriage, the wife complied with the husband's demands, fulfilling his longing for "kindness" and "attention," the husband would inevitably seek to satisfy *her* wishes.[17]

"On Conjugal Affinities," it seems clear, is a very one-sided essay. The only "affinity" that is valuable is the wife's effort to be whatever her husband wants her to be. This *mentalité* precludes reciprocal "affinity," or attempts at cooperation and empathy between partners. Only the woman is required to strive to "read the man's mind," so to speak, and identify and sympathize with his longings; a reciprocal effort is not expected from the man. The wife's only hope of gratification or reward is the fortuitous one that, out of "gratitude," her husband would bestow his "affection" upon her. Surely this is a far cry from the demands for mutual fondness and reciprocity that appeared in many of the *American Museum*'s articles.

Although the *Lady's Magazine, and Repository of Entertaining Knowledge* survived for only one year (1792 to 1793), it is of special interest because women were ostensibly its targeted audience. It has received little attention from Mott and other scholars on early journalism. It published selected articles, printed engravings, and in most ways was like other magazines of the period. At the outset its editors announced that they "submitted with all deference to the . . . fair daughters of Columbia [an early name for the United States]." On the other hand, the *Lady's Magazine* did not adopt an uniform policy on whether women should be encouraged in literary and intellectual pursuits and in seeking a higher education. Some of its writers advised women to confine themselves to reading "genial" fiction rather than getting involved in the sciences. This in itself was a relatively liberal stance. Many conservative thinkers, believing that women, too immature to distinguish fiction from reality, might be encouraged to imitate the example of passionate, impulsive young women found in novels, proposed to deny them such provocative reading matter. Indeed, some writers in the *Lady's Magazine* even charged that female writers were unfeminine.[18]

To a greater degree than the other two magazines we have considered in this chapter, the *Lady's Magazine* expounded an enlightened proto-feminist view, similar to the essays by John Witherspoon and other supporters of female equality and cooperation between the sexes that the *American Museum* published. An essay by "A Matrimonial Republican" bears sharp contrast with the pieces in the *Massachusetts Magazine* and the *Columbian*. It is unclear whether the writer is male or female. The author aggressively contended that some women displayed "superior judgment" as compared with men, reiterating Witherspoon's remarks. Like other liberals, "A Matrimonial Republican" insisted that mutual "gratitude" was the basis for a stable marriage. S/he conceived of marriage more as a business partnership than as a relationship embodying emotion, affection, and sexuality. "Marriage ought never to be considered as a contract between a superior and an inferior, but a reciprocal union of interest, an implied partnership of interests, where all differences are accommodated by conference," "A Matrimonial Republican" counseled. "A thousand little instances will arise, wherein obedience may be manifested from the husband to the wife, and from the wife to the husband, founded too on the best of all possible foundations of obedience, on gratitude; for what is natural obedience but the gratitude of each party for former instances of obedience." Unlike Mr. Griffith in the *Massachusetts Magazine*, "A Matrimonial Republican" insists that women as well as men are entitled to enjoy the benefits of "reciprocity" and "gratitude." Since obedience rests on gratitude for past kindnesses, both genders must receive equal treatment in order to have an incentive for future obedience toward their spouses.[19]

Summary

On the whole, American magazines during the 1790s espoused two antagonistic depictions of women: the independent, self-disciplined house-keeper and regulator of her children and (albeit to a lesser degree) her husband, and the passive, loving servant of her mate, who was (or should be) compliant with all his commands and anticipate his wishes. Most students of American male views of women choose to emphasize the latter point of view. At times, scholars express rage at eighteenth-century women's victimization by their husbands' virtually unlimited power over them. In addition, contemporary accounts imply male infidelity.[20] As we have seen, articles in the *Columbian Magazine* and the *Massachusetts Magazine* tend to deny the woman (wife) a separate identity or, at best, peremptorily assert her subordination to the male/husband. The *Lady's Magazine*'s contributor sought to steer more of a middle ground between the genders, arguing that each was entitled to the same amount of respect and gratitude for kind acts. But this essay seemed to drain sensuality and passion from relationships between men and women, and transmuted marriage into a business partnership.[21]

Our analysis of the *American Museum* reveals that, far from adopting an extreme attitude of opposition to the idea of equal social rights, personality and identity for women, its predominantly male writers usually accepted these rights as a matter of course. In addition, they acknowledged female sexuality as a positive force, not incompatible with the possession of charm and education. Indeed, the *American Museum* was more outspoken in favor of women's intellectual and emotional equality than many female spokespersons in both Great Britain and America, such as Maria Edgeworth, Hannah More, and Judith Sargent

Murray. Hannah More, for instance, considered the "fair sex" vain and selfish by nature, an opinion which only the most extreme misogynists among the *American Museum*'s contributors would have dared uphold.[22] This is not to deny that some of the journal's writers resented what they perceived as the increasing power of women within the family, their threat to male identity and hegemony, and their attempts to embarrass or disparage their husbands. But essays that convey this message are in the minority, and their intent is often humorous or satirical—even pro-feminist in a backhanded way—rather than hostile.

A handful of historians have noted the print media's significance in crystallizing public attitudes toward gender roles in the early Republic.[23] As Mary Beth Norton says of post-Revolutionary War magazines: "The pages of these journals constituted the single most important public forum for the voicing of radical opinion on women's status and role. There male and female authors alike addressed directly the same issues that confronted them privately in their daily lives." Though Norton, Kerber, and other scholars praise woman's role as the "Republican Mother" who taught her children (especially her sons) the values of virtue and patriotism, they downplay the obvious fact that in so doing women were merely following the dictates and ideals of their male overlords.[24] On the other hand, man-woman relationships, primarily pertaining to matters of courtship and marriage, are covered far more often in the pages of the *American Museum* than those between mother and child. It was in these adult relationships that the woman was able to occasionally exhibit her autonomy in rebellion against the man/husband's rule(s).

Many feminist historians agree that the 1790s was a seminal period in American thought about women's right to an autonomous sexual role. But they are not clear about why this decade was important. Patricia J. McAlexander views it as a time of bright promise, ending in frustration and disillusionment for those who hoped it would issue in an improved status for women. Whether woman was inherently passionate or reasonable was among the questions asked. But, as McAlexander notes, "There was a strong disagreement regarding the proper role for women; indeed, America seems to have participated fully in an intense cultural dialogue on the subject occurring throughout the western world." She argues that the origins of the nineteenth century's "cult of true womanhood" may be found in the debate of the late 1790s on "female" passion vs. "male" reason, especially as revealed during the controversy over Mary Wollstonecraft's revolutionary book, *A Vindication of the*

Rights of Woman, published in the United States in 1792. The public reaction against the violence of the French Revolution and the Reign of Terror were also factors militating against increased support for women's equality. McAlexander concludes that the more open-minded, liberal and "passionate" concepts of women's rights and freedoms were defeated by the conservative and traditional forces that stressed woman's humility, self-discipline, asceticism, and submissiveness to her spouse in domestic and sexual matters. The image of "the conservative's delicate, domestic, spiritual female" predominates during the first half of the nineteenth century, but its roots may be found in the late 1790s, when the "ideal woman was described in American fiction, letters, periodicals, [and] conduct books."[25]

Although after 1820 woman's role became largely that of moral guide and restraint on male sexuality, in the 1780s and 1790s this was only one of many feminine identities delineated by the *American Museum*. Indeed, the 1790s were a formative period for the new nation, whose sex roles and sex stereotypes were in a state of flux. McAlexander thinks it was regrettable that no compromise resolved the conflict between the "two extreme images" of women—the conservative's pure, overprotected "lady" and the radical's ideal of the passionate, unpredictable "free woman." She views the 1790s, the first years of which we have examined in this study of the *American Museum*, as a turning point in the concretization of public opinion on women's rights. Unfortunately, she concludes, the eventual outcome favored the conservatives. "So widespread was the resurgence of the old conservative view of the nature and role of women in nineteenth-century America that the cultural dialogue in which it provided but one alternative seems all but forgotten," she writes. "Nevertheless, the literature of the 1790s recalls that dialogue in all its intensity."[26]

As we have seen, Mathew Carey's *American Museum* was a major participant in that dialogue. But its views could not be easily pigeonholed within any one faction. On the contrary, its selections reflected all the diversity of gender experiences within early America, rural and urban, though probably the latter locale predominated. Though not as ardent in promoting women's equality as we in the late twentieth century might wish, the *American Museum* respected the "fair sex" and its divergence from the mold of submissive humility in which some truculent spirits—male and female—would have liked to sequester it.

Notes

1. Frank L. Mott, *A History of American Magazines, 1741-1850* (Cambridge, Mass.: Harvard University Press, 1966), 50.

2. Mott, *American Magazines*, 94-99.

3. Lawrence J. Friedman, *Inventors of the Promised Land* (New York: Knopf, 1975), 112-113, 116.

4. "How to Prolong the Happiness of the Marriage Union," in *Columbian Magazine* 1 (June 1787): 473-475, quote at 473.

5. "How to Prolong the Happiness of the Marriage Union," 474.

6. "How to Prolong the Happiness of the Marriage Union," 474.

7. "How to Prolong the Happiness of the Marriage Union," 474.

8. "Rules and Maxims for Promoting Matrimonial Happiness," *Columbian Magazine* 4 (Jan. 1790): 24.

9. "Rules and Maxims for Promoting Matrimonial Happiness," 24.

10. "Chariessa: or, a Pattern for the Sex," *Columbian Magazine* 4 (Jan. 1790): 40-45, quotes at 40-41, 42. "Chariessa" may also be found in *Representative American Short Stories*, Alexander Jessup, ed. (Boston: Allyn and Bacon, 1923), 1-8. For the greater tendency of twentieth-century male-dominated media to view "old maids" as un(re)productive, contemptible, and effete objects, see Sharon R. Ullman, *Sex Seen: The Emergence of Modern Sexuality in America* (Berkeley and Los Angeles: University of California Press, 1997), 20-23, 145-146, and Germaine Greer, *The Whole Woman* (New York: Knopf, 1999), 255-262.

11. "Chariessa," 45.

12. See Carole Shammas, Marylynn Salmon, and Michel Dahlin, *Inheritance in America from Colonial Times to the Present* (New Brunswick, N.J.: Rutgers University Press, 1987); Gordon S. Wood, *The Radicalism of the American Revolution* (New York: Alfred Knopf, 1992), 183-184; Marylynn Salmon, *Women and the Law of Property in Early America* (Chapel Hill: University of North Carolina Press, 1986); Salmon, "Republican Sentiment, Economic Change, and the Property Rights of Women in American Law," in *Women in the Age of the American Revolution*, Ronald Hoffman and Peter J. Albert, eds. (Charlottesville: University Press of Virginia, 1989), 448-452.

13. "Chariessa," 40.

14. "Chariessa," 45.

15. Mott, *American Magazines*, 108-111.

16. Mott, *American Magazines*, 110-111.

17. "On Conjugal Affection," *Massachusetts Magazine* 6 (June 1794): 343-349. Jay Fliegelman, *Prodigals and Pilgrims: The American Revolution Against Patriarchal Authority, 1750-1800* (Cambridge: Cambridge University Press, 1982), 26, 93-106, 177, 214-219, 233, 250-254, stresses the significance of the concept of gratitude—between children and parents and colonies and mother country—in the literature, philosophy, and political thought of the eighteenth

century Anglo-American world. The feeling of gratitude, and the ensuing urge to perform benevolent acts, was considered a contagious emotion by Scottish "common sense" philosophers like Adam Smith and Francis Hutcheson. According to Henry Home, Lord Kames, one gained moral pleasure by imitating the virtuous acts of others. Praising the benevolent effects of moralistic novels in his essay, *Elements of Criticism* (1762), Kames explained: "A signal act of gratitude produceth in the spectator or reader not only love or esteem for the author but also a separate feeling . . . of gratitude without an object, a feeling which disposeth the spectator or reader to acts of gratitude." Quoted in Fliegelman, *Prodigals and Pilgrims*, 26.

18. Mott, *American Magazines,* 37, 65-66, 789, is the source of the information on the *Lady's Magazine* in this paragraph.

19. "A Matrimonial Republican," "On Matrimonial Obedience," in *Lady's Magazine and Repository of Entertaining Knowledge* 1 (July 1792): 64-66.

20. See, e.g., Jan Lewis, "The Republican Wife: Virtue and Seduction in the Early Republic," *William and Mary Quarterly*, 3rd Ser., 44 (Oct. 1987): 689-721, and Wendy Martin, "Women and the American Revolution," *Early American Literature* 11 (1976-1977): 322-335. On women as the exemplars of self-control within the family and their connection with republican ideals, see Linda K. Kerber, *Women of the Republic: Intellect and Ideology in Revolutionary America* (Chapel Hill: University of North Carolina Press, 1980), 206, 245.

21. Kerber, *Women of the Republic*, 241-249, 258-264, argues that middle-class women appreciated the vicarious sense of passionate identity they gained from reading Romantic novels by Jean-Jacques Rousseau, Samuel Richardson, and Susanna Rowson, in which women were often protagonists.

22. Janet Wilson James, *Changing Ideas About Women in the United States, 1776-1825* (New York: Garland, 1981), 193-204. Patricia McAlexander, "The Creation of the American Eve," *Early American Literature* 9 (Winter 1975): 256-266, notes the triumph of a "conservative strain in American thought" regarding women by the end of the 1790s. Public opinion was willing to sacrifice women's sexual and political freedoms to the sanctity of marriage and the social order, as the widespread reaction against the lifestyle and writings of Mary Wollstonecraft and her anarcho-socialist husband William Godwin vividly demonstrated. By the the late 1790s the climate of opinion dictated that "women were again to be submissive, domestic, pious, and thereby re-establish their delicacy, spiritual superiority, and—most important—their restraining power over men" (263). McAlexander fails to cite the *American Museum* to support her thesis that there was a reaction against female sexuality and the "cult of the passion" in the media in the late 1790s. In any case, Carey's magazine had ceased publication by the end of 1792.

23. On the importance of newspapers and magazines in delineating women's role in the early republic, see Karen K. List, "The Post-Revolutionary Woman Idealized: Philadelphia Media's Republican Mother," *Journalism Quarterly* 66,

no. 1 (Spring 1989): 65-75; Mary Beth Norton, *Liberty's Daughters: The Revolutionary Experience of American Women* (Boston: Little, Brown, 1980); Susan J. Branson, "Politics and Gender: the Political Consciousness of Philadelphia Women in the 1790s" (Ph.D. dissertation, Northern Illinois University, 1992), 35-42; *Women's Periodicals and Newspapers from the Eighteenth Century to 1981,* James P. Danky, ed. (Boston: G. K. Hall, 1982); David Paul Nord, "A Republican Literature: Magazine Reading and Readers in Late-Eighteenth-Century New York," in *Reading in American Literature and Social History*, Cathy N. Davidson, ed. (Baltimore: Johns Hopkins University Press, 1989), 114-139; and Cathy N. Davidson, *Revolution and the Word: The Rise of the Novel in America* (New York: Oxford University Press, 1986).

24. Norton, *Liberty's Daughters*, 247-249, quote at 247. Norton, *Liberty's Daughters*, 247-249, and Linda K. Kerber, "The Republican Mother: Women and the Enlightenment—An American Perspective," *American Quarterly* 27 (Summer 1976): 187-205, convey an optimistic view of women's empowerment in the 1790s *via* their educative, maternal role. For the view that the Revolution and the idea of the republican mother did not improve women's condition, see Elaine F. Crane, "Dependence in the Era of Independence: The Role of Women in a Republican Society," in *The American Revolution: Its Character and Limits*, Jack P. Greene, ed. (New York: New York University Press, 1987), 253-275. Rosemarie Zagarri, "The Rights of Man and Woman in Post-Revolutionary America," *William and Mary Quarterly*, 3d Ser., 55 (April 1998): 203-230, argues that women eventually employed the Revolution's natural rights ideology to gain equality. The value of the concept of the "Republican Mother" as a force for social change is minimized in Nancy F. Cott, "Passionlessness: An Interpretation of Victorian Sexual Ideology, 1790-1850," *Signs: A Journal of Women in Culture and Society* 4 (Winter 1978): 219-236.

25. McAlexander, "Creation of the American Eve," 263-264. For a similar interpretation, see Wendy Martin, "Women and the American Revolution," *Early American Literature* 11 (1976-1977): 322-335. The value of Martin's article is limited by the small number of sources she used. She concentrates primarily on that famous husband-and-wife team, John and Abigail Adams.

26. McAlexander, "American Eve," 264.

About the Author

Arthur Scherr teaches United States history in the Department of Social and Behavioral Sciences at Medgar Evers College of the City University of New York. He has taught history at Kingsborough Community College, Bernard Baruch College, and Touro College. He has served on the editorial staffs of major historical projects connected with the political and social history of the United States during the era of the American Revolution and the early national republic, among them *The Diary of Elizabeth Drinker* and *The Papers of Robert Morris.* He holds a B.A. in history from Brooklyn College (Phi Beta Kappa), an M.A. in history from Columbia University, and a Ph.D. in history from the Graduate School of the City University of New York. He has published articles in diverse journals in history, the humanities, psychoanalysis, and the social sciences, including *The Historian, The Psychoanalytic Review, The Psychohistory Review, Mid-America: An Historical Review, The Midwest Quarterly, The Pennsylvania Magazine of History and Biography, Pennsylvania History, American Imago, The American Journal of Psychoanalysis, Names: Journal of the American Name Society, West Virginia History,* and *The South Carolina Historical Magazine*. "*I Married Me A Wife*": *Male Attitudes Toward Women in the* American Museum, *1787-1792*" is his first book.